CHARLES PURTON COOPER

A BRIEF ACCOUNT OF SOME OF THE MOST IMPORTANT PROCEEDINGS IN PARLIAMENT RELATIVE TO THE DEFECTS IN THE ADMINISTRATION OF JUSTICE IN THE COURT OF CHANCERY THE HOUSE OF LORDS AND THE COURT OF COMMISSIONERS OF BANKRUPT

Elibron Classics
www.elibron.com

Elibron Classics series.

ISBN 1-4212-3560-9 (paperback)
ISBN 1-4212-3559-5 (hardcover)

This Elibron Classics Replica Edition is an unabridged facsimile of the edition published in 1828 by John Murray, London.

A

BRIEF ACCOUNT

OF SOME OF THE MOST IMPORTANT

PROCEEDINGS IN PARLIAMENT,

RELATIVE TO

THE DEFECTS IN THE ADMINISTRATION OF JUSTICE

IN THE

COURT OF CHANCERY,

THE

HOUSE OF LORDS,

AND

THE COURT OF COMMISSIONERS OF BANKRUPT:

TOGETHER WITH

THE OPINIONS OF DIFFERENT STATESMEN AND LAWYERS,
AS TO THE REMEDIES TO BE APPLIED.

By C. P. COOPER, Esq.

LONDON:
JOHN MURRAY, ALBEMARLE STREET.
MDCCCXXVIII.

LONDON:
PRINTED BY C. ROWORTH, BELL YARD,
TEMPLE BAR.

TO

MICHAEL ANGELO TAYLOR, ESQ.
M.P.

My Dear Sir,

It was my intention to publish a short account only of what took place in the House of Commons on your motion, on the 12th of February last, for a return of the arrears of business in the Court of Chancery. The time which the Court has lately devoted to bankruptcy has, however, given me an opportunity of extending my plan, so as to give a concise statement of the most important proceedings which have at different times taken place in both Houses of Parliament, as to the evils so long felt in the administration of justice in the Court of

Chancery, the House of Lords, and the Court of the Commissioners of Bankrupt, together with the sentiments of some eminent individuals on the measures most proper to effect their removal or mitigation. I have been induced also to subjoin a sketch of my own notions of the reform which ought to be introduced into those important parts of our judicial establishments. The work claims no merit of originality. It is a hasty compilation made, as you know, in a very short space of time, and in the midst of the severe labours of an Equity Draughtsman. Some portions of the early chapters were first written as notes to the debates, and subsequently enlarged and incorporated with the text, as you will probably discover from the incoherency of those parts of the work. But, imperfect as these pages are, I am in hopes they will be found not altogether useless to yourself and other members of parliament, as they bring together in a short compass, information which otherwise could be obtained only by research in a great variety of books and documents not always at hand. After this avowal of the nature of the following pages, I could not venture to dedicate them to you, did I not know the partiality with which you view every attempt, however humble, to advance a temperate reform in the great equity tribunals of this country.

I remain, my dear Sir,

Your's, very truly,

C. P. COOPER.

LINCOLN'S INN, 14*th April,* 1828.

ERRATUM.

In the Note at page 230, in enumerating the works on Hindu and Mahommedan Law, the following paragraph has been accidentally omitted :—*The Institutes of Hindu Law, or the Ordinances of Menu, according to the Gloss of Cullúca, verbally translated from the original Sanscrit, with a Preface, by Sir William Jones;* first published in 1796, and since reprinted in Sir William Jones's works.—*Al Sirájiyyah, or the Mahommedan Law of Inheritance, with a Commentary, by Sir William Jones;* first published in 1782, and since reprinted in Sir William Jones's works :—and *A Digest of Hindu Law on Contracts and Successions, with a Commentary, by Jagannát'ha Tercapanchánana, translated from the original Sanscrit, by Colebrooke;* first published at Calcutta, and reprinted in London in 1801.

CONTENTS.

CHAPTER IX.

CHAPTER X.

CHAPTER XI.

CHAPTER XII.

CHAPTER XIII.

CHAPTER XIV.

CHAPTER XV.

APPENDIX A.

APPENDIX B.

APPENDIX C.

APPENDIX D.

CHAPTER I.

THE COURT OF CHANCERY PRIOR TO THE YEAR 1810.

THE delays experienced in the Administration of Justice in the Court of Chancery, have, from a remote period, been matter of complaint both in and out of Parliament.* Even as long since as the reign of Henry VIII. the slowness of the proceedings of this tribunal had passed into a proverb, so that Sir Thomas Moore, when, by ex-

* The publication of Mr. Parkes's History of the Court of Chancery makes it necessary to state, that this Chapter was written from notes made long before that work appeared; indeed much of what is contained in it will be found in the Letters on the Court of Chancery. Mr. Parke deserves great credit for his industry and research. If, in a second edition, some important omissions in the early history of the Court be supplied, and some of the numerous and long extracts thrown into an Appendix, and others altogether suppressed, and recourse be had in every instance to the Authors cited, the class of readers for whom the book is evidently intended, will have little to desire on the subject it treats.

traordinary industry, he had succeeded in disposing of all the causes that were ready for hearing, and on his desiring the registrar to call the next cause, he was told that none remained on the list, himself ordered the fact to be entered on record, and a poet of the day celebrated so unusual an event by an epigram,* which has come down to us.†

The bills in Chancery still remaining in the Tower, the particulars of which have been lately published by the Record Commissioners, show that the number of suits brought into the Court in the time of Queen Elizabeth must have been considerable; and from anecdotes which have been preserved of those who held the seals during that reign it seems dispatch was as rare then as at a subsequent period.

In the reign of James I. we find that even Lord Bacon was unable to judge the causes brought before him, until they had been set down for years; and when the seals were in commission after Lord Bacon's dismissal, a Member of the House of Commons stated in Parliament, that he

* When More some years had Chancellor been,
No more Suits did remain,
The same shall never more be seen,
Till More be there again.

† It has been said, but I know not upon what authority, that Sir Thomas Wriothesley, who was Chancellor from 1545 to 1547, got through every suit that was ready for hearing.

had a suit that had been depending thirty years;* and Sir Edward Coke also stated in the House of Commons, that there were more causes than the Lord Chancellor and the Master of the Rolls could get through.† It is true, that Bishop Williams, (the last churchman who held the seals,) by commencing his sittings earlier, and continuing them later‡ than had ever been done before, or than ever could be done for a continuance, succeeded in achieving what Lord Bacon could not. Of all the causes which were set down, it is said, he left none unheard at the end of the term. It is probable, however, that, notwithstanding Williams was a most accomplished statesman and scholar, the suitors preferred having their causes heard by a judge, who, to other qualifications, added a knowledge of the Law.§ Sir Julius

* During the Chancellorship of Cardinal Wolsey, there were many causes which had been depending in Court more than twenty years.

† In this Reign a Bill was introduced into the House of Commons to appoint two assistant Judges in the Court of Chancery, but it went no further.

‡ In winter he sat by candle light, two hours before sunrise, and continued to sit until eight or nine at night.

§ Equity at this period really consisted in a prudent mitigation only of the rigours of the Common Law. No one had yet attempted to reduce it to fixed rules or principles. We have but few reported Chancery cases of an older date than Lord Nottingham's time. The reader may form some notion of the

Cæsar, an eminent civilian, had been then for seven years Master of the Rolls. Most of the new causes were probably carried before him; and it is not likely there were many appeals from the decisions of Sir Julius, who was familiar with the principles and practice of the Court, to the Lord Keeper, who knew nothing of either; and if any were made, it may be conjectured the decrees of the Court below were affirmed, and future appeals effectually discouraged. In this way it may easily be conceived that Lord Keeper Williams, having once got through the arrears left on the lists of the Court by Lord Bacon, would have no difficulty in dispatching in the Term, the business appropriated to it.

Upon the Great Seal being taken from Williams it was delivered to Lord Coventry. We are told that, in his time, the Chancery "was swelling and ready to burst with causes," and their number does not seem to have diminished

grounds on which the Chancellors of that day built their decrees, from the conclusion of the Report which a learned Serjeant has given us of a case before a very eminent lawyer, (Lord Chancellor Ellesmere,) the predecessor of Lord Bacon. "The pitiful cries of the father and the mother, dying as is aforesaid, *(they had died of the plague,)* and of the poor orphans, called to God for relief, and moved the heart of the Chancellor to take compassion upon them, and to take such order as he hath done." This suit was of moderate duration, it only lasted *eleven* years.

the expense of prosecuting them. "I have heard," says a writer of that time "of two brethren, who contended in Chancery for a chain of gold, worth sixty pounds. The elder, being executor, kept the chain. The younger had proof that his father often said in his life time that the chain should be his. The suit proceeded until they had spent above a hundred pounds."*

Towards the† end of the reign of Charles I. we find Maynard and Selden, and other eminent lawyers, active members of a committee to reform the Court, the expense and delay in its proceedings appearing to have increased in proportion with the trouble of the times.‡

* The same Author tells us he had heard of two men who fell at variance about a hive of bees, and went to *law*, until he that had spent least had spent five hundred pounds.—See *The Present State of England, &c., by Walter Carey*. 1627. 4to. containing twenty-one pages, reprinted in the Harleian Miscellany.

† The first preparations for the civil war suspended for a time all legal proceedings; a circumstance which, as it created considerable dismay amongst the lawyers, seems to have afforded much merriment to another portion of the public. The author of an Anonymous Pamphlet, written in 1642, describes "the prime Court of Chancery" "in that year of disasters," to be "as silent as a Puritan Conventicle when the lights are out." See *St. Hilary's Tears, shed upon all professions from the Judge to the Pettifogger, &c.*, for *want of a stirring Midsummer Term*. 1642. 4to. containing six pages, reprinted in the Harleian Miscellany.

‡ In the Sister Kingdom the disturbed state of public affairs seems at one time to have caused the Court of Chancery almost to discontinue its sittings. The following passage is extracted

During the Commonwealth the clamours raised against the Court, did not abate.* We find Whitelocke declaring "that the office of Commissioner of the Great Seal had the greatest and most constant labour in it of any other place in England; that this shop of justice must be always open,—nullus recedat à Cancellariâ sine remedio; —that the business of the Chancery was certainly more than that of any other court, and the trouble must needs be greater, and the burthen the heavier, too heavy for him to bear."

from the *Journals of the Irish House of Commons*, 7th June, 1641. "It is ordered that the undermentioned committee shall, at two of the clock this afternoon, join with a committee of six of the Lords to attend the Right Honourable the Lords Justices, and declare unto their lordships the sense of this House in the following particulars: First, that the Court of Castle Chamber did not sit this term, and the Court of Chancery but once this term, and that the Court of Wards did sit but very seldom this term."

* "Why," says a writer of that period, "under a pretence of Equity, and a Court of Conscience, are our wrongs doubled and trebled upon us, the Court of Chancery being as extortionous, or more so than any other court?" Notwithstanding this invective against the Chancery, the author says in another place: "Who knows not that the web of the law intangles the small flies and dismisseth the great, so that a mite of equity is worth a bundle of law?"—See *The Corruption and Deficiency of the Laws of England soberly considered, &c. By John Warr.* 1649. 4to. containing eighteen pages, reprinted in the Harleian Miscellany.

The same writer notices that there was a suit in Gloucestershire between two families, which had been then lately composed, and had lasted since the reign of Edward IV.!

The Parliament resolved that the Court should be abolished, and a Committee* was appointed to consider of the mode in which matters in Equity should be determined.† It was, however, found

* It was probably about this time that a burlesque Pamphlet was published, entitled, "*The Proposals of the Committee for Regulating the Law, both in sense, form, and practice*," &c. One of the proposals was, "that the Court of Iniquity, alias the Chancery, (where a man may be suspended and demurred in his just right from generation to generation by the power of the purse,) may be judged no more by the keepers of the liberties and privileges of England," &c.

The Pamphlet is in 4to. containing eight pages, and without date. It is reprinted in the Harleian Miscellany.

† Several Bills, intended to carry this resolution into effect, were brought into the House, but they seem all to have been abandoned after having been read a first and second time. In the *Parliamentary, or Constitutional History of England, from the earliest time to the Restoration of Charles II.* vol. xx. of the edit. of 1763, it is observed, that no historian had given any of the arguments offered on the occasion of voting down the Court of Chancery in August, 1653, in which, it appears, the House was unanimous. The authors of that work endeavour to supply the defect from other sources published at the time. The following passage is drawn from one of them, being a relation by an anonymous Member of the Parliament, of their proceedings:

" In the course of the debate the Court of Chancery was called by some members the greatest grievance in the nation. Others said, that for dilatoriness, chargeableness, and a faculty of bleeding the people in the purse vein, even to their utter perishing and undoing, that Court might compare with, if not surpass, any court in the world. That it was confidently affirmed, by knowing gentlemen of worth, that there were depending in that Court twenty-three thousand causes, some of which had been there de-impossible to destroy the equitable jurisdiction, without a total change of the law of the country, and Cromwell soon afterwards brought out

pending five, some ten, some twenty, some thirty years, and more; that there had been spent therein many thousand pounds, to the ruin, nay, utter undoing, of many families; that no ship almost that sailed in the sea of the law but first or last put into that port, and, if they made any considerable stay there, they suffered so much loss, that the remedy was as bad as the disease; that what was ordered one day was contradicted the next, so as in some causes there had been five hundred orders and more; that when the purse of the clients began to empty, and their spirits were a little cooled, then, by a reference to some gentlemen in the country, the cause, so long depending at so great a charge, came to be ended; so that some members did not stick to term the Chancery a mystery of wickedness, and a standing cheat, and that, in short, so many horrible things were affirmed of it, that those who were, or had a mind to be advocates for it, had little to say on the behalf of it, and so, at the end of one day's debate the question being put, it was voted down."

Amongst *Thurloe's State Papers* is to be found an intercepted Letter, dated the 4th November, 1653, mentioning one of these bills. "Our state here," says the writer, "is very vigilant to cut off those exorbitances that formerly oppressed the good people of this nation, and to that purpose have yesterday voted the bill for abrogating the Chancery, to be brought in on Monday next, appointing a committee to determine the causes depending, and likewise that a bill be brought in for contriving a new body of the laws by the 1st of January next. And it wanted not much that the caterpillars of the land had been all banished the town, as formerly the poor cavaliers were, one voice only reserving them for a time, which will not be long."

The following extract, which I believe is nearly in the language of the Journals of the Parliament, is from the *Account of the Parliament of* 1654, taken from *the Journal of Guibon Goddard, Esq.*

his celebrated ordinance for regulating the Court. One of the regulations contained in it was, that every cause should be heard the same day it was set down, and that the Lords Commissioners should for that purpose sit, when requisite, both in the morning and in the afternoon.* It is well known that the ordinance was the cause of Whitelocke the principal commissioner's resignation; and although it continued in force for several years, it does not seem to have effected what was

M.P., prefixed by way of Introduction to the *Diary of Thomas Burton, Esq. Member in the Parliaments of Oliver and Richard Cromwell, from* 1656 *to* 1659, recently published.

" Resolved, that the High Court of Chancery of England shall be forthwith taken away.

" That it be referred to the Committee of the Law to prepare a Bill for this purpose, and report it to the House.

" That it be referred to the same Committee to consider how the causes now depending in Chancery may be determined, and likewise a provision for the determining in future matters of Equity, and putting in order other matters of law, which are within the jurisdiction of that Court, and forthwith to bring in a Bill for that purpose."

* The draft of an Act, prepared by the Commonwealth Law Committee in 1653, reprinted in Mr. Parkes's work from the New Edition of Lord Somers's Tracts, provided, that the Judges of the Court of Chancery should sit constantly, as well in vacation as in term, until all causes and motions in the register's books should be heard and determined; and the Judges were in all cases to pronounce their decree presently in court at the hearing, save in cases of very great difficulty, and then not to exceed ten days. The part of Mr. Parkes's book relating to the Commonwealth is beyond all comparison the best.

expected from it. In 1659* we find the Parliament still occupied with the reform and regulation of the Court of Chancery, and that at this time the Lords Commissioners did not themselves hear Equity suits, but a commission was issued under the Great Seal to the Master of the Rolls, and certain of the Judges and Masters in Chancery, to hear causes at the Rolls and in Chancery.†

* A well-known Anonymous Pamphlet, entitled, "*A Rod for the Lawyers, &c.*" appeared in this year. The author gives the following account of the Equity proceedings in the time of the Commonwealth. "And when either party sees he is like to have the worst by Common Law, then they have liberty to remove into the Chancery, where a suit commonly depends as long as a buff coat will endure wearing, especially if the parties have, as it is said, good stomachs and strong purses; but when their purses grow empty their stomachs fail. Then, when no more corn is like to be brought to the lawyer's mill, it is usual to ordain some men to hear and end the business; but, alas! then it is too late; for then, probably, both parties, or at least one of them, are ruined utterly in prosecuting the suit, want of his stock, and following of his calling."

The Pamphlet was published in 4to., and contains twenty pages. It is reprinted in the Harleian Miscellany.

† Commissions of this kind were not uncommon at an earlier period. The first instance of such a commission being issued was in Wolsey's time. The commission is set forth from the Parliament Roll in the *Discourse of the Judicial Authority of the Masters of the Rolls.*

Lord Southampton, who was Chancellor on the accession of Edward VI., was deprived of his office for issuing a commission of a similar nature, without any warrant from the Lord Protector. It was judged a high presumption in the Lord Chancellor to devolve on others that power which the law had trusted in his

Soon after the Restoration the Court had regained its ancient character for administering slow justice. In 1661, and the three following years, various bills were proposed to prevent unnecessary delays, expenses, and grievances, in our Equity as well as Common Law Courts, but all of them were successively laid aside. In 1670 Sir Orlando Bridgman, who, although he had been a very good Common Law Judge, made a very bad Chancellor, held the Seals, when a similar bill was proposed and read, and in like manner abandoned.

The Lord Bridgman was succeeded by Lord Shaftesbury, who, possessing no talents except for intrigue, seems nevertheless to have entertained the project of reforming the Court. "After he was possessed of the Great Seal, he was in appearance the gloriousest man alive, and no man's discourse flew so high as his did against the tribe of the Court of Chancery, officers and counsel,

hands. The commission was addressed to Sir Richard Southwell, Master of the Rolls, and three Masters in Chancery. It recited, that the Chancellor was so employed on affairs of state, that he could not attend the hearing of causes in the Court of Chancery, and empowered any two of the persons, to whom it was addressed, to execute the Chancellor's office in that Court in as ample a manner as if he himself were present, but their decrees were to be brought to the Lord Chancellor to be signed by him before they were enrolled. See *Burnett's History of the Reformation*, vol. ii. p. 15. Fol. edit. Burnett gives the original commission in the Collection of Records in the Appendix.

and their methods of ordering the business of the Court. He would teach the bar that a man of sense was above all their forms:"* "but he was soon reduced; he came like the month of March, as they say, *in* like a lion and *out* like a lamb."† This profligate nobleman did not hold the seals quite twelve months.

Lord Nottingham was as subtle a lawyer as Lord Eldon, and not more celebrated for the promptitude of his decisions. It never occurred to him "that unreasonable delays were the same in the mean as injustice was in the end; and that it often made the suitor quit his right rather than live upon the rack in pursuing it;" he "gave way to all sorts of motions, supposing that if he split the hair, and with his golden scales determined reasonably on one side of the motion, justice was nicely done, not imagining what torment the people endured, who were drawn from the law, and tossed in a blanket in his Court.‡" We find, that during the time he was Chancellor, the defective constitution of the Court for the administration of justice came more than once before Parliament. The House of Commons resolved, upon the report of a Committee of Grievances, that the extraordinary power and jurisdiction of the Court of Chancery,

* *North's Examen.*

† *North's Life of Lord Keeper Guildford.*

‡ Ibid.

and other Courts of Equity, in matters determinable at Common Law, was grievous to the subject; and a bill to redress the grievance was read, but afterwards laid aside.*

His successor, Lord Keeper North, succeeded for a time in keeping down the arrears of the Court, but in a few years the paper became loaded with remanets, which we are told so afflicted him, as to be the principal cause of the disease of which he died.†

Burnet tells us, that on the accession of William

* A whimsical description of what a chancery cause was in Lord Nottingham's time, is to be found in Lord Somers's Tracts,—" a suit in Equity, where one order shall beget another, and the poor client be swung round (like a cat before execution) from decree to re-hearing, from report to exception, and *vice versâ*, until his fortunes are shipwrecked, and himself drowned, for want of white or yellow earth to wade through on."—*The Character of an Honest Lawyer*, 1676.—*Lord Somers's Collection of Tracts*, vol. iv. p. 307. Edition 1748.

† So says his brother, Roger North. But Burnet gives a different account of the matter.—" An appeal of his had been brought before the Lords in the former session, and it was not only reversed with many severe reflections on him that made it, but the Earl of Nottingham, who hated him because he had endeavoured to detract from his father's memory, had got together so many instances of his bad administration of justice, that he exposed him severely for it. And it was believed that gave the crisis to the uneasiness and distraction of mind he was labouring under. He languished for some time, and died despised and ill thought of by the nation."—*Burnet's History of his Own Time*, vol. i. p. 665. folio edit.

and Mary, the great increase of Chancery business had made many apprehend it was too much to be trusted to one person, and so it was resolved to put the Chancery in commission. Upon Lord Nottingham's declining to be the principal commissioner, that office was singularly enough given to Serjeant Maynard, then more than ninety years old; and the commissioners, as it might have been expected, gave little satisfaction. In 1691 the seals were still in commission; but the delay and expense attending Equity proceedings do not seem to have been diminished. In that year, a bill passed the Lords, and was read in the Commons, which had for its object to remedy some of the evils complained of, but it was afterwards laid aside. Even the great Lord Somers* seems to have been unable to accomplish all that was expected from him; during his chancellorship, a bill was prepared and read in the House of Commons, to reform the proceedings in the Court of Chancery, but, like many others of the same na-

* I cannot forbear transcribing from the *Biographia Britannica*, now before me, what *Walpole*, in his *Catalogue of Royal and Noble Authors*, says of this great statesman and judge.—"It was no inglorious part of this Chancellor's life, that, when removed from the administration, his labours were still dedicated to the service of the government of his country. In this situation, above all the little prejudices of a profession, (for he had no profession but that of Solon and Lycurgus,) he set himself to correct the grievances of the law, and to amend the vocation he had adorned."

ture, both in prior and subsequent times, it was abortive.*

Lord Harcourt was Chancellor during the last seven years of the reign of Queen Anne, and it appears that on one occasion he disposed of all the business depending before him that was ready to be heard; but there was at that time a great arrear at the Rolls, and his Lordship caused a part of the suits set down there to be transferred to his own paper. The cause that enabled Lord Harcourt to get rid of the arrears of his Court does not appear to be known, but it seems to have been temporary.

Lord King held the Great Seal from 1725 to 1733. He had had considerable practice at the bar, but does not seem to have possessed those rare qualities that are necessary for the performance of the various and laborious duties of Chancellor. An inscription on his monument informs us, he took such extraordinary pains in the discharge of the business of his office, that he im-

* In 1707, during the chancellorship of Lord Cowper, an anonymous pamphlet appeared, entitled "*Reasons humbly offered to both Houses of Parliament, for passing a Bill for preventing Delays and Expenses in Suits in Law and Equity.*" The author thus speaks of equity proceedings at that period.—"He must be perfectly senseless who seeks for redress in a Court of Equity, since, as the practice now stands, his adversary may make him spend twice his debt before he can recover it." The pamphlet was published in 4to. and contains 22 pages. It is reprinted in the Harleian Miscellany.

paired his constitution, and brought on at last a paralytic disorder, of which he died.*

Lord Talbot succeeded to Lord King. Few chancellors have possessed learning and talents better suited to that high office. He was not, however, more fortunate than his predecessor. The labours of the Great Seal were beyond the strength of one man. His biographer observes, "that the great increase of business† in the Court after the seal was put into his hands, is an evident proof of that confidence which the suitors reposed in him, and will do immortal honour to his memory, though it proved fatal to his life; for the constant fatigue of his employment was one of the principal causes of his death, and therefore he may be truly said to have fallen a martyr to the public good."‡

Lord Hardwicke presided in the Court of Chancery from 1736 to 1756. One, who professes to have known his Lordship well, describes the state of the court, during the time he presided there, in terms not inapplicable to that in which we have seen it in our days. "His decrees were very few, in comparison to the many causes that came

* *Biographia Britannica, art.* King.

† It was about this time that Sir Joseph Jekyll observed, that the suits determined every year in the Court of Chancery were of much greater value with respect to the subject's property, than the suits that were determined in all the other courts.

‡ *Biographia Britannica, art.* Talbot.

under discussion in that court in his time. The hearings, re-hearings, references to masters, reports, and exceptions to those reports, exorbitant fees to counsel, and the length of time to which every cause was protracted, made the suitors weary, and glad to submit to any decree suggested and agreed upon by their counsel, in which neither party could complain of being aggrieved by the judge of the court."*

During all the above period, the business of the Court was increasing progressively with the wealth and commerce of the country; and although in the time of James I. two judges could not get through the business then depending in Chancery, not only were no measures ever taken by the legislature to remedy the grievance, but the business in bankruptcy, originally altogether foreign to the Great Seal, and given to it, for the first time, by a statute of Elizabeth, was, by subsequent acts of parliament, so annexed to it, that the public are now taught to believe, that it can be administered by no other judge than the Chancellor.

The business in bankruptcy, too, does not constitute the only additional burthen that has been imposed upon the Chancellor. It was during the above period that the House of Lords usurped

* See *Cooksey's Sketches of an Essay on the Life and Character of Philip, Earl of Hardwicke.*

to itself the right of hearing appeals, which it exercises to this day, although to a much more limited extent than formerly.

No permanent improvement took place in the administration of justice in the Court, as regards the quicker decision of causes, in the period that elapsed from Lord Northington succeeding to the Seals, to the appointment of a Vice Chancellor. Appeals and causes were set down before the Chancellor, for years before they were heard, and every Chancery suit was a violation of one of the most sacred articles of the Great Charter, by which the sovereign promises there shall be no delay of justice.

The following pages will show whether there be not still such a delay in the Court of Chancery, as ought not to be suffered to exist in any country where the principle is acknowledged, that justice ought to be equally accessible to rich and poor, and that the price of it ought not to be made so dear, and the period at which it is to be attained be placed so remote as to make it more prudent that a man should sacrifice his right, than undergo the expense and care attending the prosecution of it.

It is believed that the above statement, short and imperfect as it is, notices all the periods at which the delays of the Court have been the subject of discussion in parliament, previous to Mr. M. A. Taylor's first motion in 1810.

In the Letters on the Court of Chancery, it is suggested, that the delay formerly existed rather with the clerks in court, or solicitors and the parties, than with the judges; as there have been Chancellors who have succeeded in getting through all the arrears; but it may be doubted whether this view be correct. When those Chancellors have been eminent lawyers the business has soon accumulated again, as in the case of Lord Keeper Guildford; and if the same thing did not happen to Chancellors, who were not distinguished by a knowledge of the laws they were appointed to administer, it may, as in the case of Bishop Williams, be attributed to other causes.*

* Sir Christopher Hatton, Vice-Chamberlain to Elizabeth, although no lawyer, is supposed to have been equally successful with Bishop Williams, in keeping down the business of his Court. Hatton was a man of greater abilities than learning. It has been said, "his place was above his law, but not above his parts, which were so very pregnant and comprehensive, that he could command other men's knowledge to as good purpose as his own." See *Lives of the Lord Chancellors*. No one can doubt, that if there were no arrears of business in his time, it must have been owing to a cause not unlike that which, it is suggested, enabled Bishop Williams to master the business of his Court. A keeper of the royal wardrobe is to be found in the Catalogue of Chancellors. Should it please his Majesty to deliver the Great Seal to Lord Mountcharles, it would be the most effectual way of diminishing the number of appeals. On the other hand, should another Silvester de Everton, "cunning in customs of Chancery," arise, and the Seals be delivered to him, it may as surely be predicted, that the number of appeals will increase, and especially if they be heard and decided within a moderate time after they are set down.

CHAP. II.—PART I.

THE COURT OF CHANCERY FROM THE YEAR 1810 TO THE PASSING OF THE VICE CHANCELLOR'S BILL IN 1813.

PARLIAMENTARY DEBATES.*

Mr. M. A. Taylor.—Mr. Perceval.—Sir Samuel Romilly.—Mr. Leach.

1810.

On the 25th of May, 1810, *Mr. Michael Angelo Taylor* moved, that a Committee should be appointed to inquire into the arrears of causes remaining for hearing in the Court of Chancery, and to report the same to the House, with their opinion as to the best mode of relieving the suitors,

* I have not ventured to alter any passages in the Speeches, as reported in the Parliamentary Debates, although they obviously contain many inaccuracies. My object has not been to give any connected account of the discussion, but merely to bring into more prominent notice the sentiments of some of the members on the subjects treated in these pages. Mr. Taylor's opinions are so well known, that I have not thought it necessary to make extracts from the many able speeches delivered by him.

and that the said Committee should inspect the Journals of the House of Lords to ascertain the number of appeals and writs of error.

This motion was founded upon an uncontradicted statement that suitors had been waiting many years for the decision of the Court, and that the delay had become so proverbial, that no man began a suit with the expectation of finishing it in less than ten years.

The Chancellor of the Exchequer (*Mr. Perceval*) observed, that it must be obvious to every one that there were very great arrears in the Court of Chancery. He assured the house that government had taken the subject into serious consideration. There appeared to be no way of remedying the evil complained of, but by bringing the subject before the House. In consequence of this assurance, Mr. Taylor withdrew his motion.

1811.

On the 7th of March, 1811, *Mr. Taylor* brought forward his second motion respecting the delays that occurred in the hearing of appeals in the House of Lords, and in the hearing of suits in Chancery.

The Chancellor of the Exchequer (*Mr. Perceval*), in the course of that debate, stated, that he could not deny that great grievances did exist, that there was a deficiency in the power of administering justice in various points, and, consequently, that it became the duty of the legislature to see that deficiency supplied.

Sir Samuel Romilly observed, it was notorious that great and crying grievances really existed, and it would be a denial of justice not to inquire into them; that from the great pressure of business within the last two years, causes had stood for that time in the Lord Chancellor's paper for hearing, without having yet been heard. The House divided, when there appeared for the motion 47, against it 87;—majority 40.

On the 17th of May, 1811, *Mr. Taylor* moved, that a Committee should be appointed to inquire into the causes that retarded the decision of suits in the High Court of Chancery. The debate was adjourned to the 5th of June following.

Sir Samuel Romilly, in the course of that debate, stated, that the whole system of equity in this country was founded on the decisions of successive Chancellors, from Lord Nottingham down to the present time, and it was necessary that those who had to administer the equity laws of this country should be in the constant habit of deciding original causes in the Court of Chancery. If the duties of the Lord Chancellor were too great for him to perform, it would be better to separate from his office the duties of the Speaker of the House of Lords, or the decision of bankrupt cases, though he saw considerable objection to either, than to take from him the decision of original causes, and that jurisdiction which constituted the very essence of his office. He knew it might be said that to separate bankrupt cases from the jurisdiction of the Lord Chancellor would diminish his emoluments too much. He did not think it would: but even if it should, that ought not to stand in the way, for a moment, of an arrangement necessary for the public interest.

The House divided, when there appeared, for going into a Committee 36, against it 36. The numbers being equal, the Speaker gave his casting vote in favour of the proposed inquiry, and a Committee was appointed.*

1812.

On the 27th of February, 1812, the Committee was re-appointed. It was proposed, in the Committee, that barristers and solicitors should be

* The motion for an Address for Commissions to inquire into the Duties, Salaries, and Emoluments of the Officers, Clerks, and Ministers of our Courts of Justice, was, if I recollect right, carried by a majority of only one vote. All the world knows that the benefits expected to result from these commissions were frustrated by the manner in which they were composed. When Sir Samuel Romilly saw who were the members that Mr. Taylor's political opponents contrived to have placed on his Committee, he instantly predicted that all their proceedings would be abortive. I trust, the time is, at length, come, when the distinction of Whig and Tory, if any such still exist, will be lost, in all questions that relate to so sacred a subject as the administration of justice.

examined on the subject of their inquiry. This proposal was rejected by a majority of the members, and Mr. Taylor, in consequence, on the 6th of May, 1812, moved the House, that it should be a special instruction to the Committee to examine persons practising at the Bar, as well as solicitors, touching the causes of the delay. The House divided, ayes 20, noes 84. Of course, all further proceedings of the Committee were rendered nugatory.

In December, 1812, the Vice Chancellor's Bill was introduced into the House of Lords.

1813.

On the 11th of February, 1813, the second reading of the Vice Chancellor's Bill was moved by Lord Castlereagh in the House of Commons.

Sir Samuel Romilly said he could not content himself with giving a silent vote upon this question, which, if agreed to, would effect a complete change in the character of future Chancellors; and the country would never again see such men as Somers, Camden, or Hardwicke. He conceived that the present Bill would alter materially the constitutional course of the business of the Court of Chancery, and the office of Lord Chancellor. After a few successions of Vice Chancellors, there would be no more men found to discharge the high office of Lord Chancellor in the manner it had hitherto been discharged by so many illustrious men. If he were called upon to suggest a remedy to the evil complained of, he should say, that what appeared to him the least objectionable mode would be to separate the bankrupt business from that of the Chancery. Sir Samuel Romilly then expressed the opinions with regard to the transfer of the bankrupt jurisdiction to another judge, which will be found in a subsequent part of these pages. He stated he could not avoid quoting here the opinion of their Committee, that it was highly objectionable that judges should be paid from fees,* especially from fees ostensibly belonging to their secretary or some inferior officer. By this report it appeared, that the fees of bankruptcy, which were paid to an officer for the bankruptcy, were accounted for by that officer to the Lord Chancellor. This, in his opinion, was decidedly wrong: a judge ought never to be paid by fees; he should therefore most earnestly recommend, that these fees should be abolished, and the salary of the Lord Chancellor proportionably increased, if it should appear that the other emoluments of his office did not afford him a sufficient remuneration. Next to taking away the bankrupt business, he thought the separating of the office of Speaker of the House of Lords from that of Chancellor, would be a far better mode than that proposed by the present Bill.

* See Part II. of the present Chapter.

On the 15th of February, 1813, Lord Castlereagh moved the order of the day for the House going into a Committee on the Vice Chancellor's bill.

On the question for the Speaker leaving the chair being put, *Mr. Leach* (now *Sir John Leach, Master of the Rolls*) rose to oppose the motion. In the course of his speech, he said he opposed it because it appeared to him to tend, in its consequences, to disengage the Lord Chancellor from a great portion of his judicial functions, and to render an office, which was primarily judicial and secondarily political, primarily political and secondarily judicial. If the Chancellor's situation were considered as primarily political and secondarily judicial, would not the judicial seat be likely to be conferred on those who had most aptitude for the primary duties? If the choice were thus to be directed by political consequence and political connection, the effect would be, that when a lawyer saw that it was not legal eminence, but other talents and other qualities, which led to the judicial seat, all persons of talent would be drawn from the law to seek after political distinction. Lawyers observing that eminence was to be obtained, not, as theretofore, by professional learning and skill, but by other qualities, would withdraw themselves from the acquisition of legal knowledge, and apply themselves to the attainment of political science, character and influence.

Thus would a most material change be effected in the whole judicial constitution of the country, a change which all must allow would be a very serious evil. The Court of Chancery, as an appellant court, would lose its consequence in the eyes of the country. If the Chancellor did not live with lawyers, if he was himself a politician, would not he make choice of politicians rather than lawyers for judges? The magnitude of the evil therefore was, as he had already said, nothing less than a change of the whole judicial constitution of the country. When it appeared to those who had the command over the Chancellor that there was an assistant who had sufficient time on his hands to ease him of part of his judicial duties, was there not reason to dread that he would be involved still deeper than he had hitherto been in political business, and in intrigue not known to belong to his office. No rational man could look at the present measure with attention and not see that, if adopted, the Chancellor would at some time or other, and he presumed to think at no great distance, be withdrawn from all except his appellant duties; and would not that lead to all the evils to which he had alluded as likely to result, in respect to all our other judicial situations?

Sir Samuel Romilly, in the course of this debate, repeated his opinion, that a much readier and safer way to relieve the Lord Chancellor from the pressure of business of which he complained, would be to separate from his high office the bankruptcy cases, which took up so much of his time; nor was the idea so novel as some gentleman had affected to represent it. The bankrupt causes, of which it had been proposed to strip the Chancellor, had been said, on the other side of the house, to be essential to his office. These causes, however, were a modern excrescence on the office, after the first statute concerning bankrupts in the time of Henry VIII. Bankrupt causes were subjected to three commissioners, on the present footing, in the time of Queen Elizabeth. These commissioners were at first supposed to determine bankrupt causes without appeal, and there was no appeal until the time of Lord Chancellor Nottingham. Lord Chancellor Nottingham hesitated for some time to entertain jurisdiction in bankruptcy, and stated, as a reason, the possibility of the inconveniencies which have since arisen. He at last consented, and was the first to exercise the jurisdiction: but during the time of Lord Talbot, Lord King, and Lord Macclesfield, there were so few interferences of this kind, that there were not twenty before the time of Lord Hardwicke, when a great increase took place in consequence of the statute of the 5th of George II. It was from this period that bankrupt causes came exclusively to be brought before the Lord Chancellor, and therefore it would be no innovation to detach from that office, that which had never been entailed upon it by statute.

On the 11th of March, 1813, *Mr. M. A. Taylor* moved that the House should resolve itself into a committee of the whole House, to consider of such parts of the statute of the 13th of Elizabeth, c. 7, and other subsequent statutes as give the jurisdiction in matters of bankruptcy.

Sir Samuel Romilly, in the course of the debate, said, at present the Chancellor received the bankrupt fees— fees received by the Secretary-for-bankruptcies, to whom he paid a salary. No judge ought to be paid by fees, not that any judge could be influenced by them, but they were in this case levied on misery and insolvency. He approved of the proposed measure, because it would leave the Chancellor at liberty, and not take him out of his own court. It was particularly worthy of observation that out of twenty bankrupt cases, no more than one, perhaps, would comprise a question of equity; and where such a question did arise the Chancellor formerly ordered a bill to be filed, that it might be brought before him in the regular and ordinary way. The danger which would arise from the measure* introduced by the Noble Lord (Lord Castlereagh) struck him most forcibly, when they made the Chancellor, by the proposed

* The Vice Chancellor's bill.

bill, a political instead of a judicial character; it would operate a most mischievous change in the whole system of the profession. It would be the means of withdrawing the Chancellor from his court, to attend to his political duties. If the bill were carried into effect, it would be the means of taking the Chancellor from his court almost entirely; he would cease to be acquainted with it, he would be an absolute stranger to it,—he would no longer reside in that part of the Town where the professors of the law were to be found, he would become an inhabitant of the political part of the metropolis. The person filling the situation of Chancellor, ought to be a man perfectly well acquainted with the law of real property—a law which was to be acquired only in the course of practice; which must in the first instance, be understood by deep and sedulous study, before a Lawyer commenced his career in that branch of the profession. He should be a perfect master of the doctrines of equity, which were, in fact, *dicta* emanating from the Lord Chancellor: not from him who immediately exercised the functions of the Office, but from his predecessors, extended and enforced by himself.— And it was most important that the Chancellor should also be acquainted with all the persons who practised the law; this was necessary because the whole patronage of the law was in the hands of the Lord Chancellor. Why then should such a power as this be placed in the hands of a man ignorant of the Court of Chancery, incapable of judging of the individual merit of lawyers, and who would be only important as a great political engine? The person elevated to the rank of Chancellor should have a practical knowledge of the state of business in this court, that he might be able to expedite it, to correct any abuses which might be observable, and to bring back the practice to what it was in former times. At an earlier period it was customary for the Lord Chancellor, when he first took his seat in the court, to enter into a brief view of the situation in which he found it, and to state what course he intended to adopt for the reform of evils, and the general dispatch of business. The great Lord Bacon and others the glory and pride of the profession, had done this. The inauguration speech (if he might be allowed the term,) of Lord Bacon, was still preserved; and in it he pledged himself as to the line of conduct he would pursue, thus laying down certain principles, by which an accurate judgment might be formed of the manner in which he fulfilled his covenant with the public. But was this course to be expected from some Lord Shaftsbury, some mere intriguer, some common public debater, some hackneyed politician, ready at the nod and beck of those in power? And yet such would probably be the Chancellors hereafter to be formed under this bill—as making the Lord Chancellor less a judge, and more a political character, and therefore as tending to induce him to make appointments on the ground of political connection, rather than of professional excellence.*

* Sir Samuel Romilly wrote two Pamphlets on the subject of the Vice Chancellor's Bill. The first was entitled, "*Objections to the Project of Creating a Vice Chancellor of England.*" The second was written in answer to a pamphlet of Lord Redesdale, and was entitled "*A Letter to a Noble Lord from the Author of Objections, &c.*" He states himself, that they were written merely for the purpose of inviting explanation and discussion, and not with a view of pointing out the specific remedy for the evils occasioned by the delays in the Court of Chancery and in the Appellate Jurisdiction of the House of Lords, although he suggests a measure since adopted, that the House of Lords should sit longer and more frequently, to hear appeals. His speeches on the Vice Chancellor's Bill contained little more than a repetition of what he had already stated in these pamphlets.

CHAP. II.—PART II.

OPINIONS OF COMMITTEES OF THE HOUSE OF COMMONS, OF THE CHANCERY COMMISSIONERS, &c. AS TO THE EXPEDIENCY OF GIVING TO THE LORD CHANCELLOR, MASTERS IN CHANCERY, AND COMMISSIONERS OF BANKRUPT, FIXED SALARIES INSTEAD OF FEES.*

ONE of the stains upon our judicial system, which it is hoped the legislature will soon obliterate,† is, that the Lord Chancellor, Masters in

* It would not be difficult to illustrate the subject of this chapter, and some other topics noticed in the course of this work, by authorities drawn from the writings of authors of almost every age and country, who have treated upon the principles to be adopted in the formation of the judicial establishments of a nation, but this would be altogether foreign to the object of the present publication.

† As long ago as the time of the Commonwealth, the legislature saw the impropriety of judicial officers being remunerated by fees. An ordinance was passed, appointing salaries to the Judges and Commissioners of the Great Seal, and disabling them from receiving any other profit or perquisite by occasion of their offices. A subsequent resolution prohibited them under a penalty, either directly or indirectly, by themselves or their servants, from taking any fee, perquisite, or reward except their salaries. In

Chancery, and their clerks,* and the Commissioners of Bankrupt, are remunerated for their services by fees.

Nearly seventeen years have elapsed since the Committee of the House of Commons, appointed to inquire into the causes that retard the decision of suits in Chancery, introduced into their Report the following recommendation:—"A considerable part of the emoluments of the office of Lord Chancellor is, and, as your Committee understand, has been for a long course of years, derived from fees nominally paid to the Secretary of Bankrupts, but who accounts for such fees to the Lord Chancellor himself, and is allowed by the Lord Chancellor a certain fixed salary in lieu of such nominal fees. Your Committee cannot see this without observing, that it appears to them highly inexpedient that the emoluments of any judicial officer should be constituted in part of fees not ostensibly payable to himself, but to an inferior officer. If more

April, 1732, the House of Commons resolved, on an elaborate Report of their Committee, that the interest which a great number of officers and clerks had in the proceedings in the Court of Chancery had been a principal cause of extending proceedings to an unnecessary length, to the great delay of justice and the oppression of the subject.

* There are not twelve barristers at the Chancery bar who derive emoluments from their practice equal to the fees of a Master's clerk. It was matter of complaint, as far back as the time of the Commonwealth, that they received expedition-money and other unjust rewards from the clients.

than the proper fees should be alleged to have been taken by the ministerial officer, the complaint must be made to his superior, the Judge of the Court, who would in that case have to sit in judgment upon such alleged abuses, from which, if they existed, he would himself derive a benefit. If it should be thought that any alterations might be made in this respect; and if the salary and other emoluments of the Lord Chancellor, exclusive of such fees, should be deemed insufficient for the office, your Committee would suggest the propriety of increasing the salary, and abolishing altogether the fees in question, which, though they do not appear to be of great amount in each commission, yet can be considered in no other light than as a tax upon distress and insolvency."

The sentiments of *Sir Samuel Romilly* on this subject are given in a former page. What was said by *Mr. Baring*, in a debate respecting the fees in bankruptcy, in the year 1826, must not be omitted.

Mr. Baring observed, that when he recollected what had taken place in the discussions upon the subject of granting increased salaries to the judges, he could not but remember, that one of the arguments principally relied on in support of that measure, was the necessity of taking away the fees that were then paid to the judges, and that were supposed to create an idea that those learned persons might feel an inclination to encourage litigation for their own advantage. Now surely if such an argument could with the least propriety be applied to the common law judges, with how much more force did it apply to the Lord Chancellor, who was a judge sitting to administer equity without the intervention of a jury—whose power was in no instance equalled among the other judges—whose fiat was conclusive; since from his decisions, there was no appeal but from himself in his own Court, to himself in the House of Lords? Surely when the House were deliberating upon the fees received by such a person, they could not but agree, that it was of the utmost importance that his judgments, and the whole administration of his most important office, should be free from the slightest suspicion of interest; for let men talk as they pleased about the high characters of individuals, there would be suspicions entertained by the people whenever public and private interests seemed to clash together. For that reason, he was of opinion that the Lord Chancellor's salary should be put on the same footing as those paid to the judges of the common law; that was to say, that it should be fixed at a certain sum, and rendered totally independent of fees. By putting it upon that footing, the House would be conferring a benefit upon the Chancellor; since they would prevent him from becoming, night after night, the subject of such discussions as the present.

The Commissioners appointed to examine the duties, salaries, and emoluments of officers in courts of justice, in their First Report, as to the Court of Chancery, dated the 9th of April, 1816, stated it to be an object of national importance, to protect the administration of justice from the imputations cast upon it by the manner in which the Masters in Chancery are paid, and submitted it to the King's consideration, whether the system of fees, as to those officers, should not be assimilated to what has been done in the case of the judges of the courts of common law, and an equivalent provision conferred upon them by other means.

On the 30th of June, 1817, the then Masters addressed a letter to the Chancellor, stating that if the King should think proper to abolish the system of remunerating their services by official fees, and assimilate their situation to that of the judges by granting to them, as a substitute for all fees, such salaries as should be adequate to the dignity and importance of their offices, it would be a change very gratifying to their feelings; and on the 7th of July, 1824, the then Masters addressed a letter to the Chancery Commissioners, stating that they adhered to the sentiments expressed in the former letter, and that such for more than seven years had been, and still was the wish of all the Masters, and they expressed their hope that the Commissioners would approve of and recommend that long-desired improvement.

The Chancery Commissioners were of opinion that it was expedient that the Masters should be in future paid partly by salaries and partly by fees, and that when experience should have ascertained the average annual amount of the fees to be retained by the Master, under the new system of practice, they should receive such addition, in the way of salary, as with those fees would make up a sum equal, upon the whole, to their present average emoluments.

The Select Committee appointed by the House of Commons to consider on the Bankrupt Laws, by their Second Report, dated in May, 1818, stated there was a necessity for a considerable alteration in the mode of remunerating the services of the Commissioners of Bankrupt. They observed, a fee of twenty shillings is paid to each commissioner for each public and private meeting, which is such an insufficient compensation for the time and attention necessarily occupied, that many meetings are held before the same list of commissioners at the same time. The practice seemed to be highly objectionable, as the commissioners might be imagined to have an interest in finding a person bankrupt, in order to increase the number of fees; and though the Committee were persuaded that this consideration had in no instance influenced the conduct of any commissioner in any London list, yet it was certainly calculated to withdraw from the board that respect, on the part of individuals, which was important to the public interest; and for the same reason, the Committee felt it to be highly indelicate, that gentlemen who sit as judges should personally receive fees in open Court for the administration of justice, and in circumstances which not unfrequently rendered some degree of vigilance necessary, in order to secure the payment of their own fees; while, at other times, their right, and the means of payment, became subjects of dispute: circumstances like these must be equally offensive to the feelings of the commissioners, and derogatory to the character which their Court ought to maintain.*

* The following passage, from the evidence of Mr. Montague, given before the Select Committee, containing similar sentiments to those found in the Report, is not (considering the quarter from which it comes) entitled to have less weight with the public.

"It appears to me also, that the mode of payment of commissioners is deserving of consideration. At present, in the finding of a bankruptcy, the commissioners have always an interest in declaring that the person is a bankrupt;† and it is to be

† The bankrupt system, even in the most minute parts, is framed on an erroneous principle. It seems to have been assumed, that the commissioners will not be affected by the same motives that influence the conduct of most other men, that a commission under the Great Seal can confer moral virtues as well as judicial authority, and that those to whom it is addressed are immediately endued with an integrity and disinterestedness unknown in them before.

On the 15th March, 1826, *Sir Robert Wilson* moved, that there should be laid before the House an account of all Tavern Expenses incurred by Commissioners of Bankrupt, executed in the country, for the last three years.

Mr. Abercromby reprobated the wanton accumulation of expense which these illegal indulgences of the commissioners occasioned. He held in his hand the Bill of Costs of a Bankrupt Commission, in which there were dinner bills to

On the 28th May, 1818, a motion was made in pursuance of the recommendations contained in

remembered, that this declaration is at a private meeting, when all the proceedings are *ex parte*. I do not mean to say that this motive warps the minds of gentlemen who act as commissioners, but I submit it to be deserving consideration, whether the legislature should suffer any judge to be placed in a situation where, by possibility, he may be so influenced. It appears to me also, that the payment is objectionable, from its appearing to be wrong; it is by payment in Court to the judge, as if he were a counsel. I have repeatedly seen, what I have felt to be very painful, altercations by whom the fees should be paid to the commissioners; and I once heard commissioners refuse to proceed until their fees were paid."*

the amount of £47. Now this was a serious abuse. He was aware that if the commissioners participated in the abuse, they were disqualified from acting; but what he complained of was this, that the commissioners themselves were made judges of their own conduct, for the bills of costs in which these expenses were charged, were positively taxed before the commissioners. So much for the legal redress. The whole amount of costs in the commission to which he alluded, was £2,000.

* In two debates respecting the Court of Chancery, last year, *Mr. D. W. Harvey* is reported to have said, he was sure that if the Right Honourable Secretary opposite, whose exertions to amend the Criminal Law had earned for him the applause of the country, would walk into the Court adjoining Guildhall, and see how the Commissioners of Bankrupts were paid—if he could witness the disgraceful scenes of quarrelling, haggling, and contention, between those commissioners and the solicitors who tendered their one pound notes, he was sure that a scene so indecent and improper would call for the right honourable gentleman's immediate interposition. These commissioners were not paid, as they ought to be, by permanent and adequate salaries, but by fees, arising from their ingenuity in making out business for themselves, to the injury of the bankrupt's creditors. The manner in which they ran after their fees—the impatience with which they looked at their watches, to provide against their staying longer than their two hours—and the anxiety with which they sought to pocket another guinea, by devising another meeting in Quality Court, was one of the most disgusting scenes that any professional man could witness.

The writer, for several reasons, with which it is unnecessary to trouble the public, has always declined appearing as counsel before the tribunal of the commissioners, and, in consequence, cannot judge of the fidelity of the above descripthe above-mentioned Report, that the House should resolve itself into a Committee of the whole House, to consider of granting salaries to Commissioners of Bankrupts, in lieu of fees, and of defraying the expense of purchasing or erecting a suitable building for the meetings of the said Commissioners; and *Mr. William Dundas*, by command of the *Prince Regent*, acquainted the House that His Royal Highness, having been informed of the subject-matter of the motion, recommended it to the consideration of the House.

On the 1st of June, 1818, *Mr. Thomas Courtenay* reported from such Committee of the whole House, the Resolutions which they had directed him to report to the House, and the same were read and agreed to by the House, and were as follows:

1st. Resolved, that provision be made out of the Consolidated Fund of the United Kingdom of Great Britain and Ireland, for defraying the Salaries of the Commissioners of Bankrupts, in lieu of Fees.

2d. Resolved, that the Lords Commissioners of His Majesty's Treasury, of the United Kingdom of Great Britain and Ireland, be authorized to issue out of the consolidated fund of the said United Kingdom, any sum not exceeding £30,000, for providing a suitable Building for holding the

tion. For the honour of the judicial character, he hopes, that indignation at the gross defects existing in the administration of the Bankrupt Laws has caused Mr. Harvey to give deeper colours to the picture, than he would have chosen to use in a more calm and dispassionate moment.

public and private meetings of the Commissioners of Bankrupts, and for the transaction of all business in Bankruptcy.

The House thereupon ordered that it should be an instruction to the gentlemen appointed to prepare and bring in a Bill to alter and amend the laws relating to Bankrupts, that they should make provision therein pursuant to the said Resolutions. A Bill was afterwards brought in and read a first and second time, and committed; great discussions took place in the Committee, on the provisions of the Bill, but on its being reported, with considerable amendments, it was ordered, on the 2d of June, that the Report should be taken into further consideration that day three months.*

* See Journals of the House of Commons, vol. 73.

CHAPTER III.

THE COURT OF CHANCERY FROM THE PASSING OF THE VICE CHANCELLOR'S BILL, IN 1813, TO THE ISSUING OF THE CHANCERY COMMISSION.

PARLIAMENTARY DEBATES.

Mr. Taylor.—Sir Robert Gifford.—Mr. John Williams.—Sir J. S. Copley.—Mr. Peel.—Mr. Canning.

1819.

On the 20th of May, 1819, *Mr. Taylor* moved, that the House should resolve itself into a committee of the whole house, to take into their consideration so much of the statute of 13th Eliz. c. 7. as gives jurisdiction in matters of bankruptcy to the Lord High Chancellor, Lord Keeper of the great seal of England, &c.

The *Solicitor General (Sir Robert Gifford)* opposed the motion, on the ground of there being no arrear of business in the Court of Chancery; that so far from causes being set down two years before they were heard, those then remaining to be heard had been all set down in the last term. He said he was surprised to hear it stated, that questions of Bankruptcy were not in their nature questions for an equitable jurisdiction. Courts of law often decided questions of fact in the course of a bankruptcy case, but the general merits fell peculiarly within the province of courts of equity; nor did he believe any man, whatever might be his learning and ability, qualified to decide them, unless conversant both with the principles and practice of those courts.—The House divided,—ayes 49, noes 151.

1821.

On the 30th of May, 1821, *Mr. Taylor* moved that a resolution should be passed, that the House would, early in the next session of Parliament, take into its most serious consideration the state of the High Court of Chancery of England, as well as that of the appellant jurisdiction of the House of Lords, with a view to the adoption of such measures as would tend in future to facilitate the general business of those courts.

Lord Londonderry moved the previous question. The House divided—ayes 52, noes 56.—Majority against Mr. Taylor's motion 4.

1822.

On the 26th of June, 1822, *Mr. Taylor* moved that the House should resolve itself into a Committee of the whole House, to consider of the act of the 53 Geo. III. cap. 24.

The *Attorney General (Sir Robert Gifford)* in

the course of the debate observed—In estimating the quantity of business got through by the Lord Chancellor, the House ought to look at the number of motions taken before that learned judge. Each motion, in many cases, amounted to the hearing of a cause. Appeals very frequently were taken in the shape of motions. A cause having been decided by the Vice Chancellor, the Lord Chancellor was moved to stay proceedings under the decree, and upon the motion the whole question of appeal was gone into.—The House divided—ayes 51, noes 108.

1823.

On the 4th June, 1823, Mr. *John Williams* moved that a select Committee should be appointed to inquire into the arrear of business in the Court of Chancery, and the appellate jurisdiction of the House of Lords, and the causes thereof.

The *Attorney General* (*Sir Robert Gifford*) opposed the motion, on the ground that there were no arrears of business in the Court of Chancery: the causes had not been set down for more than two terms. The debate was adjourned to the 5th of June, and was further adjourned to the 6th of June.

The *Solicitor General* (*Sir J. S. Copley,*) stated, in like manner with the Attorney General, that there were no arrears in any branch of the Court.

The House divided—ayes 89, noes 174. Majority against the motion 85.

1824.

On the 24th February, 1824, *Mr. John Williams moved,* that a Committee should be appointed to inquire into the delays and expenses in the Court of Chancery, and the causes thereof.

Mr. Peel observed during the course of the debate, he did not mean to deny that great delay had taken place in the discharge of business, and that great hardship was the consequence. He readily admitted, in answer to the first question put by the Honourable and Learned Gentleman, that the delays that had taken place were attended with many grievances; he admitted the fact, although it would seem that the Honourable and Learned Gentleman expected a different reply. He admitted the fact without hesitation, because, as he contended, it went to prove that the delay, which was not denied, was not to be imputed to the Lord Chancellor, or to any individual, as matter of crimination. He could adduce for it other causes, which would demonstrate to honourable gentlemen, if they would give him their attention but for a very short time, that the delay was to be attributed to an increase of business in the Court of Chancery, with which, under present circumstances, no intellectual and no physical strength could entirely cope. Let honourable gentlemen look at the attendance of the Lord Chancellor in the House of Lords. On this point he would cite two cases only, the Berkeley and the Roxburgh Peerages. What was the nature of the Noble and Learned Lord's attendance in the Berkeley case? The Committee of Privileges in the House of Lords sat, in one year, upon the Berkeley case, for sometime, from ten o'clock till four every day. The number of days upon which, in that single case, the Noble and Learned Lord was called on to attend was thirty-four. The Roxburgh case required the same Noble Individual thirty-six days attendance for the hearing, the matter lasting forty-four days altogether. So that two cases alone called for the Lord Chancellor's attendance on no less than seventy days. What he had now stated appeared to him to amount to a complete vindication of the Lord Chancellor, as far as related to the question of delay on his part, and to demonstrate that such was the state of business in the Court of Chancery that it was impossible for abilities however great, or a constitution however strong, to bear the fatigues which the country imposed upon the individual who presided over it, (*hear.*) He was proceeding step by step, and was always glad, in the course of an argument, to hear how far those to whom he might happen to be opposed concurred with him, and he therefore hailed the cheers that proceeded from the other side with pleasure. If

Gentlemen on the opposite side would admit, that what he had stated was a complete vindication of the Noble and Learned Judge, he would admit to them that they had made out a case of complete justification for inquiry and consideration in respect to his court. It was quite impossible for him to deny, upon a review of all that had been said, as to the constitution, the proceedings, and the delays of the Court of Chancery, that the time was now come when the whole of these matters should be thoroughly inquired into. Now, having stated thus much, he was further prepared to say, that his Noble and Learned friend (Lord Eldon) had himself recommended the adoption of some alterations. That Noble and Learned Lord had advised, that a Commission from the Crown, under the great seal, should issue for the purpose of considering and inquiring into the present condition of many important matters connected with the Court of Chancery; that it should examine into the state of its jurisdiction, and into many of the points to which the proposed Committee of the Honourable and Learned Gentleman was to address itself: indeed, into all of those, with one exception only—that was the political powers and the political character of the Lord Chancellor, a point which he (Mr. Peel) considered to be a great one, and such as neither the Honourable and Learned Gentleman's Committee, nor the Commission that had been just adverted to, was properly competent to discuss. Sure he was, however, that the Honourable and Learned Member would agree with him, that to divest the Lord Chancellor of the political duties of his office would be to do an act that ought not to be determined upon except upon the gravest and most careful deliberation. But the Honourable and Learned Gentleman proposed that a Committee should inquire into the expenses of the Court of Chancery, and into its delays and the causes thereof, and he had no hesitation in saying, that he believed very great benefit might be derived from such inquiry. He (Mr. Peel) himself had frequently been the occasion of withdrawing the Lord Chancellor from the court over which he presided, to attend to the Recorder's report, on which it was the duty of the Lord Chancellor to give his advice to his Majesty. The Noble and Learned Lord was in this manner very frequently withdrawn from the contemplation of equity causes, to the consideration of those cases in which was involved the question of life or death. It had fallen to his lot to send to the Lord Chancellor, at the rising of his court, to inform him that on the ensuing morning his Majesty would receive the Recorder's report, containing probably forty or fifty cases. On proceeding from the Court of Chancery, the Noble and Learned Lord would, as was his uniform practice on such occasion, apply himself to the reading of every individual case, and abstract notes from all of them; and he (Mr. Peel) had known more than one instance in which he had commenced this labour in the evening, and had been found pursuing it at the rising of the next sun. Thus, after having spent eight hours in the Court of Chancery, the Noble and Learned Lord often employed twelve or fourteen more in the consideration of cases which involved the life or death of the unhappy culprits.*

* The Constitution, and, as I presume, the ancient Charters of the City of London, having imposed this painful duty upon the Chancellor, there is none to which he ought to devote so much attention and deliberation. It may be permitted, however, to inquire upon what consistent or rational principle of criminal jurisprudence a malefactor, convicted of a capital offence committed in the City of London, is entitled to have his case considered by his Majesty in Council, whilst those found guilty of similar crimes in most other parts of the kingdom are executed without any further formality than a note, not undersigned, written by the Judge in the margin of the Calendar, before he leaves the town where the assizes are held. Let it not, however, be imagined I would deprive the above class of condemned criminals of the privilege of having their cases brought under the eye of their king; I would rather give a similar benefit to all others in the same unhappy situation: but I would not make it the peculiar office of the Chancellor to advise his Majesty upon so anxious and melancholy a subject, unless his other functions were diminished. Who but Lord Eldon could do justice to the forty or fifty unhappy beings whose life or death depended upon his report, if his avocations were such that he could find no other time but one sleepless night to devote to the consideration of the offences for which they were doomed to die, and their numerous circumstances either of aggravation or excuse?

Mr. Canning said, as the speeches of two of the honourable and learned members, who had followed his right honourable colleague the Secretary for the Home Department, appeared to turn almost entirely upon the effectiveness and sincerity of the proposed Commission, he thought that it would be satisfactory not only to the House, but also to the country at large, to have an assurance, not only on the part of the Noble Lord, who was thought to be most interested in this question, but also on the part of others of His Majesty's Ministers,—an assurance which, for his own part, he most willingly gave, that the inquiry into which that Commission was to enter should be as sincere, as impartial, and as effectual as it was possible for man to make it. Even if any disposition existed to trifle with so important a subject, honourable gentlemen must be aware, that no Government, in the present enlightened state of the age, could, after consenting to institute an inquiry, conduct it in such a manner as to prevent it from arriving at a salutary and beneficial result. He could never wish to see the legal and political character of the Lord Chancellor of England made distinct and separate, considering, as he did, that in the appointment to that high office, one of the proudest distinctions of the British Monarchy had long existed. He thought that it was one of the noblest and most valuable prerogatives of the Crown of England, that it could take from the walks of Westminster Hall the meanest individual, and when he used the word meanest, he used it not with reference to talents and intellectual endowments, but to birth and original station in society, and place him, at once, in the head and front of the Peerage of England; and he never wished to see the day when the Crown was deprived of that beautiful prerogative, which, though it formed the very essence of the Monarchy, was, at the same time, the surest support and bulwark of the democratic part of the Constitution. When the advocates for their separation told him that they saw a great objection to the making a political character a judge, he was inclined to ask them, what the situation of the country would be, supposing that there were placed at the head of the hereditary magistracy of the land an individual unacquainted with its laws and institutions.

Mr. Williams withdrew his motion, in consequence of the declaration of Ministers of their intention of issuing the Chancery Commission.

CHAP. IV.—PART I.

THE COURT OF CHANCERY FROM THE REPORT OF THE CHANCERY COMMISSIONERS IN MARCH, 1826, TO THE TIME WHEN LORD ELDON RESIGNED THE SEALS.

PARLIAMENTARY DEBATES.

Sir J. S. Copley.—Mr. Peel.—Dr. Lushington.—Mr. Taylor.—Mr. D. W. Harvey.

THE Chancery Commissioners made their Report in March, 1826.

On the 18th of May, 1826, the Attorney General (*Sir J. S. Copley*) moved, that leave should be given to bring in a Bill to regulate the practice of the Court of Chancery. He observed,* that, ac-

* Sir John Copley, in the course of a very long address, announced the intention of putting an end to a most absurd and inconvenient practice prevailing in the Court, by which the senior Barristers are entitled to make all their motions at once, so that it rarely happens that a junior Counsel can make a motion. He said it was proposed to introduce the same regulation as prevails in the common Law Courts, where no barrister can make more than two motions following, which would give the juniors an opportunity of moving more frequently. Lord Lyndhurst has forgot what Sir John Copley said. As far back as Lord Bacon's time, the illiberality and injustice of this practice was felt. That great man, in his speech on taking his seat in Chancery, is re-

cording to the system as it now existed, a pretty sufficient share of previous study, preparation, and long experience was required in those who were to preside in the Equity Courts of this country, and, under the circumstances of the country, the system of our Equity Law had become so refined, that it depended also very much on decided cases and precedents, and its principles and practice were equally difficult to be mastered with those of the Common Law. He would ask, therefore, whether it was at all probable that the two systems of Equity and Common Law could be properly or beneficially administered by one Court; in fact, had honourable gentlemen no rule to guide their judgments on this question? Indeed, so greatly were the inconveniences of the union of the two jurisdictions felt, that an honourable and learned gentleman, accustomed to vote upon the other side of the House, brought in a Bill to effect their separation for that very reason. The consequence of this proceeding was, as gentlemen

ported to have said, "I know there have used to attend this Bar a number of lawyers that have not been heard sometimes, and scarce once or twice in a term, and that makes the client seek to great counsel and favourites, as they call them, for every order that a mean lawyer might as well dispatch, a term fitter for kings than judges; and, therefore, to help the generality of lawyers, and therein to ease the client, I will constantly observe, that every Tuesday, and other days of orders, after nine o'clock strucken, I will hear the Bar until eleven, or half-an-hour after ten at least."

already knew, that the Equity Jurisdiction of the Exchequer devolved on the Chief Baron entirely, while the Common Law one was administered by the other three Barons.*

Mr. Secretary Peel contended, that the conduct of the Lord Chancellor, in the administration of his Court, was such as to entitle him to lasting honour. When he heard the learned lord blamed for not having made the reforms in his Court which were now recommended, he would say, that nobody would have given his time to such a pursuit more readily than his Lordship, had he had any time to bestow upon it; but absorbed, as he was, in the various duties of his office, he had not the leisure to consider such reforms with the necessary deliberation.

Dr. Lushington, after having expressed the opinion, upon the present mode of administering the Bankrupt Laws, which will be stated in another part of these pages, observed, that upon a review of the whole business done in the Court, it was evident, on the face of the Report, that the delays prevailed to an extent grievous and ruinous to the suitors of the Court. For these delays he saw one only effective and necessary measure, the separa-

* What was said by Lord Lyndhurst, on this occasion, is evidently misreported. The other Barons sit with the Chief Baron to hear motions and pleas, demurrers and exceptions to answers in Equity causes; nay, they occasionally venture to hear, and decide them, too, in his absence.

tion of the political from the judicial character of the Judge presiding in the High Court of Chancery. It was in vain to deny, that his political avocations must be a distraction to him, effectually preventing him from the due and efficient fulfilment of his judicial duties. It was not, perhaps, so much a matter of blame, as it was of excuse, to the Noble Lord, that he had too much to do; that he was obliged, by his political duty, to be in one place, when his judicial duty required of him to be in another; that he was now there, when he ought to be here; that he was one day obliged to attend the presenting of the Recorder's Report, and on another day to attend the Cabinet Council. Again, he was engaged in hearing Appeals before the House of Lords, and these, with a variety of other occupations, allowed him little or no time to attend the efficient discharge of his judicial duties in the Court over which he presided. Amongst other disadvantages of these various avocations to which his Lordship was subjected, the suitors had to experience this material and important one, that the Lord Chancellor could not attend continuously, at any one time, to hear the whole of a case, so as to be able to take a full view of it, and to decide, at the moment that all the arguments on both sides were fresh upon his mind, but by being now called off here, and again called off there, he was only able to collect the case, as it were, by piecemeal, and to decide (when he did decide) upon it, after that disjointed and disconnected hearing of it. These various distractions realized the observation which was so familiar in the House, about ten years ago, in discussions on this question, that on account of the political and judicial functions of the Lord Chancellor interfering with each other, "the judicial year was diminished, not by minutes or hours only, but by days and weeks and months;" so it was now, and would continue to be, until the judicial was separated from the political character of the Lord Chancellor. There had been no former instance of such injury being entailed upon the suitors of the Court of Chancery by the union of the judicial and political character of the Lord Chancellor, and without the separation of which it was idle to expect any effectual reform in the abuses of the Court of Chancery—abuses greater, and more flagrant and enormous than those by which the people of any country had been aggrieved by a tribunal instituted for the purpose of administering equity and justice.

Leave was given to bring in the bill, but none was brought in during the Session of Parliament.*

* I have not noticed any of the debates which are not to be found in Hansard. I cannot, however, forbear to mention, that on the 7th of December, 1826, Mr. Spence moved for certain returns of equity business, and that he prefaced his motion by the

1827.

On the 27th of February, 1827, Mr. *Taylor*, being called upon by the Speaker to make his motion on the subject of separating the jurisdiction in matters of bankruptcy from the Court of Chancery, stated he withdrew it in consequence of the Master of the Rolls having expressed his intention of presenting to the House that night his bill for the improvement of the administration of justice in the Court of Chancery.

The *Master of the Rolls (Sir J. S. Copley)* observed, that when he had last addressed the House on the subject, he had said that there was no growing arrear of business. He had admitted that there was at that time an arrear of two years, which had arisen from a variety of causes. One of these was the illness of Sir Thomas Plomer; and the illness of the Vice-Chancellor *(Sir John Leach)* had also contributed much towards it. He knew, however, that there had been no increase for the last four or five years; and it followed that from the increased facilities which it was proposed to provide, that arrear of which they had so long heard complaints would be

declaration of his conviction that the number of judges was not sufficient for the due dispatch of the business of the Court of Chancery. Considering Mr. Spence's experience in the Court of Chancery, this expression of his sentiments is entitled to great weight.

speedily got rid of.* The House would not expect him to state what was the form of legislation proposed upon the one hundred and eighty-eight propositions of the Chancery Commissioners, to many of which it was right the House should know, that the Lord Chancellor might have given the force of the law by his mere fiat,† [cries of "hear" from the opposition benches] and many of them must have had the sanction of Parliament before they could have had that force. Some honourable gentlemen opposite had cheered, when

* If any decrease in the arrears of business had taken place, if the causes now come on to be heard in a quicker succession than during the chancellorship of Lord Eldon, I believe the public would be unwilling not to ascribe so gratifying a change to Lord Lyndhurst, although from what Sir John Copley is here reported to have said, it would have originated with Lord Eldon.

† Whatever may be said to the contrary, such still are, or a few days since were, the sentiments of Lord Lyndhurst. The Orders which he is about to promulgate, have been framed (as he states) by the present Lord Chancellor of Ireland, and the Master of the Rolls, and Vice-Chancellor, and revised by himself. To the first and second series he can give the force of law by his own fiat. The last series he announces must be made effectual by a legislative enactment. His Lordship is reported to have said the forthcoming Orders had been approved of by the bar. I presume this to be a mistake, as I believe no King's counsel practising in the Court of Chancery has been yet favoured with a sight of them. One or two King's counsel have, indeed, very recently had the honour to receive a communication from Lord Lyndhurst, on the subject of the Orders, but not until everybody knew they were in the hands of the printer.

he said that the fiat of the Lord Chancellor could have given to many of these propositions the force of law; but he had to inform the House, that though the Lord Chancellor might have done this, it had been considered that it would have been unwise if he had done so. It was certainly better to call in the authority of Parliament for the whole.

There was another subject of great and paramount importance connected with this subject,—he meant the jurisdiction in bankruptcy cases. Feeling as he did how deeply it affected the interest of the commercial portion of the community, he had maturely considered it, and had consulted others upon it; and the result of his own deliberation and that of others was, that it would not be advisable to adopt the recommendation of the Commissioners as part of the bill he proposed, and that it ought not to be blended with any other matter whatever, it ought to be well and maturely considered by itself; and if the House would go with him, *he would pledge himself to bring in a separate measure*, when it might have the full consideration of the House, in as deliberate a manner as it was entitled to.—(Hear, hear.) Did the House go with him? Were they persuaded that the regulation of the Court of Chancery was enough for one bill? It should be understood, that the Lord Chancellor did not sit as Chancellor in bankruptcy, but as Keeper of the Great Seal, holding a special jurisdiction delegated to him by various acts of parliament; that he did not decide upon bill and answer, but upon petitions presented to him in the way pointed out by those acts. Being, therefore, entirely separate, it was not necessary —it was not, he thought, even expedient, that on this occasion it should be included in the proposed bill; and he *pledged himself, if it should be allowed to pass over now, to bring it forward without delay, in such a shape as must ensure its full consideration and decision.* The Right Honourable and Learned Gentleman then coucluded by moving, "That leave be given to bring in a bill for the improvement of the administration of justice in the Court of Chancery."

Mr. M. A. Taylor said, the Lord Chancellor, after refusing and neglecting for so many years to do anything towards the redress of the grievances which were everywhere complained of, could no longer prevent the appointment of the Chancery Commission. He was inclined to believe, that the Commissioners had never intended to do much; and the little they had intended to do they had been frightened out of.*

* The Commissioners, for reasons sufficiently known, could effect no more than they have done. Their Report contains a mass of valuable information as to the practice of the Court, and the mode in which different parts of it may be improved; and it is probable many of the suggestions it contains will before long be carried into effect. The profession give Sir John Leach the credit of having originated the most important of the propositions.

He was sure the measure proposed would not expedite the business of the Court of Chancery. A variety of expedients had been resorted to, but all of them rather for the purpose of keeping off the reform which was sought than of effecting it.*

Mr. Peel said, it was impossible for him or for any other man to deny that the system of the Court of Chancery presented great impediments to the administration of justice, and entailed a grievous expense upon the suitors. He had proposed the commission with a full sense of those evils, and from a conviction that a commission so constituted could devise the most effectual means of relief. He was not one of those who thought the Lord Chancellor—the first lawyer in the kingdom—ought to be excluded from all connection with the cabinet. He did not think that the first law officer in the realm should be precluded from giving his opinion upon those cases of criminal law which came before the government, and if there were any who thought that the Lord Chancellor had not done enough in his six hours a day, let them recollect the various other avocations which required a share of his attention.

Leave was given to bring in the bill. It was brought in and referred to a Committee, and afterwards reported to the House.

On the 23d of March, 1827, the Master of the

* See Part II. of this Chapter.

Rolls *(Sir J. S. Copley)* moved the further consideration of the report of his bill for improving the administration of justice in the Court of Chancery, when *Mr. Abercromby* said, he hoped the honourable and learned gentleman would not press the proceedings on the bill in the absence of so many honourable and learned gentlemen, then on the circuit, who had taken a deep interest in the measure, and who were best qualified to judge of its practical effects.

The *Master of the Rolls* said, he would postpone the further consideration of his bill to an early day after the recess; but he hoped that when it was brought forward, every facility would be given to its progress, lest, if it should be brought into the other House at a late period of the session, that circumstance should afford the means of completely frustrating the measure. He feared there might be found those who were not very cordial supporters of the bill; and it might be alleged that a measure of such vital importance should not be brought before the legislature, at a period when there was not a sufficient opportunity for its due consideration. The right honourable gentleman concluded by postponing his motion to the 4th May.

On the 5th of April, 1827, Mr. *D. W. Harvey* moved, that there should be laid before the House certain Returns of Equity business.

In the course of the debate, *Mr. Peel* said, the honourable member (*Mr. Harvey*) in his speech had stated, that his object was to separate all political functions and feelings from the duties of a Lord Chancellor. This might be a very legitimate and proper object—whether an active partisan and political functionary ought to hold the Great Seals was a constitutional question, which certainly ought not to be discussed upon the present occasion.

The House divided:—ayes, 66, noes, 132; majority against the motion, 66.

CHAP. IV.—PART II.

IT IS NOT POSSIBLE FOR NEW ORDERS TO REMEDY THE GREAT DELAY THAT OCCURS IN SOME BRANCHES OF THE COURT, BETWEEN THE SETTING DOWN AND THE HEARING OF CAUSES.

GREAT fears may reasonably be entertained lest the forthcoming Orders should deserve to be characterised in the same way as the Chancery Commission, and the other expedients alluded to by Mr. Taylor in the preceding debate.

At present, years pass away, during which causes in their different stages remain on the list awaiting their turn to be heard, the Court being so overloaded with business that it is impossible that they should be heard at an earlier period. *

* The evidence of Mr. Bickersteth before the Chancery Commissioners upon this subject is deserving of notice. He states, that in many cases the delay which happens between the setting down of the cause and the hearing exceeds the amount of all the other unnecessary delays put together, and it is a delay of which the suitors and the public have great reason to complain. When a cause is prepared for a hearing and set down for that purpose, he conceives the suitors are then making a direct demand upon the Court for justice, and that every unnecessary delay which afterwards takes place, and which is not occasioned by the parties themselves, is a violation of the laws, which forbid the delay of justice.

Orders of the Lord Chancellor, founded on some of the most useful propositions contained in the report of the Chancery Commissioners, may expedite the cause prior to its being set down to be heard, or when it is in the Master's office, or may retrench some useless expense, but they cannot advance the causes one day when they are once set down to be heard. Such orders, by hastening the time of the original hearing and the hearing on further directions, would rather aggravate than diminish the present grievance, as the causes must remain on the list during a longer period before they could be heard. * It would be absurd to retrench a few weeks in the intermediate stages of a cause, by new modelling certain parts of the practice, when, by the inadequacy of the Court, as at present constituted, to dispatch the business that comes before it, years must pass away during which the causes slumber on the lists for hearing. It would be a mockery to tell the

* It is also not unworthy of remark, that new Orders, however skilfully and carefully drawn will probably give rise to numerous applications to the court as to their meaning and effect. The practice will become unsettled, and a considerable time will elapse before it can be fixed again. Besides, every question upon the new procedure must be resolved by the Chancellor himself, which Lord Lyndhurst, knowing nothing of the details of equity practice, will, notwithstanding his great quickness, find no easy task. The expediency of producing new Orders at the present moment appears to me, much as I desire to see the Court effectually reformed in all its parts, very doubtful.

suitor thus deprived for years of perhaps his only means of subsistence, that orders regulating the practice have passed the Great Seal, which will save him a few miserable shillings. When the causes are once ready to be heard, they should be heard and decided within such a period of time as is consistent with a good administration of justice. It is obvious from these pages that this can only be attained by appointing an additional judge, and that the separation of the business in bankruptcy from the Great Seal would not alone suffice.

CHAP. V.—PART I.

THE COURT OF CHANCERY DURING THE CHANCELLORSHIP OF LORD LYNDHURST.

PARLIAMENTARY DEBATES.

Mr. Taylor.—Sir James Scarlet.—Mr. D. W. Harvey.—Dr. Lushington.—Mr. Brougham.

1827.

LORD Lyndhurst became Chancellor in April, 1827.

On the 22nd of May, 1827, *Mr. M. A. Taylor* moved, that the House should resolve itself into a Committee of the whole House to consider of the statute of the 13th of Elizabeth, and such subsequent statutes as give to the Lord High Chancellor of England jurisdiction in matters of bankruptcy.

The *Attorney General* (*Sir James Scarlet*) said, he should proceed to state a few facts from which he would deduce this inference, that, with three efficient judges (and such they had,) there was not the least necessity for subtracting from the Court of Chancery any part of the jurisdiction which it possessed, nor would the public have any cause to complain, that the bankruptcy cases were not separated from the Great Seal. He did not mean to say that if the legislature chose to disjoin these powers, no person could be found adequate to the fair adjudication of bankruptcy cases. He entertained no superstitious fear that they could not find an individual calculated to perform the functions of a separate judge in those cases; but before they adopted such a course of policy, he thought it was necessary that its expediency should be established. The question was whether it was necessary when they had three judges (of one of whom they had had full experience, and with respect to two of them they had no reason to despair,) to re-model the Court of Chancery, and to place additional burdens on the public? In his opinion the judges whom they had at present, were more than equal to do the whole business of Chancery. He admitted that the Lord Chancellor had to attend to the lunatic petitions and to appeals in the House of Lords. But with respect to lunatic petitions, if they would look even to those which found their way on the papers, they would not amount to more than ten or a dozen in the year. The *quantum* of labour was not so very considerable, and a Chancellor, with the benefit of youth, health and activity, would be able to accomplish all that his office required. It was in the contemplation of the present Lord Chancellor, assisted as he was by the experience of those gentlemen who practised in his court, to *apply himself to the introduction of some mode by which the voluminous proceedings in cases of bankruptcy might be abridged. Such a plan would be attended with the best effects; for at present those proceedings were extended to a length hardly conceivable. Let this experiment, then, be tried, before they proceeded to a new field, before they attempted to re-model the whole form of the Court of Chancery. He was happy to state that such a plan as he had adverted to was in contemplation, and he felt most confidently that it would succeed.* His honourable and learned friend had asked what had become of the bill, which the present Lord Chancellor had introduced, founded on the report of the Chancery Commissioners? He begged to remind his honourable and learned friend, that the bill was not brought in during the last, but in the present session, when the Lord Chancellor held the situation of Master of the Rolls. That learned Lord gave notice of his intention to bring in a bill, and he introduced it with an elaborate speech. Now, if the House would permit him, he would state, that in his opinion, the bill in question would always disappoint the public. He did not disagree with the Commisioners on any material points, and he approved of many of their suggestions, though not of all; but he certainly felt, that, to make those suggestions the subject of a cumbersome bill in parliament, was a proceeding not only useless in itself, but one that would disappoint the public. The present Lord Chancellor, who was the organ of the Commissioners, felt, he knew, as he (the Attorney General) felt on that question. The present Lord Chancellor was of opinion, and it was his opinion also, that the specific points of improvement, noticed in the report of the Commissioners, did not require any act of parliament for carrying them into effect,* but might be made by the authority of the Lord Chancellor, in his own court. He knew nothing further about the bill. He was not aware that the learned Lord who introduced it had requested any other individual to take it up. He put it to his honourable and learned friend, whether, under the present circumstances of the government and the country, to which he would not allude more particularly, it would not be more decorous to pause before he called upon the House to take this matter, important as it was, out of the hands of his Majesty's government. He owned that the motion of his honourable and learned friend would appear to him, even though he were to approve of it much more than he did at present, to be premature and uncalled for, under existing circumstances. He felt no alarm lest the duties of the Court of Chancery should be found too great for the performance of the head of the Court, and the

* Lord Lyndhurst, as it is before stated, considers the sanction of the legislature will be requisite for the last series of his intended Orders.

two learned judges by whom he was assisted. He was also of opinion, when they had infused fresh vigour into that Court, and had introduced more celerity into its proceedings, the business of it would be performed, not only by three angels but by three men of ordinary talent and industry.

Mr. D. W. Harvey said, it would appear, from what had fallen from His Majesty's Attorney General, that, in the ensuing recess, the noble Lord, who was now at the head of the Court of Chancery, was to concoct a small neat system, which was to put an end to the ruinous expense complained of; and was to devise some intelligible code of official arrangement, by which all the clamours of the country were to be stilled. The judge was to be changed, but the practice of his Court was to remain almost unaltered, and all the splendid denunciations, which had thrilled through every bosom in that House and in the country, were only to be considered as party tactics, and to be looked upon as the result of disappointed ambition. Now that the object of professional advancement was obtained, those who had been most loud in their attacks had become the eulogists of the late Lord Chancellor's merits. And the House was now told, that if, in the vehemence of debate, any thing had been said which was calculated to injure his character, it amounted to nothing, and was only to be considered as the accidental effusion of party spirit.

Suitors were now to be satisfied that the Court would in future move on with the utmost celerity and harmony, that they would no longer have their hopes withered, their prospects blasted, and their comforts destroyed, by the delays and expenses. A greater insult than such a declaration could not easily be imagined. The abuses of the Court of Chancery still reigned in all their pristine deformity. It was a mockery to the House and to the country, to say that this branch of the law was as it ought to be, and that a few petty regulations were all that was wanted to make causes be dispatched with promptitude and justice. If the administration thought that the country was to be so deluded, they were deluding themselves, and would discover their error when, perhaps, it was too late. Though there were some questions which might be deferred without injury to the public interests, the present question was not one. It was his opinion, that, if the new administration had not been formed, the bill which the present Lord Chancellor had introduced into that House for the Improvement of the Court of Chancery would have been carried by acclamation. But now that it was formed, Parliament was told that it was an useless measure, that scarcely one of its provisions were advantageous; that the one hundred and eighty-eight propositions of the Report, which had one hundred and eighty-eight eulogists, were to be abandoned; and that all that was necessary to simplify the Court of Chancery was, for the Lord Chancellor to make certain regulations, under which all expenses and delays were to cease.

Dr. Lushington said he perfectly agreed with those who thought the question ought to undergo complete revision, who thought that the property of the subject was wasted by the expensive nature of the processes of the Court, who thought the delays of the Court of Chancery equally unnecessary and indefensible. The bill which was brought in by Lord Lyndhurst had been since abandoned, and they had been told to wait until they could see what his Lordship and his two coadjutors could do, by the force of their own regulations. He was ready to give Lord Lyndhurst every confidence, but he must doubt whether any exertions which the noble Lord might make, notwithstanding his advantages of being earlier in life, and more bold and fearless in disposition, than his predecessor, could ever reduce the business of the Court of Chancery within those limits of dispatch and accuracy which were requisite to do justice between all parties. He was of opinion, that much more must be done than his honourable and learned friend, the Attorney General, seemed to anticipate. He was ready to wait until the next session of Parliament; but when it came it would be necessary to lay on the table of the House forthwith plans to alter the law of the

Court of Equity, and also the law of real property; and when those objects were attained by legal enactments, he entertained hopes, though he had also doubts, that the three judges would dispatch their business with all requisite celerity. One thing above all others he deprecated—he deprecated any attempt to diminish with undue celerity the present number of arrears. He did not say that Lord Lyndhurst would pursue that course of proceeding;—but he hoped that nothing would be said in that House which would lead to an expectation that his Lordship would do more than any man could do, for if any such expectations were raised, it would be equally inconvenient to the public and to the noble Lord. Let the noble Lord proceed steadily in his course, and if he should happen to find that the mass of the arrears was too great for him to put down, let him not be ashamed to confess it. He should conclude by stating, that he should always support any measure that tended to reform our jurisprudence, and that he conceived to be productive of public advantage. He was convinced, that every branch of our law required to be investigated, and that alterations might be made in most of them, which would tend greatly to the public benefit.

Mr. Brougham said he begged to remind the House, (for he was on his defence, and called on to prove the consistency of his opinions,) that the

Vice Chancellor's Court had not had fair play. Instead of having an efficient Chancellor, Vice Chancellor, and Master of the Rolls, there had always been either an unfit Vice Chancellor, or an unfit Master of the Rolls, which left the Court in the same situation as before the Vice Chancellor's bill passed. His (Mr. Brougham's) argument was this—" Do not tell me the system is in fault, when the men are in fault; give the bill fair play, and then consider of further alterations." He said, on the present question, they had, in the first place, one of the most efficient Equity judges who had ever sat in the Court, the present Master of the Rolls. Of this individual he would only say, that what had been said that night, and upon previous occasions in his praise, was quite inadequate to do justice to his talents. There was no man who had witnessed his conduct in his arduous and difficult, in some respects unpleasant, situation, who was not satisfied, who was not impressed with wonder, and in some cases with unbelief, when it was known what struggles he was making with a severe and distressing complaint. That conduct had excited the highest respect. Here, then, was as efficient and as proper a Master of the Rolls as could be required. Of Sir Anthony Hart—and he spoke in the hearing of his friends—he would say, that he had been one of the oldest and most experienced practitioners in the Court of Chancery.

To the extent of his professional knowledge, he could not speak; but he was admirably calculated to get through business, which would compensate for other qualities in which he might be deficient. Here, then, was another good Equity judge. Did any one doubt that the present Lord Chancellor, though not educated in the Equity Courts, was a man of great legal talents, and of a strong, manly, and independent mind? He possessed a remarkable power of simplifying and dealing with the most complicated questions. It was the remark of those who had the greatest experience in Westminster Hall, that no man knew so well how to split the nut, throw away the husk, and get at the kernel.* He would undertake to say, that what was predicated of the Lord Chancellor was that he was a man qualified for reforming the Court, and anxious to save its time; it was the general opinion that he excelled in this, and that he would make up for that defect in his education, in not being brought up in a Court of Equity, which was not his fault, but his misfor-

* No judge ever sat on the bench superior to Lord Lyndhurst in this important judicial quality. Lord Lyndhurst has shown so much urbanity and attention to the bar, that I do not believe (although he may have many public opponents) he has a single personal enemy amongst the gentlemen practising in his Court. If, however, he had a thousand enemies, not one could venture to deny the justness of this praise.

tune. That he would in a short time make up for that defect, he entertained a most sanguine expectation. This was a ground of his confidence in the present arrangements. But he did not therefore say, "attach the bankruptcy to the Great Seal for ever—marry them—link them eternally"—but he said wait a year; give time to the Court of Chancery, which now had three and not two judges, for the introduction of practical and effectual reforms. Then, he said, leave the Lord Chancellor to make these experiments. The noble Lord thought he could do something with the aid of his two efficient coadjutors. Let the House wait and see what effect their united endeavours would produce.* They had now *judices a judicando*, not *judices a non judicando;* they could now try the experiment in the Court of Chancery, where there were not two judges, but three; but it should be fairly tried, and if, at the end of a year, the case should appear hopeless, then he would admit, that the bankruptcy experiment should be adopted, and he would support a proposition, which he now deemed mischievous, or at least premature. This was his opinion; and he believed it was consonant with the opinion of the Lord Chancellor. *That noble and learned Lord was of opinion, that if, after trial, it*

* See Part II. of this Chapter.

should be found that the three judges did not (it would be because they could not) get through the business of the Court, he would have no objection to sever the bankruptcy from the Great Seal.

The House divided: for the motion 37, against it 134; majority 97.

CHAP. V.—PART II.

SOME REMARKS ON THE RETURNS LATELY MADE TO THE HOUSE OF COMMONS RELATIVE TO THE CHANCERY AND BANKRUPTCY BUSINESS.

THE year of trial alluded to in the preceding debate has nearly elapsed, and the Returns of business depending in the Court, lately moved for by the Solicitor General, show that the fair expectations that appear to have been entertained must be disappointed.

It appears from these returns, that, in 1825, the Vice Chancellor and Master of the Rolls disposed of 1082 causes, further directions, and exceptions; whilst, in 1827, only 887 causes, further directions and exceptions were disposed of in their branches of the Court; so that 195 more causes, further directions and exceptions were disposed of in 1825 than in 1827. No more bankrupt petitions were disposed of in 1827 than in 1825. The comparison between the quantity of business done in 1826 and 1827 will not be found more favourable; for, although 26 more causes, further directions and exceptions were disposed of in 1827 than in 1826, yet more bankrupt petitions were heard in 1826 than in 1827—the number heard in the former year being 613, whilst the number heard in the latter is only 532.

There is (as was lately stated by Mr. Taylor in the House of Commons) a diminution in the number of appeals pending before the Lord Chancellor at the beginning of Hilary Term, 1828, when compared with the number pending when Lord Lyndhurst received the Seals; but this is easily accounted for, from the little time given to motions, and the other reasons mentioned in a subsequent page. The number of bankrupt petitions depending before the Lord Chancellor has also decreased, and for similar causes.

On the other hand, the number of bankrupt petitions depending before the Vice Chancellor has considerably augmented. The number standing for hearing in that branch of the Court at the beginning of last Hilary Term was 258, whilst the number standing for hearing at the commencement of Hilary Term, 1826, was only 131, being little more than half. The number at the beginning of Hilary Term, 1827, was 217. What was the number when Lord Lyndhurst was first appointed to the office of Chancellor, I am not informed.

Lord Lyndhurst has ascribed this increase in the number of bankrupt petitions to the *acci-*

dent that the late Vice Chancellor was able to devote eight days only, instead of sixteen, to the hearing of this description of business. This is an *accident*, however, of very frequent occurrence in the Court. Hardly a week passes, that the matters appointed for particular days are not postponed in consequence of the Court not having been able to dispose of those fixed for hearing at an earlier period.

But it is not by the quantity of business inscribed on the lists for hearing, alone, that we are enabled to judge of the extent of the arrear. The time that has elapsed since the causes and bankrupt petitions were set down, affords the best criterion for forming an opinion on this subject. The original causes standing at the head of the Vice Chancellor's paper to be heard the first day of Hilary Term, 1828, were set down previously to Easter Term, 1826; and the further directions and exceptions, at that time at the head of the same paper, were set down previously to Trinity Term, 1826. So that here are nearly four years wholly lost to the suitors, during which their causes advance slowly on the list, with the probability of a retrograde movement: for if any of the parties happen to die, or become bankrupt or insolvent, or if in any other way the interest of a party is devested or altered, (and every body knows that events of this nature are very common occurrences during the long pendency of Chancery suits,) the cause cannot be heard, and it frequently happens that the proceedings must be begun *de novo*.

The bankrupt petitions standing at the head of the Vice Chancellor's paper the beginning of last Hilary Term, must have been set down more than twelve months. A petition now before me, and which, notwithstanding the time of late devoted to bankrupt petitions, to the prejudice of the other business of the Court, has not yet come on to be heard, was inscribed on the list for hearing in March, 1827.

It appears singular that the Solicitor General, when he moved for a return of the business done by the Vice Chancellor and Master of the Rolls in each of the years 1825, 1826, and 1827, omitted to move for similar returns of the business done by the Lord Chancellor. The returns show us a diminution of business in the Lord Chancellor's Court, and if it be the intention to ascribe this diminution to Lord Lyndhurst having disposed of more business than Lord Eldon, the Solicitor General ought to have moved for returns of the *special* orders made by the Lord Chancellor during the last three years, as the bar in general ascribe the decrease in the number of appeals and bankrupt petitions pending before the Lord Chancellor to a very different cause.

Some account of the business done by Lord Lyndhurst will be found in a subsequent page.

No one can feel surprised that Lord Lyndhurst has not done more. Considering his inexperience as an Equity judge, and the political events that have marked his Chancellorship, we can only wonder that, even with his great judicial talents, he has been able to get through any business at all.

Lord Lyndhurst has stated, that in twelve months there will be no arrear of appeals before him. This is admitted, in a subsequent part of these pages, to be extremely probable, unless indeed an inefficient judge be placed in another branch of the Court. For it is not mere experience in the business of the Court of Chancery, that will enable any man to preside there to the satisfaction of the suitors. He must possess certain qualities indispensable in a judge. He must be duly impressed with the importance of the high functions which he has to discharge; he must have quickness to seize, and memory to retain, the facts detailed to him—a mind which can either comprehend them in the gross, or divide and examine them in detail. He must not only himself feel convinced he is right in the judgment he forms, but he must have the art to produce the same conviction in the minds of others.

If a judge, deficient in these qualities, should unfortunately for the suitors at any time preside in any of the inferior branches of the Court of Chancery, there can be no doubt there would be many appeals to Lord Lyndhurst, notwithstanding the judge appealed from should have practised in the Court of Chancery all his life—and especially if those appeals should be heard in a moderate time after being presented.

Lord Lyndhurst has also stated his belief, that the arrear of bankrupt petitions depending before the Vice Chancellor will be disposed of before the end of next term. This may admit of more doubt than his Lordship's statement as to the appeals.

CHAP. V.—PART III.

SOME ACCOUNT OF THE PROCEEDINGS IN A COMMON CHANCERY SUIT, AND THE PROBABLE TIME OF ITS DURATION.

EVERY practitioner knows, that, in the present state of the Court, a common suit by legatees or creditors cannot be terminated in less than five years,* even supposing its duration be not prolonged by exceptions to the Master's report,† or appeals from interlocutory or final orders.

* The hearing of suits is often expedited by the defendant consenting to the cause being brought on out of its turn, which the Court permits, where there is to be no discussion at all, or some very short point only is to be argued. These causes are styled *consent* and *short* causes. The observations in the text are applicable to the great mass of causes which are prosecuted in an adverse manner, or involve questions of too much importance to be disposed of in a summary way.

† Exceptions to the Master's report may be taken in respect of a great variety of matters, of which the Master has cognizance in different periods of the cause. I will try to explain their nature to the unprofessional reader, by showing what they are with reference to the sufficiency of an answer put in to a bill. A creditor or legatee's bill generally calls upon the executors, who are defendants, to state what money, belonging to the testator's estate,

I will endeavour to explain this to the reader, who is not a member of the profession of the law.

I will take one of the most common suits instituted in the Court of Chancery—a suit against executors, the object of which is to recover legacies or enforce the payment of debts. In about a year after the filing of the bill, the cause will be ready to be heard, and it is then set down for hearing before the Vice Chancellor. Eighteen months must expire before the Vice Chancellor has disposed of the prior business on the list, and its turn to be heard comes, and then (two years and a half after the commencement of the suit) a decree is made, directing one of the Masters of the Court to take an account of the executors' receipts and payments, in order to see whether there are assets to pay all the debts and legacies. The making this decree does not occupy the Court five minutes. Some little delay, however, generally occurs in drawing up the decree, which is then carried into the Master's office.

they have in their possession; and if the executors do not discover the amount of the money, the plaintiffs take what are technically called Exceptions to the answer for insufficiency, in order to compel the discovery. These Exceptions are immediately argued before the Master, who reports the answer to be insufficient. The executors being dissatisfied with the Master's decision, take what are also termed Exceptions to his Report, and these Exceptions are set down to be heard in the list of Further Directions and Exceptions, and, generally speaking, all proceedings in the cause are stationary until they are disposed of.

At the end of twelve months, the Master has taken the accounts and makes his report to the Court, and the executors, upon a motion or summary application, made to the Vice Chancellor for that purpose, pay into Court the balance found due from them. Indeed it frequently happens, that executors pay money into Court upon motion made at an earlier period of the cause. This money cannot, however, in either case, be disposed of until the Court gives what are technically called Further Directions, being an order to distribute the fund amongst the creditors and legatees pointed out by the Master's report, after payment of the costs of the suit. To obtain this order, the cause must, after the Master has made his report, be set down in the list of Further Directions and Exceptions, where it remains eighteen months before its turn to be heard a second time arrives, and then, in a lucky case, an order is made to pay the legatees and creditors. The order made to pay the money into Court, the decree made upon the first hearing of the cause, and the order made upon further directions to divide the fund, may all be made the subject of an appeal to the Lord Chancellor, and afterwards to the House of Lords. The Master's report, stating the result of the accounts, may also be excepted to, and the exceptions set down to be heard before the Vice Chancellor; and the Vice Chancellor's decision upon the exceptions, in like manner, carried by appeal before the Lord Chancellor, and afterwards to the House of Lords.* In fact, almost all the minor orders, deciding points of practice and other trifling matters incident to judicial proceedings, are subject to a double appeal; and the pendency of an appeal, even on such subjects as these, renders it impossible to prosecute the suit with effect.

During all this time, the suit is liable to the delays occasioned by the events alluded to in a preceding part of this Chapter, namely, death, bankruptcy, insolvency, &c. of some of the parties; new and unexpected points arise, cross or supplemental suits are frequently rendered necessary, the pleadings increase in bulk with the lapse of time, and a cause, which, if heard when first set down, might have been disposed of at a trifling expense, swallows up a large portion of the estate, for the administration of which it was instituted.

It is evident from this statement, that if the plaintiffs use the utmost diligence in the prosecution of their suit, if the defendants be not particularly litigious, if there be no exceptions, no appeal, still great delay is unavoidable, and *that* delay is with the Court, and not with the parties; the cause, at two different stages of it, being inscribed on the list for hearing during a period of

* It is obvious many additional years must elapse, if the cause travel through the two last stages.

eighteen months, waiting its turn to be heard, and in this manner three years are altogether lost.

I am taking, however, a very favourable view of even a common Chancery suit, for the payment of a few wretched creditors and legatees, without exception or appeal, when I assume they will receive their debts at the end of five years, upon the suit coming on for the first time on Further Directions. From various causes, which it is not necessary here to explain, it seldom happens that the Court finds itself in a condition to divide the fund without directing a second reference to the Master to take some additional accounts, to make some further inquiries, to convert into money certain property still left unsold, &c. Take, for instance, the common case of debts or legacies charged upon real estate, in case of the personal estate being insufficient to satisfy them. The Court but rarely does or can direct the real estate to be sold, until the Master reports there is a deficiency of the personal estate. There must, therefore, be a second reference to the Master, to carry on the accounts, to sell the real estate, &c. He must make a second report, the cause must be a second time set down on Further Directions, it must wait a third period of eighteen months before its turn to be heard arrives, and all the proceedings in this third stage may be delayed and embarrassed by the same events and incidents as in the two former stages.

It must not be forgotten, that during all this time the widow and children of the testator, who I will suppose to be his residuary legatees, are kept out of the enjoyment of the property which the testator intended should produce to them an immediate income. The residuary legatees cannot touch a sixpence until all the prior charges of debts and legacies are actually paid, unless, by some amicable arrangement between the parties, the Court can ascertain at an earlier period of the cause, that there are funds sufficient to pay all the debts and legacies, and the costs of the suit.

Legatees of particular sums of money are not in a much better situation than legatees of a portion of the residue, as the creditors must of course be satisfied before the legacies can be paid. A daughter, to whom a testator leaves a legacy of £10,000 for her fortune, charged upon his real estate, must wait eight years before she can receive interest or principal, and during more than half this time the cause remains on the lists of the Vice Chancellor, waiting its turn to be heard.

But when I suppose that a legatee of £10,000, charged upon real estate, will receive the legacy at the end of eight years, I am putting a most favourable case. It rarely happens that a suit, to administer a large property, can be carried on without exceptions or appeal, and then the delay is presently doubled or trebled.

Two briefs in causes on Further Directions, set down before the Vice Chancellor, are at this moment on my table. The real and personal estates, in both cases, are considerable, and neither the legatees, or residuary legatees, have yet received any part of their bequests. In the one suit the bill was filed rather more, and in the other rather less, than twenty years since, and during more than half that time the causes have, in different stages, been waiting their turn to be heard.*

* Two other kinds of Chancery business frequently occur in the Returns made to Parliament, as to which it may be useful to give some explanation, namely, Pleas and Demurrers.

Pleas and *Demurrers* are nothing more than short answers, upon the putting in of which, the opinion of the Court is taken in a summary manner, whether the suit ought to go any further. If a party, for example, come for relief in equity, and it is clear, according to the case stated by the bill, that the proper course is to bring an action at law, the defendant may make that objection in a few words, in the form of a demurrer. So, if a bill be filed for an account of partnership dealings, the defendant may shortly state, by way of plea, that the accounts have been settled, or that a release has been given, or that there never was any partnership. Pleas and Demurrers are by no means numerous, and are generally heard very shortly after they are set down for hearing.

CHAPTER VI.

IT IS NOT POSSIBLE FOR THREE JUDGES TO GET THROUGH THE PRESENT BUSINESS OF THE COURT OF CHANCERY WITH CONVENIENT DISPATCH.—OPINIONS OF THE BARRISTERS EXAMINED BEFORE THE CHANCERY COMMISSIONERS ON THE SUBJECT.

WE have seen in the preceding chapter, that Sir James Scarlett and Mr. Brougham entertained sanguine hopes that Lord Lyndhurst, assisted by two efficient judges, would be able to keep down the arrears of business; and they urged the impolicy of making any alteration in the constitution of the Court, until it should be ascertained how the ancient machinery would work under more vigorous superintendence.

The Returns lately moved for, and now on the table of the House of Commons, do not permit us to doubt that those agreeable anticipations have not been realized. It is not the object of these pages to point out all the causes that have contributed to this failure. It is but just, however, to Lord Lyndhurst, to state, that they are not all (as some persons do not scruple to affirm) attributable to the circumstance that his Lordship is still in his novitiate as an equity judge. If experience in the business of his Court could have been superadded to his Lordship's other splendid judicial accomplishments, the miscarriage would probably not have been so great; but still there would have been a miscarriage.

Those learned persons who have affirmed that three judges are able to adjudicate all the multifarious business coming at present within the range of Chancery jurisdiction, assume that those judges will be all eminently qualified for the performance of the judicial functions, not only with wisdom but with dispatch. Such a constellation may throw a light over our jurisprudence once in a century, but if we reckon upon its appearance more frequently, we shall find ourselves disappointed. The great national tribunals should be so organized that the business can be dispatched within the period of time required for the due administration of justice, not by such men as Ellenborough and Grant only, but by men whose natural and acquired endowments may be less illustrious. Men will always be found at the English bar who, although not endued with those brilliant talents and that extensive learning which have given pre-eminence to some of our judges, and consecrated their names in the history of their country, yet will not be less capable of filling the judicial seat to the advantage of the public. A judge of moderate abilities and knowledge, who, fully impressed with the importance of the principle, that it is his duty not merely to decide right, but, to convince those whom he addresses of the correctness of his decision, hears patiently the arguments addressed to him, and then pronounces his judgment with deliberation and firmness, often gives more satisfaction to the suitors than one of more dazzling attainments.

The soundness of the principle that appears from the debate in the preceding Chapter to have been adopted by Sir James Scarlett and Mr. Brougham, might, therefore, in my humble apprehension, have been reasonably questioned, even supposing the three judges, who, it must be admitted, merit the eulogy pronounced on them, had accomplished that which was predicted. One cannot, however, but feel a little surprise, that gentlemen, who can be but slightly acquainted with the Court, should have entertained so confident an expectation that Lord Lyndhurst and two assistant judges could keep under the whole business, when it was well known to all the profession that the barristers practising in the Court of Chancery, who were examined before the Chancery Commissioners as to the possibility of the Lord Chancellor, Master of the Rolls and Vice Chancellor being able to transact the business of the Court with due expedition and deliberation, gave it as their opinion, that, constituted as the Court now is, and especially the time of the Chancellor being so considerably occupied by business extraneous to the ordinary Chancery business, they could not.

Mr. Bell, in his evidence, after having observed that appeals in the House of Lords necessarily took up a great portion of the Chancellor's time, particularly if it were considered that he had appeals not only from his own Court, but from all the Courts in the kingdom, and from Scotland and Ireland, expressed an opinion, that if the arrears were cleared off, and all those appeals were entirely laid out of the question, and the Chancellor had nothing at all to do but, together with the other two judges, the Master of the Rolls and the Vice Chancellor, to sit regularly and dispose of the questions in Chancery, without any reference to appeals of any sort, the three judges would be able to get through the regular business; but, he observed, there would be appeals, and more particularly when there was a person at the head of the Court whom the profession and the public looked up to as they did to Lord Eldon; so that, in all probability, with those and with bankruptcies, together with the collateral questions that arise in different ways, the time of the Chancellor would be most completely employed, without his being able to take a very effective part in the decision of causes in the regular course of hearing; thus we should be left only to two judges, which would place us nearly in the same situation we were in before the Vice Chancellor was appointed; and in answer to the question, whether if all the duties that at present attach to the office of Lord Chancellor, sitting in the House of Lords upon appeals and so forth, were continued, the Lord Chancellor, together with the Master of the Rolls and the Vice Chancellor, would be sufficient to dispatch the business with sufficient celerity and deliberation, Mr. Bell stated, that judging from the fact he should think not. In a subsequent part of his evidence he stated, that supposing the present arrear were cleared off, he thought three efficient judges would be sufficient to dispatch all the business of the Court of Chancery; but, he added, he was apprehensive, supposing even the present arrear were cleared off, that the time of the Lord Chancellor would be so taken up with appeals from other judges of his own Court, the Court of Chancery in Ireland, and the other Courts of the three kingdoms, to the highest tribunal, that he would have little time left for the common course of Chancery business and bankruptcy, and then the business would rest on two judges as before, and he thought they would not be able to dispatch it.

Sir Lancelot Shadwell stated, it appeared to him impossible that any Chancellor, Vice Chancellor, and Master of the Rolls could get through all the equity business and all the bankrupt business. His saying, that the load of business in the Court was so great that three angels could not get through it with convenient dispatch, is well known.

Mr. Roupell stated, he was of opinion that it was impossible, in the then state of business, to get through it with effect, looking at the fact that before all the Judges there was a vast accumulation of business, which, with all their diligence, they were unable to keep down.

Mr. Heald at first expressed an opinion that if the arrear was cleared off, or considerably diminished, three courts would be sufficient to dispose of the business of the Court of Chancery, with sufficient celerity to prevent injury to the suitors; but in a subsequent part of his evidence he stated, that upon reconsidering his former opinion he doubted whether the present courts, with certain additional assistance, which it was proposed should be given by the Master of the Rolls, could get through the business of the present arrear, and the accruing business of the courts, in such a manner as the suitors had a right to expect, because he was apprehensive that the business of the Court was increasing, and he could not bring himself to believe that the business of the Court could be reduced in a sufficiently short space of time to furnish any well grounded hope of having the causes disposed of as quickly as we could all wish, but he had doubts upon the subject.

Mr. Bickersteth stated, that his opinion was, that if the Judges sat during as long a time as could be reasonably expected of them, and if they exerted all possible diligence during the time of their sittings, and gave their judgments with all due dispatch, it would still be impossible for them, in their present numbers, to keep the business within those moderate limits within which it ought to be kept; that the smallest number of Judges ought to be employed, but till the experiment was made, it could not be ascertained what the smallest sufficient number would be; that there were causes, amounting even to hundreds, which were in arrear, and many of these causes were of great length and intricacy. That the suitors had a right to be heard carefully, and to have their causes decided with deliberation; and it was obvious that great dissatisfaction would be created by disposing of the arrears hastily. Fresh arrears were coming forward in continued succession, and they would, as he conceived, come forward faster and in greater numbers, if the arrears were cleared off. Under these circumstances he believed that the business of the Court could not be properly kept under by the present number of Judges. He conceived that when the cause is set down for hearing, and due time for notice is allowed, there ought to be no delay, and that any accumulation of causes in that stage is a disgrace to the Court. Having used that expression, he begged leave to add, that he conceived an accumulation of arrears might begin and increase, notwithstanding the utmost exertions of a most diligent Judge, and the Judge had no right to hurry. What he conceived to be the fault was, that assistance was not obtained as soon as the arrears began to exceed a very limited amount; a great accumulation appeared to him to be a very great evil. That he had not personally seen much of the distress and agony of mind which must arise from the delays in the administration of justice; what was obvious, however, was, that many parties died after years of litigation, but before their rights were established; and that many suits ended in compromises, by which some parties obtained advantages to which they were not entitled, whilst others sacrificed advantages to which they were entitled, in order to prevent the loss of the whole in costs. Cases had occurred, within his own knowledge, in which the whole property sought to be administered in Chancery had proved insufficient to pay the costs of the suit, and in which the last question discussed in the cause had been how the deficient fund was to be apportioned amongst the different solicitors, in part payment of their respective bills.

CHAPTER VII.

THAT THE DELAY NOW EXISTING IN THE HEARING OF CAUSES IN THE COURT OF CHANCERY AMOUNTS TO A DENIAL OF JUSTICE, SHOWN BY AN ACCOUNT OF THE BUSINESS DONE AT VARIOUS PERIODS, FROM THE YEAR 1745 TO THE PRESENT TIME.* AN ADDITIONAL JUDGE TO BE USEFUL MUST BE EFFICIENT.

THE impression of the writer is, that the delay that has always attended Chancery proceedings has, from the end of the sixteenth century, di-

* The details contained in this Chapter, as to the quantity of business depending or disposed of in the Court of Chancery, are taken from the *Reports of the Committee of the House of Commons, appointed in* 1811, *to inquire into the Causes that retard the Decision of Suits in the Court of Chancery :—The Report from the Committee of the House of Commons, appointed in the same year, to inspect the Lords' Journals :—An Account of the number of Bills filed in Chancery in the years* 1810, 1811, *and* 1812, *printed by order of the House of Commons in* 1813 *:—The Report from the Lords' Committees, appointed in* 1823 *a Select Committee on the Appellate Jurisdiction of the House of Lords :—and from the Appendix to the Report of the Chancery Commissioners.*

minished to a very great extent the number of suits, which, if there had existed a prospect of obtaining justice, in that moderate space of time required by every well regulated system of jurisprudence, would have found their way into the Court. But that this has been the case since the middle of the last century, cannot, it is apprehended, be doubted by any one who will give his consideration to the following facts.

Account of the number of Bills filed in Chancery (including bills of revivor and supplement) during the three periods of ten years each undermentioned:—

From 1745	to	1754	. . .	18,909
1760	to	1769	. . .	14,461
1800	to	1809	. . .	15,440

I am not aware that there exists any account of the number filed in the years intervening between such three periods, except the year 1799.*

* I have since discovered, in making some researches in the Journals of the House of Lords (a most difficult task, as it seldom happens that you have the benefit of an index,) that in 1811 an account of the number of bills filed from 1760 to 1810 was ordered and subsequently presented from the Six Clerks Office. I have been promised a copy, but it has not reached me. In the same year, a statement of business done in the Court of Chancery and at the Rolls from the year 1755 to the year 1800, and of the number of Decrees pronounced from the year 1760 to the year 1810 inclusive, was ordered to be laid before the House of Lords. From the inquiries I have been enabled, through the kindness of some friends, to make at the Library of the House of Peers, &c. I believe no returns were ever made in pursuance of this Order. The Registrars of the Court to whom I

Account of the number of bills (including bills of revivor and supplement) filed in each of the following years:—

In 1745 . . .	2064	In 1822 . . .	2202
1746 . . .	2241	1823 . . .	2286
1747 . . .	2138	1824 . . .	2388

In 1801, the number of bills filed was 1225, and the number appears to have gone on gradually increasing, except that in one or two instances there was a trifling diminution from the number filed in the year immediately preceding, down to the year 1809.

The increase that took place in the number of bills filed in the three following years was more rapid. There were filed

In 1810	1706
1811	1938
1812	2055

There does not appear to exist any return of the number of bills filed in the years intervening between 1812 and 1822, nor any return of the number filed in the years subsequent to 1824.

Now when we look at the increase which has taken place in the wealth and commerce of the country since the year 1745,* and the great quan-

have spoken have no recollection of such returns. Indeed, I apprehend, it would be quite impossible for the Registrars to comply with the terms of the Order in its full extent.

* The following is an Account of the Amount of the Effects belonging to the Suitors in Chancery, standing in the books of

tity of additional matter for equitable jurisdiction which has been thus created, it is impossible not to see that some cause has operated, and still operates, to prevent its becoming the subject of suits, and that that cause is the ruinous delay experienced by the parties.

Adventitious circumstances may augment or diminish, to a considerable extent, the number of bills filed in particular years, but when the immense increase of every other description of judicial business is considered, there must be some peculiar cause that has prevented the number of Chancery suits from augmenting in a similar* ratio.

the Bank of England, in the name of the Accountant General of the Court, in 1745 and 1825:—

In 1745	£ 1,723,957	10	1
1825	39,174,722	8	7

It is probable that the value of the landed and other property over which the Court exercises controul, and which is not included in the above account, has, since the year 1745, increased in a much greater ratio than the funded property. Let the increased machinery of the Court (one additional judge) be compared with the increase of the property to be administered, and its inefficiency will be seen in a moment; to say nothing of the still greater increase that it is presumed would take place in the amount of the property subjected to the jurisdiction of the Court, were it not for the appalling delay that has so long existed.

* In a debate in the year 1621, on the power and abuse of the Chancery, under which, said Sir Robert Phillips, "*we all groan,*" Sir Edward Coke is reported to have stated, that in Edward the Third's time there were not 400 causes in a year,—but then

In 1745, 1746, and 1747, Lord Hardwicke was in the middle of his judicial career, and it is not improbable that the delays which took place in his time, then began to be severely felt by the suitors; and we find the number of bills filed diminished during the succeeding years of his chancellorship, to which the return applies. The year 1753, in which there appears to have been a great increase upon the preceding year, must be excepted.

From 1760 to 1769, Lord Northington and Lord Camden held the seals. Lord Northington has lately been called a great lawyer. His contemporaries, however, thought him unqualified for the office of Chancellor. Lord Camden certainly was a great lawyer, but he is said to have been slow in his decisions. Whatever, however,

there were 35,000 ! ! ! Sir Francis Fane replied, there were not 16,000 subpœnas in any one year, as appeared by the books ! ! !

The anonymous author of the Relation of the Proceedings of the Commonwealth Parliament that abolished the Court, quoted in a Note to the first Chapter of this Work, informs us, it was said in the course of the debate there were then 23,000 causes depending in the Court ! ! ! Mr. Parkes quotes the Relation, but I was never so fortunate as to meet with any more of it than the extract in the old Parliamentary History. It is very difficult to form any correct notion as to the number of suits now depending in the Court of Chancery; but the number of bills yearly filed being upwards of 2000, and common suits by creditors, legatees, next of kin, &c. often lasting from ten to fifteen years, and family suits twenty or thirty years, it is not improbable the number of suits actually depending exceeds 20,000.

may have been the judicial qualities of Lord Northington and Lord Camden, it was not likely they should get through the business of the Court with more dispatch than so great and experienced an equity judge as Lord Hardwicke. Lord Hardwicke too, for some years after his resignation, attended the hearing of appeals in the House of Lords, and many of Lord Northington's decrees were there reversed, which of course imposed upon the latter the obligation to weigh well every case that came before him.

It is probable then, that the great delay attending suits in Chancery contributed, from 1760 to 1769, to diminish the number in the same way as in the latter time of Lord Hardwicke. That the same cause, (in conjunction perhaps with some others) operated to prevent the institution of suits from 1800 to 1809, may with greater certainty be affirmed, when we look at the gradual augmentation in the number of bills filed that has taken place since the year 1810, at which period the circumstance that the legislature intended to appoint an additional judge for the quicker dispatch of equity business was first announced, and may be supposed to have had some influence in increasing the influx of business into the court. And it may be inferred, with every probability that the conclusion is correct, that if in the time of Lord Hardwicke an additional judge had been created to assist the Chancellor and Master of the Rolls, there would not have been that diminution in the number of causes brought into the Court that seems to have taken place.

It is not unimportant to observe that, in Lord Hardwicke's time and down to a period not very remote, Solicitors drew their own bills; and until the year 1807 they only received 6*d.* per folio for drawing. Since 1807, they are allowed 1*s.* per folio for drawing, and they no longer draw their bills, but employ Counsel for that purpose, the fee they pay Counsel for drawing being allowed them as paid the Counsel for perusing, settling, and signing their names. Thus, since the year 1807, the Solicitors have been paid for the non-performance of an irksome and laborious duty double what they received in Lord Hardwicke's time for the performance of it.*

It is not to be expected, of course, that the number of decrees pronounced should be equal to the number of original bills filed, as many suits will always, for various reasons, be compromised or discontinued, even where a decision may be

* It must not be supposed that the writer entertains any notion that Solicitors are overpaid for their Chancery labours. On the contrary he is convinced, that from the length of time that elapses before they are reimbursed the monies laid out by them in the prosecution of an equity suit, nine causes out of ten yield them little or no profit. No notion is more absurd than that the law's delay is advantageous to the Solicitor. The mode, however, in which these officers of the Court are paid is extremely objectionable. No officers of courts of justice should be remunerated by fees given in respect of labours which they do not perform.

had with all reasonable dispatch and cheapness; but still the number of bills filed, and decrees pronounced, in equal spaces of times, affords no bad criterion for judging of the effect of the delay and expense attending the prosecution of suits to a hearing.

The returns made to Parliament give us ample information on this subject.

The following is an account of the number of Decrees made in the years 1810 and 1811.

1810.	General Paper.	Short Causes.	Total.
Lord Chancellor	23	14	37
		Consent Causes.	
Master of the Rolls	276	129	405
		Total	442

1811.	General Paper.	Short Causes.	
Lord Chancellor	19	17	36
		Consent Causes.	
Master of the Rolls	280	111	391
		Total	427

The number of Original Bills filed in 1810 and 1811 does not appear,* but the number of Original Bills filed in 1808 was 1588, and the number filed in 1809 was 1565.

From this statement it should seem, that shortly

* The return from which the account given in a former page of this Chapter of the Bills filed in 1810, 1811, and 1812 is taken, does not distinguish the Bills of Revivor and Supplement from the Original Bills. The number of Original Bills filed in 1810 and 1811 must, however, have been much greater than the number filed in 1808 and 1809.

before the appointment of a Vice Chancellor, it was impossible for the Court to keep down the arrears, unless more than two-thirds of the suits instituted were terminated by compromises, or in some other way, before the hearing.

We have an account also of the number of Decrees made in the following years, but without distinguishing the branches of the Court in which they were made, or the Decrees made by consent, or in short Causes, from the others.

	Decrees.	Dismissions.	Dismissions for want of Prosecution.	Total.
1800 -	266	25	88	379
1801 -	322	31	70	423
1802 -	362	20	69	451
1822 -	457	30	184	671
1823 -	446	31	168	645
1824 -	302	16	97	415

Three Terms.*

* This statement is taken from the Appendix to the Report of the Chancery Commissioners. Some returns, communicated by the Lords to the Commons in 1811, give further particulars as to the Decrees made in 1800, 1801, and 1802; but the total numbers of Causes disposed of fall short of the numbers abovementioned, from orders for dismission on hearing, or for want of prosecutions, not being included.

The statement of Decrees made in 1810 and 1811 is taken from the Second Report of Mr. Taylor's Committee made in 1812. Orders dismissing on the hearing, or for want of prosecution, are not included therein.

The number of Bills filed in the same years was as follows:—

1800	1394
1801	1332
1802	1412
1822	2202
1823	2286
1824	2338

Bills of Revivor and Supplement are included in this account. There is another account of the number of Bills filed in 1800 and 1801, by which the numbers appear to have been less.

It will, no doubt, be observed, that the number of Decrees made in the years 1822 and 1823, when there were three judges, did not much exceed the number in 1810 and 1811, when there were only two. It is probable that the total number of Decrees made in 1824 was less than the number in either of the two preceding years. In neither of those three years was the Rolls an effective Court.

By this last account, it appears, that the Decrees made in the years there specified bore a still smaller proportion to the Bills filed in those years, than the number of Decrees made in 1810 and 1811 to the number of Bills filed in 1808 and 1809.

Another circumstance that confirms the opinion that it is the tardiness of the Court that has checked the increase of suits is, the great increase that has nevertheless taken place in that description of business, which may be supposed to be less affected by the delay.

Take, for instance, the number of injunctions, which, it is well known, if they are obtained at all, are obtained immediately on the Bill being filed, or a very short time after; this description of business, from its urgency, having a preference over all other, and therefore experiencing comparatively but little delay.

The following account contains, it is believed, all that is to be found in print on the subject.

	Common and Special Injunctions.
In eight months of the year 1799 there were granted . .	34
In eight months of the year 1821 .	174
In 1800	49
In 1801	73
In 1822	240
In 1823	207

It will be seen, that the increase of the number of bills filed since the beginning of the present century bears but a small proportion to the increase that has taken place in the number of injunctions.

A more striking proof of the real source of the reluctance of parties to engage in an Equity suit, except in cases where the mischief to be avoided comes upon them too suddenly and too rapidly to admit of hesitation, can hardly be found. In other cases there is ample time for negociation and compromise, and in nine cases out of ten mutual sacrifices are made, to avoid the endless anxiety and expense of a suit. Sometimes, however, (and for the ends of justice it is to be feared too often,) it happens, that the poor man must lose his right; for how can he feed a Chancery cause, which, if it pass through its various stages of exceptions, rehearing, appeal, &c., may easily live twenty years? Not a day passes that the Chancery barrister, in the honest discharge of his duty, does not advise his client* to sacrifice hundreds, rather than embark in an Equity suit, a vessel in which few have sailed long without being wrecked.

Other proofs are not wanting in support of the above hypothesis. Men are more ready to litigate at the expense of others, than at their own. In matters of Lunacy the costs of all parties, in almost every case, come out of the lunatic's estate. In matters of Bankrupty the costs of some of the parties come out of the bankrupt's estate. Let

* "There does not,"—says *Mr. Montague*, in his *Letters to Mr. Peel on the Report of the Chancery Commissioners*,—" There does not, I can confidently say, a week elapse, without my advising some suitor to abandon his right, rather than harass his peace of mind by the certain expense and vexation attendant upon protracted litigation." Neque instituere litium actiones malebat quam controversiam tollere.

us see then whether this description of business has increased.

The following accounts fully verify the conjecture which the writer had made on this subject before he discovered them.

Petitions in Bankruptcy set down for hearing in the following years:—

	Petitions.
In 1799	212
In 1800	285
In 1801	247
Total	744
In 1821	619
In 1822	550
In 1823	498
Total	1667

Lunacy Petitions set down for hearing during the following years:—

	Petitions.
In 1799	119
In 1800	124
In 1801	147
Total	390
In 1821	245
In 1822	320
In 1823	364
Total	929

An account of the number of Orders in Bankruptcy made upon the hearing of Petitions by Hardwicke, in the following years:—

1747	135
1748	155
1749	99
1750	115
1751	126
1752	123
1753	116
1754	68
1755	106
1756	119
Total number of Orders drawn up and entered	1162

An account of the number of Orders in Bankruptcy made upon the hearing of Petitions by Lord Eldon, in the following years:—

1801	172
1802	241
1803	288
1804	280
1805	329
1806	221
1807	252
1808	265
1809	251
1810	256
Total number of Orders drawn up and entered	2555

There were 674 other Orders in bankruptcy pronounced by Lord Eldon, which were not drawn up.

An account of Orders made upon the hearing of Lunatic Petitions, by Lord Hardwicke during the years—

1737	48
1738	62
1739	36
1740	26
1741	22
1742	40
1743	62
1744	72
1745	50
1746	66
Total	484

An account of Orders made upon the hearing of Lunatic Petitions by Lord Eldon, during the years—

1801	99
1802	95
1803	104
1804	82
1805	122
1806	117
1807	129
1808	131
1809	127
1810	133
Total	1139

It seems probable too, that the appeal business of the House of Lords would be less affected by delay than the general business that comes into the Court of Chancery. The expense of carrying a case by appeal to the supreme Court of the Empire is so great, that it is seldom incurred, except in cases where the property in dispute is of great value; and in those cases the parties are generally possessed of sufficient wealth to make the pendency of an appeal to the House of Lords of much less inconvenience to them than the pendency of a Chancery suit is to the merchant or tradesman.

The following is an account of the number of appeals presented in the House of Lords since the middle of the last century down to the year 1823, with the exception of the years 1811 and 1812.

From 1751	to	1760	170
1761	to	1770	272
1771	to	1780	344
1781	to	1790	223
1791	to	1800	290
1801	to	1810	492
1813	to	1823	570

But the most convincing proof of the assertion, that it is the delay in the hearing that has been the cause of the number of suits brought into Chancery not being more numerous than they were in Lord Hardwicke's time, is the fact above alluded to, of the increased influx that has taken place since the quicker dispatch of business occasioned by the creation of the Vice Chancellor's Court. For although the arrears are greater now than in 1812, when a Vice Chancellor was first appointed, yet the causes have not been so long on the list for hearing as at that time. It may be safely asserted too, that a greater proportion of the bills filed are productive of business that comes before the judges of the Court than formerly: the greater the delay and the more the patience of the suitor is tried, the greater the probability of a compromise. But when there is a prospect of a speedy hearing, a party, satisfied of the justice of his cause, prefers to wait the decision of the Court. Where the causes have been set down for several years it not unfrequently happens that the greater part of the twelve causes (the number usually placed in the daily list for hearing) are struck out, neither counsel or solicitors appearing. In most of the causes so struck out, a compromise has taken place, or some of the parties interested have died, and there has been no opportunity to bring their representatives before the Court.

The opinion of the writer is, that the delay which exists at present, notwithstanding the relief afforded by the creation of a Vice Chancellor, amounts to a denial of justice; not merely to the poor man, but to every man, who has the wisdom to discern that it is better to make a present sacrifice than to undergo years of anxiety, not unaccompanied by considerable expense. The author thinks, in common with many of his professional brethren, that there ought to be an additional judge, and feels convinced that even with such assistance it would in a few years be found difficult to keep down the arrears of the business that would be brought into the court, although it is possible (especially if the judge appointed should have judicial qualities at all resembling those of Sir John Leach,) that at first the whole of the business ready for hearing would be got through. As soon however as it should become known to the solicitors and their clients, that a Chancery suit could be heard immediately on its being set down, thousands of questions that are now compromised or decided, very little to the satisfaction of the parties, by arbitration, would be submitted to the decision of the judge.

Much must, however, depend upon the learning and judicial talents of the new judge. If the person chosen to fill that office should happen to be of advanced age, and fitted by his habits and character to the transaction of a small quantity of judicial business, and that with unusual slowness and deliberation; above all, if that person should have expressed himself incapable of performing more extensive duties than those which he now discharges, it may safely be predicted that an additional Court, with such a judge at the head of it, would not afford any relief to the suitor. An additional burthen would be imposed on the country and the delay would be the same as before.*

* It is deeply to be regretted that (for what reason I know not) much less attention has been generally paid to the fitness of the individuals selected to fill the judicial seat in our Courts of equity, than in our Courts of common law. It is true, that men of respectable abilities and attainments have always been appointed; but it has not unfrequently happened, that other individuals were to be found, of much greater talents and learning, and notoriously more competent to the quick and efficient discharge of the laborious and difficult functions of a judge. The public are not perhaps sufficiently aware of the great difference in the quantity of business disposed of, occasioned merely by the greater or less aptitude of the judge for its dispatch. I could easily demonstrate this by some very striking comparison of the quantity of business done by different judges during equal portions of time. I shall, however, for reasons with which it is not necessary to trouble the reader, purposely avoid bringing forward the instances which would perhaps the most strongly illustrate what I have said.

The following is an account of the number of original causes, further directions, exceptions and re-hearings, heard at the Rolls during the last seventeen Terms that Sir William Grant, and the first seventeen Terms that Sir Thomas Plumer, presided in that Court. From the beginning of Trinity Term, 1813, to the beginning of Michaelmas Term, 1817.

Causes	949
Further directions, exceptions and re-hearings . .	366
	1315

From the beginning of Michaelmas Term, 1817, to the beginning of Hilary Term, 1822.

Causes	593
Further directions, exceptions and re-hearings . .	266
Total	859

So that Sir William Grant, at the end of his career, adjudicated 356 more causes and 100 more further directions and exceptions, and re-hearings, than Sir Thomas Plumer was able to dispose of in the same space of time. Sir Thomas Plumer was a slow and laborious man, with a very moderate knowledge of the principles and practice of the Court over which he presided, and capable therefore of doing well only a small portion of business; and yet when he was first elevated to the bench, many individuals might have been found at the Chancery bar not unwilling to accept office, who, possessing equal perseverance with Sir Thomas, were at the same time endued with those other qualities that would probably have enabled them to dispose of nearly as much business as Sir William Grant.

CHAPTER VIII.

THAT THE QUANTITY OF GENERAL BUSINESS OF THE COURT OF CHANCERY, DISPOSED OF BY THE LORD CHANCELLOR, HAS GREATLY DIMINISHED SINCE THE YEAR 1745.—COMPARISON OF THE BUSINESS DONE BY SIR JOSEPH JEKYLL AND SIR WILLIAM GRANT, IN EQUAL SPACES OF TIMES.—UNION OF THE POLITICAL AND JUDICIAL FUNCTIONS IN THE LORD CHANCELLOR.

By the general business of the Court of Chancery, I mean that over which jurisdiction is given by the Constitution to the person holding the Great Seal of England, and which is now exercised upon bill filed, to the exclusion of bankruptcy, lunacy, and some other matters foreign to the office of Chancellor, and in which he has no authority, except by special delegation from the Crown, or under particular statutes.

The following is an account of the quantity of business done by the Lord Chancellor, from Michaelmas, 1745, to Michaelmas, 1755, and from

Michaelmas, 1800, to Michaelmas, 1810, with the exception of motions.

1745 to 1755.		1800 to 1810.	
Causes	1638	Causes	685
Exceptions, further directions, and equity reserved .	712	Exceptions, further directions, and equity reserved .	411
Rehearings and appeals	58	Rehearings and appeals	91
Pleas and demurrers	274	Pleas and demurrers	190
Petitions	1653	Petitions*	2718

Lord Hardwicke was Chancellor during the first period, and Lord Eldon during the second, with the exception of the short Chancellorship of Lord Erskine, who does not appear to have despatched more business than Lord Eldon did in the same space of time, both in prior and subsequent years. The 685 causes disposed of during the second period comprise 115 in which decrees were made by consent; whether any of the 1638 causes decided by Lord Hardwicke were consent causes does not appear.

I have taken no notice of the number of orders made on motions during the above period, as the motions of course are included in the account; and to state the number of motions, without dis-

* See *Report of a Committee of the House of Commons, appointed in the year* 1811 *to inspect the Lords' Journals.*

tinguishing special motions from motions of course, would only mislead the reader. In 1810, the Lord Chancellor made 6730 orders on motion. How many of those were special motions, we do not know. From returns made to the House of Commons, and ordered to be printed in February, 1822, it appears, that the Lord Chancellor, from the beginning of Easter Term, 1813, to the end of the year 1821, made 5,255 orders on special motions, being, on an average of nine years, 583 a year. Since that time, it is apprehended the Lord Chancellor has heard but few special motions, except appeal motions; and we learn from the Appendix to the report of the Chancery Commissioners, that during the years 1823, 1824, and 1825, such appeal motions averaged about 35 a year.

The following account of motions was delivered by the registrar of the Court to the Committee of the House of Commons, appointed in 1811 to inquire into the causes that retard the decision of suits in causes of Equity.

An Account of the Number of Motions heard before the Lord Chancellor within the period stated as under.

From 1st Jan. 1810 to 5th April, 1812 . . .	14,987
From 1st Jan. 1797 to 5th April, 1799 . . .	11,121
From 1st Jan. 1737 to 5th April, 1739 . . .	11,280

Motions of course are obviously included in

this account, and one can only regret to see such illusory statements laid before the legislature.

The only increase, it will be observed, in the quantity of business done by the Lord Chancellor, is in the appeals and rehearings, and in the petitions. The increase of the number of appeals and rehearings may be ascribed to the greater quantity of business, which it will presently appear was done at the Rolls during the latter period, when compared with the quantity done there during the former period, and to the increased wealth of the suitors, and to some other causes, which, as they have been more than once stated to the public, it is not necessary to repeat in this place. The increase in the number of petitions may be attributed principally to the difficulty and delay attending the bringing on of causes in the usual and ancient course for the original hearing, and for the hearing on further directions. Causes cannot be brought on to be heard originally, or on further directions, out of their regular turn, unless by the consent of all parties, and then only where they do not embrace any point that can lead to long discussion; but petitions in those causes may be presented eight or ten times a year, in all three branches of the Court, even where they are to be opposed; and frequent, and in general not unsuccessful, experiments, are made to anticipate by an order upon a petition part of the relief, formerly obtained only upon decree.

A large portion of the orders obtained upon petition may also be obtained in a more summary way by motion, (the parties having the choice of both modes of applying to the Court,) and the great increase that has undoubtedly taken place in the number of special motions may be ascribed to the same causes which have produced an augmentation of the number of petitions. Indeed, it is well known, that Lord Eldon, when censured for devoting his time to motions, to the prejudice of the causes on the list for hearing, always justified himself by the much greater importance attaching to motions now than in former times, as orders are frequently made upon them deciding the principal point in the suit, which is therefore no longer prosecuted.

I have compared the quantity of Chancery business disposed of by Lord Hardwicke in ten years, with the quantity of business done in the Lord Chancellor's branch of the Court in the first ten years of the present century. Some returns made to the House of Commons, and ordered to be printed, in February, 1822, enable me to make a similar comparison at a still later period.

Account of Business disposed of by the Lord Chancellor since the establishment of the Office of Vice Chancellor, in the beginning of 1813, to the end of 1821, being a period of nearly nine years; and also of the Business disposed of by the Lord Chancellor, from Michaelmas, 1745, to Michaelmas, 1754, being a period of nine years.*

1813 to 1821.		1746 to 1754.	
Causes	53	Causes	1501
Exceptions and further directions .	39	Exceptions and further directions .	646
Pleas and demurrers	26	Pleas and demurrers	248
Petitions	407	Petitions	1530
Appeals	157	Appeals	54

I am not aware that there exists any account of the Chancery business disposed of by the Lord Chancellor at any later period. The account of such business disposed of by the Lord Chancellor in the years 1823, 1824, and 1825, to be found in the Appendix to the Report of the Chancery commissioners, is too confused and imperfect to be useful.

I will, therefore, finish this part of my statement with the following *copy* of an official document, for the authenticity of which I can vouch.

* This last account is taken from the *Report of the Committee of the House of Commons, appointed in* 1811 *to inspect the Lords' Journal.*

" Between the 1st of May, 1827, when the Lord Chancellor took his seat in the Court of Chancery, and the 1st day of Hilary Term, 1828.

Heard and disposed of.

Appeals	34
Causes	6
Exceptions	5
Petitions	70

Heard, but stand for Judgment.

Appeals	16
Equity reserved	1
Causes	2 "

What is the number of bankrupt petitions, lunatic petitions, and special motions disposed of by Lord Lyndhurst during the above period, I do not know. His Lordship has, for reasons stated elsewhere, got through more of the business that appears most prominent on the lists of the Court than was probably for some years past disposed of by Lord Eldon in the same space of time. But if the total number of special Orders made by him, taken at the highest amount, were doubled, tripled, or even quadrupled, they probably would not be found equal to the number made by Lord Hardwicke in the same space of time.

The circumstance of the Lord Chancellor for many years past having disposed of so much less business than his predecessors, has given rise to the conjecture that suits in general now occupy more time than they did formerly. It has, moreover, been affirmed, and there are not wanting those who believe that there exist a prolixity and diffuseness in the arguments of the counsel of the present day which were unknown to those who practised in Westminster Hall a century ago. The increased intricacy of commercial transactions has probably rendered the pleadings in some descriptions of suits longer and more complicated than they formerly were; but these are not the causes that consume the most of the time of the Court. Most practitioners know by experience that such suits involve rather questions of fact than questions of law, and generally go off in certain inquiries and accounts, which are the subject of debate in the Master's office, and not before the Chancellor or either of his assistant judges. Cases containing points of law, to which it is supposed no former decisions apply, are those which draw most exorbitantly on the time and attention of the Court. These, however, are rare, in comparison with the number that occurred in former days. A long chain of decisions, from the time of Lord Nottingham downwards, has provided us with precedents applicable to almost every combination of circumstances, and which are at once received and acknowledged as containing the principle by which all similar cases must be adjudicated. A suit which a century ago would have occupied some days in arguing is thus determined by the mere mention of the analogous case decided by a former Chancellor, or if there be any discussion, it is probably a vain attempt to draw some distinction between the case before the Court and that by which it is supposed to be governed.*

From a very early period of my professional studies, I imbibed the notion that although the charge brought against the modern bar of tautology and irrelevancy in their arguments is not without foundation, yet that nothing can be more unjust than to reproach them with having a greater propensity to these errors than their predecessors. The frequent reprimands which it appears the judges in former times made to counsel for repetitions and digressions in their speeches, the Orders to be found in the Lords' Journals that the Chancellor should direct the counsel to be concise and pertinent in their arguments, and that the second counsel should not repeat what the first had said, are convincing proofs that the faults imputed to the present race of barristers existed in those of a former age. Whoever, indeed, will take the trouble to look at the old Reports, from the interminable Plowden downwards, where anything like a full account of what took place at the hearing of a cause is given, will find the speeches of the ancient counsel not

* The numbers of modern Reports may seem irreconcileable with this statement. But there is more of the husk than of the grain of the law to be found in them. If no steps be taken by the bench or bar, some legislative enactment must be made to abate so intolerable a nuisance.

only full of quotations from the writings of common lawyers and civilians, but stuffed, according to the pedantic custom of the times, with citations and allusions drawn from every species of ancient and modern learning. Some persons, who know the author's ideas on this subject, have asserted that they are too conjectural to be relied on, and have expressed a conviction that if returns could be had of the business done by two Masters of the Rolls, possessed of similar judicial qualities, the result would be the same as in the case of the Lord Chancellor, and that it would turn out that the supposed unimportant nature of suits a century ago, together with the brevity and relevancy pervading the arguments of the ancient barristers, enabled the Master of the Rolls of that day to dispose of a much larger portion of business than his successors are now able to get through in the same period of time. It is obvious that the notions of these gentlemen are equally founded on hypothesis with mine, and it is therefore satisfactory to be able to apply to both assertions the test of experience; and this, from some returns made to the House of Lords in the year 1811, and which seem from some unaccountable cause to have hitherto escaped the attention they deserve, I am fortunately enabled to do.

Sir Joseph Jekyll and Sir William Grant rank as two of the greatest judges that ever sat in our

Equity Courts. The following is an account of the business done by Sir Joseph Jekyll whilst Master of the Rolls, during a period of ten years, from Michaelmas, 1745, to Michaelmas, 1755, and also of the business done by Sir William Grant whilst Master of the Rolls, during a period of ten years, from Michaelmas, 1800, to Michaelmas, 1810:—

1745 to 1755.		1800 to 1810.	
General Paper.		*General Paper.*	
Decrees	1654	Decrees	2518
Further directions .	168	Further Directions	805
By Consent.		*By Consent.*	
Decrees	642	Decrees	1065
Further Directions	187	Further Directions	462
Petitions.		Petitions.	
General Paper	1932	General Paper	4798
Consent . . .	509	Consent . . .	2164
Rehearings . . .	23	Rehearings . . .	*32

I take no notice of the motions, as few if any motions are made at the Rolls except such as are of course.

If after reading the above statement there be any person disposed to think that suits are now

* This account is taken from the *Report of the Committee of the House of Commons, appointed in the year* 1811 *to inspect the Lords' Journals.* We are indebted for this, and some other valuable information, to Returns made to the House of Lords in 1811, on the motion of Lord Lauderdale.

longer and more difficult to deal with than they were eighty years ago, or that modern counsel are more prolix than those who flourished at that period, I certainly am at a loss to know how he will reconcile with his hypothesis the immense quantity of business disposed of by Sir William Grant above that disposed of by Sir Joseph Jekyll. Both judges sat during the same days and hours; both occasionally sat for the Lord Chancellor. Sir William Grant, however, sat to hear appeals in the Privy Council, which Sir Joseph Jekyll rarely did; and when we recollect the difficult nature of those appeals, it must be admitted that Sir Joseph must have had much more leisure for the consideration of the points arising in causes in his own Court at the Rolls than Sir William Grant had. It is not unworthy too of remark, that the business carried before Sir William Grant was as important as any that comes before the Court; and that from the dispatch which he used, few of those causes were placed on his list which are instituted merely for delay, and which disappear without discussion as soon as their turn to be heard arrives. The quantity of business of this nature, which, from the inefficiency of the judges who have presided at the Rolls from the time of Sir William Grant until the appointment of Sir John Leach, has been, as I have mentioned elsewhere, a principal cause of the rapid progress which has lately been made in disposing of the arrears of that Court.

The reader will naturally inquire what is the cause that the Lords Chancellors of the present age dispose of so small a proportion of the business of the Court,* whilst the subordinate judge has been able to dispose of more than double the business got through by the most accomplished Equity lawyer, that, with perhaps one exception, ever sat at the Rolls. It cannot be the increase in the number of appeals in the House of Lords; for we shall see in a subsequent page, that from soon after the time when the House of Lords acquired the appellate jurisdiction, to the beginning of the late reign, the Chancellor devoted as much time to hearing of appeals in the House of Lords as at present. It cannot be the increase in bankruptcy business; because all the bankrupt cases, except a few appeal petitions, are heard by the Vice Chancellor: it cannot, for a similar reason, be the increased number of cause petitions or motions;

* It is probable the present Chancellor does not pronounce as many Orders as his predecessors in the sixteenth century. Lord Bacon, in a memorable letter to be found in the *Journals of the House of Lords, v. 3, p. 54, March 20th,* 1620, states, that he made 2,000 Decrees and Orders in a year. Orders upon motions and petitions of course are included in this number; and, supposing them to bear about the same proportion to the Decrees and Special Orders as in Lord Hardwicke's time, it may be concluded Lord Bacon made as many Special Orders as the present Chancellor.

and with regard to the business in lunacy, although it has greatly increased, yet it is, as was stated by Sir James Scarlett, in one of the late debates, a species of business that in general occupies very little time.

The cause is too palpable not to have been long since felt and known. But in this country, grievances must be long and severely felt; they must be the topic of incessant complaint by the people out of parliament, and repeatedly denounced by their representatives before they can be remedied.* It is in vain that for centuries every writer who has entertained sound notions on the principles to be adopted in the organization of tribunals of justice, has condemned the union of the political and judicial functions, and, above all, the dependence of the judge upon the executive power.

It is in vain that our ancestors, by abolishing the office of Chief Justiciar, have showed us, more than five centuries ago, what they would

* Not to multiply instances, I will only mention that many of the crying evils in the laws relating to bankrupts, and debtors and creditors, are to be found in two Reports of the Committees of the House of Commons; the first on the Bankrupt Laws made in 1759, and printed in *the 28th Volume of the Commons' Journals*; the second on the Practice and Effects of Imprisonment for Debt, made in 1792, and printed in the *47th Volume of the Commons' Journals*. Some of the evils there complained of have been tardily mitigated by legislative enactment, but others still exist in aggravated enormity.

have done, had the various and conflicting duties which are now centered in the Chancellor been at that time attached to his office, and that they have, in more modern times, rendered the inferior judges of Westminster Hall, independent of the crown.* It is in vain that we see in France, and most other countries of Europe, sounder principles adopted in the formation of their tribunals.† The first judge of the first tribunal in this country, who has under his controul almost all the property of the kingdom, is, in the nineteenth century, a principal member of the cabinet, bound to advise the Sovereign upon every great question, foreign and domestic, and mixed up with the intrigue hourly carrying on in the palace even of the wisest and best monarchs, and liable to see himself, by any change in the administration, divested, in a moment, of his power and patronage, deprived of his princely income, and no more at liberty to follow that honourable course which led to his elevation. For the judges of the present age cannot, like the Cokes and the Pember-

* The biographer of Lord Chief Justice Wilmot informs us, it was a frequent observation of that eminent man, that one of the greatest advantages the courts of law have over the Court of Chancery, is, that they are not affected by changes in the administration of public affairs.—See *Memoirs of the Life of Sir John Eardley Wilmot, by John Wilmot, Esq.* 8vo. edit. p. 39.

† On this subject I must refer the reader to the Letters on the Court of Chancery.

tons, descend from the bench to the bar, and the Ex-Chancellor may be left (like the late Lord Erskine) incumbered with a peerage, with no other resource than a pension, which does not, perhaps, equal one-fourth of the income he acquired during his practice as a counsel.

It requires but a slight glance at some of the memoirs, which serve to illustrate our history, to be convinced, that the inconvenience resulting to the Equity suitors, from the political character and avocations of the Chancellor, has been experienced from an early period. Not to go back to those times when all our institutions were in their childhood, when a bishop or a general was considered a fit person to distribute justice to the subject in the principal tribunal of this country, we are informed, that, immediately after the Restoration, Clarendon, who had been bred and had practised as a lawyer, found his political engagements too great to admit of his devoting that time to the investigation of Equity causes, which their growing number and importance demanded, and he was therefore compelled to have recourse to an expedient which Wolsey, Hatton, and Williams, had adopted, although for a different reason. Wolsey, Hatton, and Williams, being ignorant of the equity they were called upon to administer, wisely employed able civilians, or common lawyers, to assist them in inquiring into and adjudicating the different cases that were brought before them; and Clarendon, perceiving that the distractions arising out of his functions as a minister left him no leisure for examining the affairs of the Equity suitors, made no important order or decree without the assistance of one or two judges. Between the time of Lord Clarendon and Lord Hardwicke, more than one Chancellor died a martyr to the efforts which, to their everlasting honour, they made, that the causes of the suitors should not suffer by the political engagements of the judge.

When we recall the names of Walpole, Pulteney, and Pelham, and the history of the changes that took place in the composition of the cabinet from 1736 to 1756, and the prominent part that Lord Hardwicke acted in all the public affairs of his time, we cannot doubt, that however indefatigable he was in the various toils of his office, his political duties must have greatly diminished his efficiency and utility as a judge; and this was probably the source of the complaints of tardiness and indecision, which we have before seen were brought against him, in despite of the immense quantity of business he got through, when compared with what has been disposed of by the Lords Chancellors of the present day. Lord Hardwicke frequently sat in his Court until after midnight, and by that means, for a time, subdued the arrears of his Court. It is obvious, however, that neither the bench nor the bar could long support such extraordinary exertions, and it was soon felt and acknowledged, that nothing is gained by the suitors, by decisions made when the faculties of the judge and counsel are exhausted; and succeeding Chancellors have seldom prolonged their sittings to the late hours that Lord Hardwicke did.

We shall probably never again see a greater equity lawyer than Lord Thurlow, who succeeded to the Seals about twenty years after Lord Hardwicke: but it has been said that he disappointed the expectations that his judicial qualities had raised, and that the justice of the Court did not flourish more under his superintendence, than in prior and subsequent times, and this can be attributed to no other cause than his political distractions. In his time, the Chancellor had discontinued his early sittings at the House of Lords. One or two hours, from two to three, or four o'clock, for two or three days in the week, was all the time Lord Thurlow devoted to hearing appeals in the court of dernier resort; and although the same rule was followed, with few exceptions, by his successors, down to 1813, the Chancellors must have availed themselves of the time thus gained, rather for the performance of their political than their judicial functions, as these pages, and the records of the Court, show a diminution, instead of an increase, in the quantity of business done by the presiding judge.

Nor ought it to be deemed matter of reproach to those distinguished persons who have filled this high office, that they have dedicated themselves to the public affairs, involving the welfare of the whole community, in preference to those matters which affect only private and individual interests. The labours of a principal minister of the crown must incontestably be greater, and must demand more of the Chancellor's time than they did in former ages, and the Chancellor must not neglect the national weal for the sake of adjudicating the rights and claims of those who have the misfortune to be involved in litigation; and if there be, from this cause, a denial of justice to the subject, if the fortunes of the suitors are swallowed up in the gulph of Chancery, and they themselves often brought, by anxiety, delay, and disappointment, to a premature grave, the fault is not with the Chancellor, who does not perform the various duties attached to the Great Seal, but in the legislature, which places on the shoulders of one person a load which, for centuries, has been too great for the most gigantic strength to bear.

CHAPTER IX.

NO ARREAR OF BUSINESS AT THE ROLLS.—THE QUANTITY OF BUSINESS GOT THROUGH BY LORD LYNDHURST.—PROBABILITY THAT HE WILL KEEP DOWN THE NUMBER OF APPEALS.

VERY little doubt is entertained, that every cause now set down for hearing at the Rolls will be disposed of during the present sitting; and with persons not acquainted with the Court, this circumstance may be perhaps used as a plausible argument, to show there is no necessity for the appointment of an additional Equity judge. A very few words will suffice to show, that the Rolls Court will not be left long in this unincumbered state.

For the last ten years, the great bulk of the Equity business of the country has been thrown upon Sir John Leach, than whom a judge more distinguished for his zeal in the dispatch of business, his quickness in unravelling the most entangled facts, and his desire, in every case, to reach substantial justice, never ascended the bench. For some time after his appointment to the office of Vice Chancellor, he succeeded in keeping in check all the business that came before him; but the rapid progress made by him, and the lamentable delay at the Rolls, induced the parties to carry all their business to the Vice Chancellor's Court, and it became too enormous to be subdued even by Sir John Leach; and during the three last years that he presided in the Vice Chancellor's Court, the causes were set down from eighteen months to two years before they were heard.

Sir John Leach took his seat at the Rolls in Easter Term, 1827, and the following account will show that the conjecture, as to the bulk of the business of the Court being carried before him, is not without foundation.

From Easter Term, 1826, to Hilary, 1827, there were set down to be heard before the Vice Chancellor, (then Sir John Leach,) 259 Rehearings, Causes, Exceptions, and Further Directions; whilst from Easter Term, 1827, to Hilary Term, 1828, there were set down to be heard before the Vice Chancellor, 184 Rehearings, Causes, Exceptions, and Further Directions, only. The solicitors, finding the field of the Rolls now entirely clear, will carry their suits there in greater numbers than ever, and Sir John Leach, in a year or two, will be as much over-burthened with business, as he was during the latter part of his Vice Chancellorship.

The following is an account of the quantity of business that stood to be heard before the Lord Chancellor, Vice Chancellor, and Master of the Rolls, the first day of Easter Term, 1827, when Lord Lyndhurst took his seat.

Pleas and Demurrers	19
Appeals and Rehearings	109
Original Causes	325
Further Directions and Exceptions . .	149
Causes, Rehearings, Further Directions, and Exceptions, at the Rolls	228
Total	830*

The following is an account of the quantity of business that stood to be heard before the Lord Chancellor, Vice Chancellor, and Master of the Rolls, the first day of last Hilary Term.

Pleas and Demurrers	17
Rehearings and Appeals	69
Original Causes	351
Exceptions and Further Directions . .	158
Causes, Rehearings, Further Directions, and Exceptions, at the Rolls	230
	825

* This statement is taken from the books of causes set down for hearing, delivered to counsel at the beginning of every Term. Upon the authority of these books, Sir Samuel Romilly stated in his evidence before Mr. Taylor's committee, that there was no arrear at the Rolls. The statements immediately following, are taken from the recent Returns.

I do not know the exact number of Bankrupt Petitions that stood for hearing the first day of Easter Term, 1827. The numbers that stood for hearing the first days of Hilary Term, 1827 and 1828, are as follows:

Hilary Term, 1827.

Lord Chancellor	90
Vice Chancellor*	217
	307

Hilary Term, 1828.

Lord Chancellor	32
Vice Chancellor	258
	290

* All the business, both in Chancery and Bankruptcy, is set down to be heard before the Lord Chancellor, but the Lord Chancellor, for some years past, has directed all the business, except the Appeals, to be heard by the Vice Chancellor, and yet the Petitions in Bankruptcy and Causes are not only addressed to the Lord Chancellor, but actually answered, to be heard by himself. A party applying to the Lord Chancellor, that his case might, from the certainty of an appeal from the Vice Chancellor's decision, in order to save time and expense, be heard by his Lordship in the first instance, would, unless there were some special circumstances in his case, certainly meet with a refusal. Motions are almost the only description of business that can be taken before the Lord Chancellor in the first instance. When mention is made of the arrears of the Vice Chancellor's Court, it is therefore with reference to that portion of the business set down to be heard before the Lord Chancellor, which the Lord Chancellor directs the Vice Chancellor, as his deputy, (for by the Act of Parliament he is nothing more,) to dispose of.

It clearly appears from this statement, that there is no material diminution in the total amount of the business of the Court. The immense arrears in the Vice Chancellor's Court may, in some measure, be attributed to heavy motions being carried there, especially during the time of Sir Anthony Hart. It should not be forgotten, however, that these arrears exist, notwithstanding the small number of causes set down to be heard before the Vice Chancellor in the last year, compared with the number set down in that branch of the Court in preceding years.

But although there is no material diminution in the total quantity of business depending in the Court, yet there appears to be a considerable decrease of the number of Appeals and Bankrupt Petitions, standing for hearing before the Lord Chancellor; and this is owing to several causes. One of the most obvious is, that fewer appeals are now presented than during Lord Eldon's time. From Easter Term, 1826, to Hilary Term, 1827, there were set down to be heard before Lord Eldon, 33 Appeals and Rehearings; whilst from Easter Term, 1827, to Hilary Term, 1828, there were set down to be heard before Lord Lyndhurst, only 19 Appeals and Rehearings; and many of the last-mentioned Petitions, Appeals, and Rehearings, must have been prepared or resolved upon in the time of Lord Eldon, although not presented or set down until the accession to office of his successor.

There are also peculiar causes which have enabled Lord Lyndhurst to dispatch a considerable number of appeals. Lord Eldon considered motions as a most important part of the business of the Court, inasmuch as the decision on a motion frequently puts an end to the suit, and the pendency of a motion generally prevents the parties from prosecuting the cause with effect, until it be disposed of. For this reason, Lord Eldon always devoted a considerable portion of time to that species of business.* It is, however, one of the most difficult to be understood by a judge who has never practised in the Court. Lord Lyndhurst has devoted little or no time to motions, except such as by the ancient usage of the Court he was compelled to devote, namely, the Seal days out of Term, and one day in each week during the Term;† the consequence is, that this branch of business has been in a manner annihilated. The extraordinary time devoted to Appeals has also occasioned an arrear of opposed

* Lord Eldon frequently devoted a week or ten days at a time to the business of the Seal, as it is technically called, that is, to the hearing of special motions.

† During the present month, the Lord Chancellor has devoted several additional days to motions.

Lunatic Petitions, and of opposed Cause Petitions, set down to be heard before the Lord Chancellor, but they do not appear in the printed lists.

Lord Lyndhurst has, (as it appears from the Registrar's Book,) from the beginning of Easter Term, 1827, to the beginning of Hilary Term, 1828, heard and disposed of 34 Appeals.* He has also heard 16 Appeals which stood for judgment at the beginning of Hilary Term, 1828.

When Lord Lyndhurst received the Seals, he left 16 Causes standing for judgment at the Rolls; of these, 10 still remain on the list for judgment.

It must not be inferred from this statement, that I mean to impute the slightest blame to the nobleman at the head of the Court of Chancery. My design is simply to demonstrate that Lord Lyndhurst has not been more successful in the struggle with the various and laborious duties of his office than Lord Eldon. My firm conviction is, that the judicial functions of the Chancellor, including the hearing of Appeals in the House of Lords, are greater than any man can perform to the advantage of the community;

* I take no notice of the statement which Lord Lyndhurst, on a late occasion, authorized some members of the House of Commons to make, as to the business done during his Lordship's Chancellorship, and the business then depending. The statement shows upon the face of it that his Lordship had been deceived.

and it is therefore no reproach to Lord Lyndhurst, when it is stated that the business of the Court over which he presides is in arrear. The public has, however, a right to call upon the legislature to adopt immediate measures to remedy so great an evil in the administration of justice in the principal civil tribunal of the country—an evil which it is now manifest the greatest energy and decision in the supreme judge are not able to abate.

The writer has been frequently asked, if he thought Lord Lyndhurst would keep down the arrears of Appeals? and he has had no hesitation in stating he thought he would. Lord Lyndhurst's policy is, (and in that he shows his good sense,) to affirm the decree of the Court below. This circumstance, when once known, coupled with his Lordship's little knowledge of Equity business, will not suffer the appeals to be numerous; although, if they be heard soon after they are set down, instead of remaining on the lists for years, as formerly, it is probable their number will not be less than in Lord Eldon's time, and especially if it should ever happen that either of the assistant judges is deficient in those judicial qualities, which are not less necessary than experience in Equity business. In June, 1811, the first appeal in the list had been set down nearly three years. Such grievous delay is an effectual check to the increase of business—parties do wisely to sacrifice a great portion of their rights, rather than undergo the torment and expense occasioned by such long protracted litigation.

CHAPTER X.

THE ASSUMPTION BY THE HOUSE OF LORDS OF THE APPELLATE JURISDICTION OVER OUR COURTS OF EQUITY IN THE REIGN OF CHARLES THE SECOND A VIOLATION OF THE CONSTITUTION.

THE appellate jurisdiction at present exercised by the Lords is perhaps the most absurd and objectionable part of our judicial system; and it is not altogether unworthy of observation, that the most eminent lawyers this country ever saw have considered the exercise of such jurisdiction an infringement of the constitution,* and an assumption of an authority which belonged to the whole

* It is necessary to inform the unlearned reader, (if these pages should find one,) that the whole account of the origin of the jurisdiction of the Lords in appeals is abridged from *Mr. Hargrave's Preface to Sir Matthew Hale's Work on the Jurisdiction of the Lords' House.* Wherever it was not inconvenient, I have used the passages of Mr. Hargrave's Work, with such alteration only as was requisite to preserve a connection between the different parts of the statement.

Parliament, of which the Lords formed only a part.

The Rolls of Parliament, from the time of Edward the First down to the end of the reign of Henry the Fourth, are, as it is well known, full of judicial proceedings; but, after that period, we find no trace of the Parliament having exercised jurisdiction in civil suits until some time after the accession of James the First. During the early part of that reign, the Lords exercised, without scruple, an appellate jurisdiction over common law suits, but under the delegation of writs of error issued by the Crown, authorizing them to adjudicate the particular case;* and it is remarkable that they then thought they had no power to exercise an appellate jurisdiction over decrees in Equity, upon a petition presented to themselves; and a Committee appointed to investigate the subject reported that there was no precedent of the exercise of jurisdiction by the Lords over Equity decrees, except under the authority of some writ, commission, indorsement of petition, or other act emanating from the Crown. Towards the end of the reign of James the First, the Lords appear, however, frequently to have adjudicated between

* All jurisdiction being either mediately or immediately derived from the King, no question has ever been entertained as to writs of error being strictly conformable with the constitution. In early times they were brought in full Parliament, but this course was discontinued many centuries since.

party and party, on original petitions of complaint presented to themselves, where the matter in dispute had never been discussed before any inferior tribunal,* and yet they forebore from assuming upon such petitions the right to examine Equity decrees; and the usual mode of impugning the Chancellor's judgments seems to have been to procure a commission from the Crown, directed to certain Lords or judges to review them, or to reverse them by a bill brought into Parliament for that purpose. In one case, towards the close of this reign, a remonstrance was made against the exercise by the Lords of appellate jurisdiction over an Equity Order upon a petition to themselves, and they acquiesced in the validity of the objection, and obtained a commission from the Crown to enable them to review the particular case.

In Charles the First's second Parliament, the House of Lords acted in all respects, as a Court having authority to try original causes between subject and subject. Sometimes they heard the causes themselves, and sometimes they selected persons, whom they empowered to hear them in their stead. In this Parliament, they seem first to have approached to the exercise of appellate jurisdiction over Courts of Equity, and actually ordered a cause to be argued by counsel at the bar

* The House usually referred the matter to particular Lords or common law judges, sometimes to particular courts of justice.

of the House, but the Parliament was dissolved before the cause was heard. In Charles the First's fourth Parliament, the Lords made great advances towards establishing in themselves an original and appellate jurisdiction in civil suits, both ecclesiastical and temporal; but still it does not appear that there is amongst the proceedings of this Parliament a direct precedent of any Order made by the Lords themselves upon a petition of appeal from a Court of Equity, with such a hearing of the cause as can be considered to amount to a complete unequivocal exercise of equitable appellate jurisdiction; and it is remarkable, that when this Parliament was dissolved, three bills for reversing three different decisions of the Court of Chancery were depending before the House of Commons.

The first direct petition from an Equity decree, and the first Order of the Lords, reversing an Equity decree upon such petition, without any authority delegated to them by the Crown, are stated by Lord Hale to be in the year 1640, during the sitting of the Long Parliament, in the time of the Commonwealth. Lord Hale, if I recollect right, observes, that the trouble of the times caused parties to throng to the House of Lords upon all occasions; and the Lords were induced, from the difficulty the suitors at that time experienced in obtaining relief in the ordinary tribunals, to extend the exercise of their jurisdiction, both original and appellate, beyond all former limits; and he argues, that Orders made by the House, during a period of general anarchy, when every member of the legislative body was disjointed, ought not to be drawn into precedents for future times; and, indeed, if the acts of the Long Parliament are to be cited as examples, they would first prove that the Lords had inherent in them the privilege of exercising the judicial functions in almost every case, and in the next place that the order of the peerage did not exist as a component part of the legislature.

Notwithstanding, however, the commotion of the times, the usurpation of original and appellate jurisdiction by the Lords did not pass wholly without notice. The cases of Maynard and Lilburne occurred in 1646 and 1647, and gave rise to a discussion as to the extent of the judicial authority of the Lords, and every lawyer in Westminster Hall (except Prynne, who, after having been mainly instrumental in effecting the abolition of the Star Chamber, now with singular inconsistency exalted the judicature of the Lords to an independence on Parliament) seemed to think that the Lords had assumed a most unwarrantable jurisdiction, and wholly inconsistent with the constitution. It is worth while also to observe, that Fairfax, and the council of the parliamentary army, in August, 1647, agreed upon certain heads of a proposal to be addressed to the Commissioners of the Parliament residing with the army, some of which touched this question of the Peers' claim of jurisdiction, and demanded a declaration that the original and appellate jurisdiction in Parliament were in the Lords and Commons jointly, and that the Lords could not exercise either jurisdiction without the concurrence of the Commons.

Little seems to be known as to the judicature in Parliament from the abolition of the regal office and the House of Peers until the Restoration. Cromwell appears to have seen the absurdity of a Court whose members were ignorant of the law they were to administer; and it is conjectured that the ordinary mode of examining judgments and decrees of the Courts of law and Equity, was by issuing writs of errors and commissions, delegating to particular persons authority for that purpose. The ordinance, however, for regulating and limiting the jurisdiction of the Court of Chancery already mentioned,* gave a very satisfactory appeal from the decisions of that tribunal by granting the privilege of a rehearing before the Lord Chancellor or Lord Keeper, joined by six judges, of whom two were directed to be taken out of each of the three great common law Courts, and of whom also one was to be a chief justice or chief baron.

During the Convention Parliament, the Lords acted as if there were an illimited jurisdiction, ori-

* See the First Chapter of the present Work.

ginal and appellate, inherent in the peerage, and they would not allow that the concurrence of the Lower House was requisite to give effect to their judicial acts.

The House of Commons protested against this usurpation of exclusive jurisdiction; but as any discussion of the subject was likely to cause a rupture between the two Houses, which at that period would have been productive of consequences most calamitous to the nation, the Commissioners, by the advice of Sir Matthew Hale and Sir Heneage Finch (afterwards Lord Nottingham), declined engaging any further in the dispute of judicature, but reserved the point to be discussed at a more proper season.

It was during the following Parliament that the principal contests between the two Houses respecting the right of judicature arose. In the great case of Skinner and the East India Company, the Lords claimed the right to adjudicate between party and party in the first instance, and not by way of appeal. The votes of the House of Commons, however, soon proclaimed to the people of England that the exercise by the Lords of original jurisdiction in civil causes was an usurpation. The case of Skinner and the East India Company ended in a compromise between the two Houses, but such a termination of the contest was a blow fatal to the claim of the Lords, and they have ever since relinquished the exercise of original jurisdiction in civil causes.

In the fourth session of the Long Parliament of Charles the Second, a new quarrel of the two Houses arose on another branch of judicature, and the event was different. The great question in this dispute was respecting the appellate jurisdiction exercised by the Lords over decrees in Equity, upon a mere petition presented to themselves; and the House of Commons came to a determination that the Lords had no such privilege as they claimed, and passed a Resolution *that any person soliciting, pleading, or prosecuting any appeal against any commoner of England before the House of Lords, should be deemed and taken a betrayer of the rights and liberties of the people of England, and should be proceeded against accordingly.* After such a resolution, it may seem extraordinary that the Lords have been left in quiet possession of this privilege; but the King siding* with the Commons, the latter began to open their eyes to the consequences of their depriving the Lords of appellate jurisdiction over Equity, which would be a return of such jurisdiction to Commissioners named by the King, whose decision would be final, unless the entire Parliament interfered as the Court of last resort. The Commons, therefore, seemed to have thought they had done enough for the public weal by securing a victory over the claim of the Lords to

* In the quarrel as to the original jurisdiction, the King had espoused the part of the Lords.

original jurisdiction in civil suits; and that however unfounded their claim to appellate jurisdiction over Equity decrees might be in principle, it was rather an affair between the King and the Lords than between the Lords and the Commons,—and that to gain a victory over the Lords on this point would be only to win a prize for the Crown, under circumstances which made it more safe for the constitution that the power should continue with the peerage.

The Commons seem to have been persuaded, that, in the instance of appellate jurisdiction over equity causes, however clearly the strict doctrine of the Constitution might be with them, their assertion of it was to struggle against their own interest, and to prefer confidence in nominees of the Crown to confidence in the Upper House; and consequently that success in their pursuit would be to enlarge the sphere of Royal influence at a time when, from the ambitious schemes of the misguided monarch, the contraction of the kingly power was deemed the true policy.*

"But," as the learned writer, from whom the foregoing pages on the subject of our present consideration, are extracted or abridged, observes, "whatever were the reasons which induced the change of disposition in the Commons, the effect

* See *Hargrave's Preface to Hale's Jurisdiction of the Lords' House*, p. 163, 164, and 165; from which many of the foregoing passages are taken almost verbatim.

of the change was leaving the Lords in quiet possession of the object, which had been so warmly contested for with them in the former session; and though the Long Parliament of Charles II. was permitted to subsist for two other sessions, yet the acquiescence of the same House of Commons continued in that unequivocal way, which imported, that the appellate jurisdiction of the Lords was not intended to be questioned:" and "Thus," continues the same author, "the issue of the fight for the appellate jurisdiction became in effect as much a decided victory to the Lords, as the issue of the previous fight for original jurisdiction was in effect a victory to the Commons. But there was this difference between the two victories. The point gained by the Commons was carried against the united efforts both of King and Lords; but the point gained by the Lords seems at last to have been a voluntary concession of the Commons, from a discovery, that, if they prevailed, the Crown would be fixed in the exercise of a discretion equally formidable to both Houses. Nor was this the only difference. The victory of the Commons appears to have been gained upon principles of the Constitution approved by Lord Hale, by Lord Nottingham, by Lord Vaughan, by almost the whole of Westminster Hall, except that Champion of aristocratical power, in its most excessive latitude, the memorable Mr. Prynne. But the victory of the

Lords appears to have been effected by the fear of the Commons, that unless they, by their acquiescence, sanctioned what in principle some of the first lawyers of the country, as well as themselves, held an unauthorized assumption by the Lords, it would leave the Crown and its Ministers with more power over appellate judicature than, from the want of confidence in the Crown and some of its advisers, was thought to be compatible with the public interest. So to be defeated was to the Commons in the nature of a second victory, not indeed over the Lords, but over themselves and their own pride, in respect of the arduousness on the part of such an assembly to sound a retreat, after being seemingly pledged to fight the battle out; and also over the secret views of the Crown, if really there was any deep scheme of making the Commons a mere instrument for increasing regal influence under the mask of preventing an unconstitutional mode of administering appellate justice."

There are no subsequent occurrences with respect to the question of the jurisdiction of the House of Peers, which it is necessary to notice in this short narration. The parliamentary judicature rests nearly on the same basis as it did in the reign of Charles II.* The Lords had claimed

* The exercise of appellate jurisdiction by the Lords seems, however, to have been questioned by some as late as the reign of William and Mary. The following passage is taken from an

an original jurisdiction in civil suits and an appellate jurisdiction over all courts and all causes; and had insisted that their judicative power was primitive and inherent in the peerage by the Constitution; and that they had authority, as the court of last resort, to exercise parliamentary judicature singly and solely, and without the concurrence or authority of the King or Commons. The claim of original jurisdiction has been abandoned, and the right to judge appeals from the ecclesiastical and maritime courts and in prize causes, and from the colonies,† has been, in like manner, relinquished by the Lords, although they have, with singular inconsistency,

Essay on Popular Discontents, written by Sir William Temple, probably about the year 1690:—"I have not heard any part of our ancient constitutions so much complained of, as the judicature of the House of Lords, as it is of late and usually exercised; which, if carried on a little farther, and taken notice of by the House of Commons, as much as it seems to be resented by many of their members, may, for aught I know, at one time or other, occasion a breach between the two Houses: an accident that would be, at all times, pernicious, but might in some conjunctures prove fatal to the public affairs and interests of the kingdom."—*Sir William Temple's Works*, vol. iii. p. 42.

† It has been well observed, that it is impossible to found the original exercise of appellate jurisdiction by the Privy Council upon any principle consistent with the constitution, except that of a commissionary delegation of the Crown, which is the essence of the appellate jurisdiction of the Lords over the Common Law Courts under writs of error; although it is true, that such delegation of royal authority to the Privy Council took place in a manner less solemn than by a writ of error.

retained the jurisdiction over appeals from Courts of Equity.*

The resolution of the House of Commons, in the year 1675, that any person soliciting, pleading, or prosecuting any appeal against any commoner of England, from any Court of Equity, before the House of Lords, should be deemed and taken a betrayer of the rights and liberties of the people of England, and should be proceeded against accordingly, has never been rescinded; but there has been too long an acquiescence both of the Crown and the Commons in the appellate jurisdiction of the Lords over Equity decrees, upon a mere petition to themselves, to admit of that jurisdiction being now called in question;† and, indeed, several acts of parliament have been

* Another inconsistency in the conduct of the Lords will not fail to strike the reader; that claiming, as they did, the right of appellate jurisdiction, as inherent in the Peerage by the constitution, they, nevertheless, declined to exercise appellate jurisdiction over the Common Law Courts, except under the authority of writs of error.

† It was not until the year 1726, that the jurisdiction of the House of Lords on appeal from interlocutory orders and summary proceedings was completely established. It is remarkable, that the oldest precedent brought forward by the Lords' Committee appointed to inquire into the subject was not more ancient than the year 1721. In the same year (1726) a petition of appeal was presented to the House of Lords from two orders of the Lord Chancellor granting the custody of a lunatic's estate, and it was only after a long debate that the Lords decided not to assume an appellate jurisdiction in matters of lunacy.

passed, which must be taken to acknowledge that the House of Lords are fully entitled to the privilege they enjoy.

It is not with the remotest notion of raising any doubt as to the right of the Lords to exercise the appellate jurisdiction over Equity decrees in the manner in which they now do, that the foregoing narration is made, but with the view of diminishing the force of some objections urged against the proposal that has been made to effect no less a change in our judicial system than that the Lords should divest themselves of the appellate jurisdiction, and the same should be conferred on a tribunal composed of judges versed in the laws which they are called upon to administer.*

* The proposal alluded to is contained in the Letters on the Court of Chancery. The Letters which treat on this subject will be found in the Appendix.

CHAPTER XI.

OF THE HEARING OF APPEALS IN THE HOUSE OF LORDS, FROM THE RESTORATION DOWN TO THE YEAR 1811.

The Calendar of the Journals of the House of Lords professes to give an account of the times when appeals were brought in and adjudged, and also of the material proceedings in them, from 1660 to 1807; and from the dates there given, it should seem that appeals seldom moved on more slowly to a hearing than soon after the House of Lords had acquired the appellate jurisdiction. From one to two years seems to have been the period that usually elapsed between the time when an appeal was presented and the time when it was decided. From the reign of James II. down to the year 1807, it does not appear, at least from the Calendar, that the general body of appeals remained longer on the roll before they came on to be heard. It is true that we meet with causes that were depending in Parliament from five to thirty years before they were determined, or otherwise disposed of; but in those instances there must have been some peculiar circumstances that retarded their termination, and it was probably the fault of the parties, and not of the tribunal, that their rights were not sooner adjudicated. On the other hand, it is evident that many appeals were advanced or appointed for bye days, and thus disposed of at an earlier period after they were presented than usually happened. The supposition, however, that the appeals during the latter part of the above-mentioned period were generally disposed of in so short a period of time after they were presented, is not quite consistent with some anecdotes preserved in the memory of the profession, and from which it may be inferred, that the causes lingered not two, but six or seven years in the House before their turn to be heard arrived.

However this may be, it is quite clear, that the House of Lords, during the first sixty or seventy years of the last century, devoted a much larger portion of time to the hearing of causes, than during the forty or fifty succeeding years; and yet the number of appeals brought during the latter period must have been more than quadruple that brought during the former. I believe, indeed, it will be found, that a century ago the House of Lords set apart as many days and hours to the adjudication of the appeals as they do at the present time, although the number now presented must be as 10 to 1 to the number then presented.

From notes which I have at different times transcribed from the Journals, I find that in 1690 and 1692 the House sat at nine o'clock in the morning to hear causes. In February, 1698, the House resolved, that for the future, when any cause should be appointed to be heard, the counsel should be called in, and the cause proceeded in after twelve o'clock, and that no other business should intervene. In 1701, counsel were called in at ten o'clock. In December, 1703, it was ordered, that on the days causes were appointed to be heard, the cause should be called in precisely at ten o'clock, and that no other business should intervene. In January, 1705, an order was made, forbidding the reading of any private bill before the hearing of a cause. An order of June, 1715, directed causes to be called in precisely at eleven o'clock, and that no other business should intervene. In May, 1717, the two orders of January, 1705, and June, 1715, being read, and considered, it was ordered, that for their better observation the House would (after the causes then appointed to be heard) appoint Tuesdays, Thursdays, and Saturdays only, for the hearing of causes during that session of parliament, upon which days the causes should be called in at the first sitting of the House, and nothing should intervene.

It appears from a Report made in the year 1720 by a Committee of the Lords, appointed to examine into the state of the several appeals depending before the House, and also to consider of some proper method for the bringing on and determining appeals not determined in the session in which they were first brought, that the Committee had examined into the state of the appeals as they then stood, and found that a great many had been depending ever since the beginning of the year 1702, (a period of eighteen years,) on some of which no proceedings at all had been had since they were first brought in, and that the rest were not determined; and that no proceedings whatever had been had in any of them that session. Two orders were made upon the foundation of this Report, the one dismissing thirty-five appeals that had not been duly prosecuted, and another directing that appeals not determined during the session should stand dismissed, unless the parties should take the necessary steps to have the same brought on the succeeding meeting of Parliament, by applying to the House to appoint a day for hearing the same.*

In November, 1724, it was ordered, in regard to the number of appeals depending in the House,

* The standing order of the 5th April, 1720, still in force, is a portion of this order, as afterwards amended.

that Saturday* should for the future be added to the cause days usually appointed, which appear at this time to have been Mondays, Wednesdays, and Fridays. In 1725, the House sat on Mondays, Wednesdays, and Fridays, to hear appeals; and, in 1726, Thursday was appointed an additional cause day. In 1727 and 1728 Mondays, Tuesdays, Wednesdays, and Fridays, were appointed days for hearing causes. From 1729 to 1739† the House heard causes on Mondays, Wednesdays, and Fridays. An order of the Peers, made in 1734, directed that the appeals not determined in the preceding session should be heard and determined in the next session, without any new application being made to appoint a day for hearing the same.‡ In 1742, the

* Lord Mansfield, at one time, would sit on Saturdays to hear Scotch appeals, and counsel remonstrated with him upon it.

† In 1730, an order of the nature alluded to in a former page was made, which, notwithstanding what has been said, might not be altogether useless in the present day. Notice being taken in the House, that the counsel, at the hearing of causes, very frequently argued foreign to the point, by reason whereof the hearings of causes were extended to an unreasonable length; it was ordered, that the Lord on the woolsack should acquaint the counsel that they should speak as concisely as the nature of the case would admit, that they should keep close to the matter, and that the second counsel should not repeat what the first had said. A similar order appears by the Journals to have been made in December, 1703.

‡ This order was afterwards amended, and is the present standing order of the 8th of June, 1749.

order of June, 1715, was altered, by directing that the causes, instead of being called on precisely at eleven o'clock, should be the first business proceeded in after prayers. In 1744, the causes seem to have been called on at eleven o'clock. In 1762, the two orders of January, 1705, and June, 1715, were read, and ordered to be strictly observed for the future; but I am disposed to think that the period during which such orders were strictly observed was short. The appeals were often postponed to other business, and counsel frequently not called in before one or two o'clock.

Lord Thurlow was Chancellor, with the exception of an interval of eighteen months, from 1777 to 1791; and during the time he had the seals, he seldom, if ever, sat in the House of Lords longer than from two to four o'clock on the appellate business, or oftener than two or three times a week. During several years, however, of Lord Thurlow's Chancellorship, Lord Mansfield sat repeatedly to hear Scotch appeals, particularly in 1780 and 1782, and the two succeeding years. He used generally to go to the House punctually at one o'clock, and he sat until about four o'clock, when the noise arising from the public business of the House compelled him to give it up. It was very rare in his time that a Scotch appeal lasted more than two or three days, which comprised only three hours each.

From 1777 to 1791 there were presented 410 appeals; and 236 appeals were determined in the same time.*

In 1788, the trial of Warren Hastings commenced, and occupied so considerable a portion of the time of the House in that and the seven succeeding years, that very little time could have been bestowed upon the appeals, and yet the number of appeals determined during those years bears nearly the same proportion to those presented, as in the years immediately preceding, the number determined being about half the number presented.

During the Chancellorship of Lord Loughborough, the House rarely proceeded to the hearing of causes before two o'clock. His Lordship sat until one or half-past one in the Court of Chancery, and then proceeded to the House of Lords, where he heard appeals until four o'clock, at which time the public business began; but from the frequent interruptions by messages from the House of Commons, it was not an uncommon thing for the House not to be occupied more than an hour in hearing a cause; nor, as I believe, did Lord Loughborough hear causes every day.—

* See the Appendix to the first *Report from the Committee of the House of Commons*, appointed in 1811 *to inquire into the causes that retard the decision of causes in the Court of Chancery*, for an account of the number of appeals presented and determined in the House of Lords from 1750 to 1810.

Mondays, Wednesdays and Fridays were the regular cause days; Tuesdays and Thursdays (which used in ancient times to be appointed bye days, for hearing causes which it was supposed would not last more than one day) being generally appropriated to claims of peerage, or any other business going on before the House.

After the termination of Warren Hastings's trial, Lord Loughborough made some extraordinary efforts to get through the appeals in arrear, and occasionally sat at eleven o'clock; and we find for two or three years he succeeded in disposing of nearly as many appeals as were presented. The House, however, soon resumed the habit of sitting only twice or three times a week, for one or two hours at a time; and notwithstanding the immense increase in the number of appeals that took place after the Union, no more time was devoted by the House to the discharge of its judicial functions, until the year 1813. From 1791 to 1800 there were presented 290 appeals, and 152 appeals were determined, whilst from 1801 to 1810 there were presented 492, and only 130 were determined.

I am not aware that we have any account of the number of appeals presented, or determined, or depending, in any of the years prior to 1751; but whoever will take the trouble to compare the account of the number of appeals presented, with the number determined in every year, from 1751 to 1800, will perceive, that during that period the number heard bore but a small proportion to the number preferred. The total number of appeals presented from 1751 to 1800 appears to have been 1299, whilst the total number decided during that period did not amount to more than 714. Some portion of the appeals which did not undergo the examination of the House were undoubtedly presented for the mere purpose of retarding the final success of the opposing parties, and were abandoned by the appellants as soon as there was a prospect of their being heard, but the greatest part must have disappeared from the roll, from very different causes. The lives and affairs of men do not stand still during the pendency of an Equity suit, carried by appeal to the Court of last resort. Plaintiffs or defendants die, or become bankrupt or insolvent, or are forced to compromise the litigated matter, by relinquishing their rights. In this manner, nearly one half of the appeals brought during a period of sixty years appears to have melted away. From 1751 to 1810 the number of appeals presented was 1791, whilst the number determined was no more than 844. From the account of appeals that stood to be heard before the House of Lords in 1811, we find that one was lodged in 1793, two were lodged in 1795, one in 1797, one in 1799, two in 1801, two in 1802, one in 1803, four in 1804, and the rest in 1805 and the succeeding years. The total number of appeals and writs of error then lodged was 266. The time that elapsed between the presenting and the determining of the general body of appeals seems to have been six or seven years.*

* This, as I have already suggested, would not, from the calendar to the Lords' Journals, appear to have been the case. The Appendix to the *Report of the House of Commons*, made in 1811, already cited, and the evidence of Mr. Chalmers, leave no doubt, however, of the fact. The following are the questions put to Mr. Chalmers, and his answers to them:—"Have you observed that there has been any increase of Scotch appeals in consequence of the delay? I know that there has been a great increase of appeals, and I know that appeals are entered many of them only for the purposes of delay; there was a remarkable instance of it this session, to prevent a person paying £1000 into Court; it was in the House seven years; I had orders to withdraw the appeal as soon as it could be called on, and when it came to the last moment, I took it away upon paying the costs.

"Do you think that appeals for delay form a considerable proportion of the present appeals? I believe they do.

"Do you think that proportion is greater than it used to be? I can have no doubt of that.

"Do you mean greater in proportion to the whole number of appeals? Certainly. I mean that the very circumstance of the number of appeals is the cause of entering such appeals as those which are never meant to be heard, but for delay."

CHAPTER XII.

RESOLUTION OF THE HOUSE OF LORDS IN MAY, 1813, THAT THE HOUSE SHOULD SIT THREE DAYS IN EVERY WEEK DURING THE SESSION, FROM 10 O'CLOCK TO 4, TO HEAR APPEALS.—REPORT FROM THE LORDS' COMMITTEES, APPOINTED IN 1823 A SELECT COMMITTEE ON THE APPELLATE JURISDICTION OF THE HOUSE OF LORDS.

On the 5th March, 1811, *Lord Eldon* moved in the House of Lords for the appointment of a Select Committee, to consider and report what measures it might be most expedient to adopt, for the purpose of expediting the hearing and determining of appeals and writs of error in the House of Lords. His Lordship observed, that he should not attempt to anticipate what the recommendation of the Committee might be. It was clear, that some measure was necessary, there being then upwards of 270 appeals and writs of error before the House, and it being quite impossible, unless more time was devoted to hearing them than had hitherto been employed for that purpose, that the arrear of business could be got through before another arrear as great, or greater, had accumulated. Neither should he then observe upon what regulation it might be deemed necessary to make, respecting the proceedings of the Courts of Equity below, in consequence of a larger portion of the attention hitherto devoted to those Courts being given to the judicial proceedings of that House, as that subject would most probably come under the cognizance of the Committee.

The Committee, on the 20th of May, 1811, reported to the House their opinion, that it was indispensably necessary that a greater portion of the time of the House of Lords should be employed in hearing appeals, than had been up to that time allotted to that part of the business of the House; and that it would be expedient, therefore, that the House should determine to sit for that purpose at least three days in every week during the session, meeting at ten o'clock at latest on each day, till the then existing arrear of causes should have been considerably reduced, and subsequently two days in the week at least, meeting at the same hour. The Committee also reported their opinion to the House, that as the above regulation would unavoidably take up a large portion of the time of the Lord Chancellor, which would have been employed in other judicial duties, it would be necessary that some relief should be afforded to him in the discharge of such other judicial duties; and the Committee suggested the expediency, in order to secure at the same time a sufficient attendance upon the House of Lords by the Lord Chancellor, and sufficient means for carrying on the business in the Court of Chancery, that an additional judge in the Court of Chancery should be appointed.

On the 30th of May, 1811, the above Report was taken into consideration, and agreed to by the House, but no measure founded upon it was introduced during that session of Parliament.

On the 6th of July, 1812, the Bill, entitled "An Act to provide for the better Administration of Justice," but better known as the Vice Chancellor's Bill, was brought into the House of Lords, and was passed and sent down to the Commons for their concurrence a few days afterwards, where it was read a first time; but it being too late in the session for the discussion of so important a measure, the second reading was put off two months, and another year passed away without any thing being done to diminish the evil arising from the daily accumulating arrear of appeals.

The Bill was, however, again passed in the House of Lords in the early part of the session of 1813; and after it had passed the Commons, and received the royal assent, a Committee of the Lords was again appointed to consider of the best means of facilitating the hearing of appeals, writs of error, and other judicial proceedings in the House, and to report to the House.

On the 30th of April, 1813, the Committee reported to the House that it was their opinion, that upon Mondays, Wednesdays and Fridays, being the days appointed for hearing causes, the House should meet at 10 o'clock, and should proceed to hear causes the first business after prayers; and should continue hearing the same, in the course and order in which they stood in the paper of causes, till a quarter before four, and that no other business should intervene.

On the 3d of May following, the Report was taken into consideration, and agreed to; and a standing order, conformable with the opinion expressed by the Committee, was made, and immediately put in force.

Lord Eldon, in the course of one of the debates on the measure to be adopted to expedite the hearing of the appellate business, stated, that according to the mode of hearing that had been adopted of late years, the last of the appeals then presented, even supposing there were no new appeals brought in, could not be decided for eleven years from that time, and taking the average number determined yearly since 1800, his Lordship's statement will be found to be correct; and with this knowledge of the time necessary to get through the actual arrears, according to the system then existing, it seems extraordinary the House should not have considered within what period those arrears could be disposed of under the new regulation. The House resolved to sit as before, three days a week, on the appellate business, but to employ on it six instead of two hours each day, being thrice the time before allotted; a measure which it is obvious could only enable the House to get through the actual arrears in one third of the time mentioned by Lord Eldon, being somewhat less than four years, instead of eleven; and during this period appeals would be yearly presented, which, upon an average of the preceding ten years, would be at least equal in number to those yearly determined upon the new system, calculating the number disposed of under the new system to be thrice that disposed of under the old.

It seems, too, altogether to have escaped the attention of the Peers, that the House formerly sat on appellate business as often and as long as they proposed to do under the new regulation; and that the Standing Order of the 3d of May, 1813, would merely revive what, according to the extracts from the Journals contained in the preceding Chapter, seems to have been the ancient habit of the House at different periods from the time of James the Second to the beginning of the late reign; and that the appeals presented for several years before May, 1813, were at least three times as numerous as they had been fifty years before. The information contained in the Report of the Committee, imperfect as it appears in some

N

respects, was nevertheless sufficient, had the slightest consideration been given to it, to convince the House of the inadequacy of the new measure to effect the object proposed. The year 1813 was not, however, favourable to the amelioration of our judicial system, and the House of Lords may be excused if, at the most eventful period of a war which threatened our independence as a nation, and the general overthrow of our institutions, they took a less accurate view of the state of their judicial business, and the machinery and time necessary to manage and dispose of it, than its importance required.

From May, 1813, the House of Lords strictly adhered to the Standing Order above mentioned, and during the sitting of Parliament, from five to six hours a day were devoted, three times a week, to the hearing of appeals; but the appeals came in much faster than they were determined, and at the end of ten years the arrears were found to be very little less than they were in 1813. The number of appeals, however, disposed of in this space of time was nearly thrice the number disposed of during the ten years from 1800 to 1810; the number heard from May, 1813, to March, 1823, being 371, whilst the number heard from 1801 to 1810 was no more than 130. The number of appeals presented from May, 1813, to March, 1823, was 570, being 199 more than the number disposed of; and there seemed to be no reason to suppose the number yearly presented would be diminished. Since 1813, there must have been increased dispatch in the decision of the causes, and the continued acceleration of the time of hearing will probably have prevented the bringing of appeals merely for delay. But on the other hand, it is to be presumed, that the possibility of obtaining the decision of the supreme tribunal in a moderate space of time, induces many parties to present appeals, who, under the ancient system of procrastination, would have been forced to acquiesce in the judgment of the inferior court.*

The House of Lords, in 1823, opened their eyes to the insufficiency of the regulation of 1813. It was now apparent, that although the arrears were in a small degree diminished, it would be impossible to prevent their rapid augmentation, unless the House sat more frequently and it was

* This conjecture is in some degree verified by a comparison of the number of appeals presented from May, 1813, to March, 1823, with the number presented from 1801 to 1810. The number of those presented during the former period has been already stated to have been 570; the number presented during the latter period was 492. The details in this Chapter, as to the numbers of appeals presented and determined, are taken from the *Report from the Lords' Committee*, appointed in 1823 *a Select Committee on the Appellate Jurisdiction of the House of Lords;* and the *First Report of the Committee of the House of Commons*, appointed in 1811 to *enquire into the causes that retard the decision of suits in the Court of Chancery.*

resolved to crush the evil before it had become too formidable.

On the 25th of April, 1823, *Lord Liverpool* called the attention of the House of Lords to the subject. His Lordship observed, that when the measure was first proposed in 1813, for hearing appeals during the whole morning, three days in the week, and which had been rigidly adhered to, it was expected that when the existing arrear of appeals was got rid of, the number would be so kept down, that one day* in the week would suffice for hearing them, and that his noble and learned friend on the woolsack would then be enabled to devote the other two days to the business of the Court of Chancery. So far, however, from this being the case, the number of appeals had actually increased since that period, the number lodged being considerably more than the number heard and decided. Under these circumstances it became absolutely necessary to consider of some other measure, not only with a view to facilitate the administration of justice in that

* The reader who has given any attention to the preceding Chapter cannot fail to feel surprised that the House of Lords could, for a moment, have entertained the notion, that one day in the week, during the sitting of Parliament, would enable them to dispose of the appeals yearly presented, which, in 1813, must have been from fifty to sixty. The hearing of an appeal frequently occupies the House several days, and every body knows Parliament does not sit more than six months in a year.

House, but also to prevent the delay of justice in other courts, arising from the present mode of hearing appeals. His Lordship concluded by moving for the appointment of a Committee to consider of the best means of facilitating the administration of justice, as connected with the hearing of appeals, writs of error, and other judicial proceedings.

The Committee were not long in reporting to the House.

The Committee, by their Report, stated, amongst the various causes which had produced the accumulation of business, it was apparent, upon the accounts referred to the Committee, that the great number of appeals from Scotland was the most prominent, there being 151 Scotch appeals out of the total number of 225 appeals remaining unheard; which, according to the average number annually heard, upon three days in the week, during each sessions since 1813, could not be disposed of in five years from that time, exclusive of the additional number of appeals which might be presented annually during the same period; and it was to be remarked, that the appeals from Scotland were not only more numerous than other appeals, but that they generally occupied a much larger portion of the time of the House. Ireland also had furnished a considerable accession to the general mass of business in the supreme court of appeal. And in England the increased business of the Court of Chancery, in which the property of the suitors had, within the course of the last reign, risen from £4,700,000 to above £33,000,000 sterling, had not only increased, of necessity, the number of appeals, but had also occupied so much larger a portion of the time and labour of the Lord Chancellor in his own court, as to preclude him from bestowing an adequate degree of attendance for the decision of appeals which come from England, Scotland, and Ireland, to the House of Lords. It was true that very considerable efforts had been made, of late years, to remedy this evil, by the establishment of the Vice Chancellor's court, and also by the Orders of the House of Lords, which, since the year 1813, had provided for the sitting of the House, on three days in every week during the session, from the hour of ten to four, for the special purpose of hearing appeals and writs of error. But all those exertions had been, at length, found ineffectual, and there was then a manifest impossibility that any person holding the great seal could find the time which was requisite for the business of the Court of Chancery and the House of Lords, and for all the other great and arduous duties of his high office.

The Committee then proceeded to state certain

improvements in the modes and forms of conducting suits in Scotland, which they conceived might be introduced with great benefit to the suitors, and to the general administration of justice; and they afterwards detailed the measures which, with the view to the then state of the appellate jurisdiction of the House of Lords, and the business of the Courts below, they thought might be highly advantageous in themselves, and at the same time tend to reduce the growing mass of appeals within narrow and more manageable limits.* And as I am not aware that their Report has ever been printed, except for the use of the Peers, and as it embraces many of the topics discussed in these pages, I have transcribed this part of the Report.

* There is one measure suggested by the Report, as applicable to the Scotch law, which I am confident might be very successfully applied to diminish the number of equity causes, in the manner in which it is most desirable to see them diminished; I mean by passing declaratory acts, to remove doubts upon some points which furnish a constant harvest of litigation. There are other points where no relief can be had at common law, but it is obtained of course upon application to an equitable tribunal. Upon these points remedial acts might be passed, to render the institution of a suit unnecessary, and to place the parties at once in the full enjoyment of their legal right. A gentleman of the greatest experience in the Court, thinks, with myself, that in this way one-fifth part of the Chancery business might be annihilated.

Extract from the Report of the Lords' Committee, appointed a Select Committee to consider of the best means of facilitating the Administration of Justice, as connected with the Hearing of Appeals, Writs of Error, and other judicial proceedings.

" WITH respect to England, the Committee have pro- " ceeded to enquire, how far the attendance of the Chan- " cellor in the Court of Chancery may be rendered more " adequate to the transaction of business in that Court, " consistently with his attendance in the House of Lords; " and it has been represented to them that this may be, " in some degree, effected in various ways. It may be " done by enabling other Courts to take cognizance of " matters at present wholly under the cognizance of that " Court; or by occasionally referring to other courts, or " other judge or judges, matters which are now subject to " the jurisdiction both of the Court of Chancery and of " such other courts or judges, but which are generally " made the subjects of application to Chancery only; and " by not allowing, in certain cases, appeals or re-hearings " from one branch of the Court of Chancery to another; " and by not allowing, in certain cases, appeals from that " Court to the House of Lords; and by the Court being " enabled (in cases in which, according to law, it may not " now have authority so to do) to alter the rules of prac- " tice in the Court; and, possibly, by other provisions " and regulations.

" The Committee are not prepared as yet to report " fully and satisfactorily upon these several matters; nor " can they probably be enabled so to do without the " benefit of a review of the practice of the Court, by the " three judges of the Court, with respect to such parts of " its practice as are hereinafter adverted to.

"Some branches, however, of the business transacted "in the Court of Chancery, it is conceived, could not be "removed from it, without great detriment to the public, "whilst others might be beneficially transferred to other "courts or judges.

"Of the first sort are matters in lunacy. These "employ occasionally very considerable portions of the "Chancellor's time of attendance in his court; they are "not matters in which the Chancellor, as such, has juris-"diction, but are committed to him by a special commis-"sion or warrant from the Crown, which may be given to "any other person. The Lords Chancellors have, how-"ever, been entrusted, for a very long series of years, "with the care of idiots, lunatics, and persons of unsound "mind, exercising, on behalf of the King, as *parens* "*patriæ*, the duty of taking care of those who are unable "to take care of themselves; and the Committee think, "that although this duty might, according to law, be "entrusted to others, the discharge of it ought not to be "withdrawn from the Chancellors, who, in their court, "have long administered the affairs and property of such "persons, according to settled rules and doctrines, and "with establishments of officers necessary for the dispatch "of business and the security and improvement of the "property of such persons.

"It has also been suggested, and the Committee think, "that the visitatorial jurisdiction, which the Chancellor "occasionally exercises on behalf of the Crown and as "Chancellor, could not properly be withdrawn from among "the duties of the Lord Chancellor.

"It appears, that when the Vice Chancellor's court "was established, persons entitled to respect, recom-"mended that the jurisdiction in bankruptcy (which "is a jurisdiction in which both equity and law are "administered, and which, from the commencement of "that jurisdiction, and centuries since, has been com-"mitted to the Lords Chancellors) should no longer be "exercised by them; and that this would be beneficial, "as allowing the Chancellor to give more attention to the "other business of the Court. To others it appeared, "that it would not be advisable to withdraw the business "of bankruptcy from that court of legal and equitable "jurisdiction, in which it had been so long administered, "and commit it to a court probably little acquainted "with equity, and without appeal from such a court, the "jurisdiction being summary; and thereupon it seemed "to the Legislature more advisable to authorize the "Chancellor to refer petitions in bankruptcy to a Vice "Chancellor, allowing appeal to the Chancellor. It has "been represented to the Committee, that the relief "afforded to the Chancellor by this arrangement has "been very considerable, a great portion of the petitions "in bankruptcy having been heard and decided by the "Vice Chancellor, in late years, and that though upon "the first institution of that office it was not unlikely "that there should be many appeals, the number of "petitions in bankruptcy finally decided by the Vice "Chancellor has been very considerable; and it seems "probable that the number of appeals will decrease. It "does not, therefore, appear to the Committee to be "advisable, or necessary, to withdraw the jurisdiction in "bankruptcy altogether from the Lords Chancellors, due "attention being given to check frivolous and vexatious "appeals. It has, however, been represented as worthy "of consideration, whether the practice, which formerly "was in use, of referring to two judges (under acts of "Parliament then in force) the hearing of petitions for "bankrupts' certificates might not be usefully revived.

"It has been further suggested to the Committee, that

"appeals ought not to be permitted, as they may now be "made, to the House of Lords, from interlocutory Orders "of the Court of Chancery; but it appears that this will "require more consideration than has been given to the "subject,—first, because appeals of this nature are very "uncommon, and also because it is suggested, perhaps "with truth, that many motions have been made before "the Chancellor, the decisions upon which the parties "agree shall be (though not in form, yet in fact and "substance) a decision of the cause, rendering formal "hearings of the cause and further proceedings unneces-"sary. Such motions always call for discussion, requiring "as much time as if the cause was regularly heard, and "prevent further proceedings in the Court; but Orders "made upon such motions, being in fact and substance "decisions of causes, the appeal from such Orders to the "House of Lords ought not to be denied.

"It has been further stated, that there are motions of "many kinds requiring instant hearing, which, in the "present state of the country, and the business which its "concerns produce, require often much of the Chancel-"lor's three days attendance in the Court of Chancery to "be devoted to them: such are motions for Injunctions, "in many cases for Writs of *Ne-exeat regno*, being in the "nature of an equitable holding to bail; and motions "against persons charged with contempts of the Court; "and such also are the motions for dissolving such Injunc-"tions, for discharging such Writs of *Ne-exeat*, for "discharging parties from imprisonment for contempts. "And it has been represented, that these motions too "are of much importance to the property and personal "liberty of the subject, and, therefore, his time is not "misspent in hearing such motions, and much expense is "thereby saved to the suitor.

"With respect to such motions, and some other parts "of the business of the Court, it has been suggested for "consideration, that it might be useful to call into "operation more frequently the Commissioners of Assist-"ance, consisting of Puisne Judges and Masters, who "under the commission may hear and determine the "business of the Court in the Chancellor's absence. But "the Committee are not enabled to state that so much "utility could be derived from this, as to express, at "present, a recommendation that this assistance should "be frequently called for.

"Amongst the measures which it may be most expe-"dient to adopt, for relieving the Lord Chancellor from "some of the business of the Court of Chancery, are the "following:—

"1st. As to matters arising out of the execution of "local and private acts of Parliament. For about thirty "years last past, by virtue partly of Standing Orders in "this House, and partly by the practice and usage of "the House, the Court of Chancery has been made an "instrument in the execution of local acts of Parliament, "relating to Canals, Navigations, Aqueducts, Avenues to "Bridges, Inclosures, Docks, Railways, Tram-roads, "opening and paving Streets, supplying Towns with "Water and Gas, and various other speculations; by "which acts, the purchase money of lands taken under "the authority of Parliament for such purposes, (where "the titles are doubtful, or cannot be immediately "completed,) is directed to be paid into the Court of "Chancery, there to remain until by proceedings in "that Court the titles can be tried, or means found by "that Court to clear doubtful titles; and it is obvious, "that in every case in which Parliament has thus "burthened the Court of Chancery, this new species of

" business operates against the despatch of the ordinary " business of the Court.

" This practice of Parliament seems to have originated " when the Court of Chancery alone had an Accountant " General, who could act with the Bank of England in " the care of the purchase money. But it has been " suggested, that the Court of Exchequer having now " an Accountant General and Masters, the Court of " Chancery might be relieved as to this business, or part " of it, by introducing into the Standing Orders of the " House and future acts of Parliament, passed conform- " ably to them, the Court of Exchequer, instead of the " Court of Chancery. And it has also been suggested " that the Court of Chancery might be further relieved " by giving to the Court of Exchequer the execution of " private acts of Parliament of different descriptions.

" In the several local acts of Parliament above " mentioned, the persons entrusted to carry such acts into " execution are not allowed to enter upon lands wanted " for the purposes of such acts, unless they observe the " regulations respecting things to be done for the benefit " of the persons whose land is to be taken for that " purpose. These regulations are, it is represented, " often not attended to, and the non-observance of them " occasions applications to the Court of Chancery for " injunctions to prevent parties from entering until such " regulations have been observed. The discussions " which take place in the Court, upon applications to " dissolve these injunctions, are represented as employing " the Court for a considerable time; in some instances, " not less than, or during a very large proportion of, the " three days per week, in which the Lord Chancellor " now attends the Court. The fact, that all the monies "which are to be disposed of in executing these acts "of Parliament were to be paid into Chancery, has "naturally led the parties concerned in the matter of these "injunctions into the same Court; and the great number "of acts passed in the last twenty years, in the execution "of which the Court of Chancery has been made an "instrument, cannot but have occasioned a very consider-"able addition to the business of that Court. These mat-"ters, it has been suggested, might be transferred into the "Court of Exchequer, by applications to be there made "for Injunctions, or Orders in the nature of Injunctions; "and it may deserve consideration, whether provision "might not be made also for enabling the Court of "Common Pleas to administer justice in such matters, "upon applications to be made to that Court for Orders "or Rules in the nature of Prohibitions, to be discharged "by that Court, or some of the judges thereof, upon just "cause shown,

"It deserves also consideration, whether, in like "manner, relief might not be given to the Court of "Chancery with respect to acts of Parliament which "create Benefit Societies, Friendly Societies, and other "Societies of a like nature, the disputes among the "members of which, as to their property, the Court of "Chancery has been, by many acts, required to hear and "determine; and which Societies either not understanding "the effect of the Parliamentary Regulations, which they "are required to attend to, or omitting to observe them, "or forming their existence upon principles upon which "they cannot continue to exist, furnish calls upon the "time of the Court of Chancery to the obstruction of the "ordinary business within its jurisdiction.

"2dly. It has been stated to the Committee, that of "late years, and not till of late years, except very rarely "indeed, parties have been brought before the Chancellor "by writs of *Habeas Corpus*, in order for their discharge, "if their imprisonment should, upon discussion, appear "to be illegal, and in cases in which formerly the common "law courts and common law judges had been almost "always applied to. This takes place generally in cases "of commitments by Commissioners of Bankrupts. It "having been doubtful whether the judges of the "Common Pleas and Exchequer could grant this writ in "vacation, an act lately passed empowering each of the "judges to grant it. It has been therefore suggested, "that as this species of application to the Chancellor was "formerly unusal and has of late occasionally employed "much time, he might be authorized to refer (in cases in "which it might appear to him reasonable so to do) the "consideration of matters of this nature to some of the "judges of the other courts of Westminster Hall.

"3dly. It has been also stated, that there is a course of "appeal from court to court in the Chancery, and from "the Chancery to the House of Lords, which, without "injury to the suitors, might be suffered no longer to "exist. The following instance may exemplify what is "meant, and at the same time show what might be an "useful change in practice. When a defendant is called "upon to answer a bill, his answer is sometimes referred "to a Master as insufficient, or as impertinent, or as scan-"dalous, the reference directing the Master to report "whether the answer is open to these objections. If the "party is dissatisfied with the Master's report, he excepts "to it; the exceptions, often very many in number, are "heard before the Master of the Rolls or Vice Chancellor. "If upon that hearing the report is confirmed, the party "may appeal to the Chancellor. If the Chancellor again "confirms the Report, the party may appeal to the House "of Lords. This last appeal, it is represented, is seldom "resorted to, but that the hearing before the Master of "the Rolls or Vice Chancellor is frequently resorted to, "and also the appeal from them to the Chancellor, and "that in hearing such exceptions upon appeal much time "is occasionally employed.

"It is suggested, therefore, that it might be reasonable "that in most cases of this nature, in which both the "Master in Chancery and the Master of the Rolls, or the "Master in Chancery and the Vice Chancellor, concur in "judgment, such judgment should be final, and that it "cannot be necessary, in all such matters, to require four "judicial discussions and decisions, and some order or "Rule of Court, stating in what cases they might be "allowed, may be framed, and with proper sanction "adopted. The same rule, it is stated, might be applied "to other proceedings in the Court, to which insufficiency, "impertinence or scandal is imputed, such as examinations, "interrogatories, depositions, affidavits, &c.

"The appeal to the House of Lords in any of such "cases, it has been suggested, could only be taken away "by Act of Parliament, and that it might be prudent, as "to the appeal to the Chancellor, to resort to the same "authority, the ancient practice of the Court being said "to form part of the law of the land.

"It has been stated to the Committee, that all the "orders made by former Chancellors, as to the practice "of the Court, are now under examination, to the intent "to have it determined which of the same are now in "force, or have been affected by subsequent practice, and "that after this shall be ascertained, it will be expedient "to determine, upon a general review of the practice of "the Court, what alterations and regulations may be use- "fully adopted with relation to other parts of the pro- "ceedings and practice of the Court of Chancery not "herein noticed; it is conceived that other alterations "might be suggested, which would be entitled to deliberate consideration, but as the extreme importance of "speedily providing the means for the hearing and determining of the appeals now depending in the House is "strongly felt by the Committee, they have not thought "it right to delay making the Report which is now offered "to the House, and the Committee may, by the House, "be enabled to report hereafter upon that part of the "subject which relates to the Court of Chancery more "largely, if deemed to be necessary or expedient."

The Committee then stated their opinion as to the measures to be adopted to dispose of the existing arrear, and as it appears to me that no words can convey so just a notion of the defective and preposterous constitution of our tribunal of last resort, as the measure and the resolutions originated and recommended by the Committee, and afterwards adopted by the House of Lords, and the debates to which they have given rise, I shall, notwithstanding the long extract already made from the Report, transcribe, in this Chapter, that part of the Report relating to such measure and resolutions; and, in the next Chapter, I shall give a short account of the debates that took place in Parliament upon the subject in the years 1823 and 1824, and again upon a temporary renewal of the measure by the present Chancellor, Lord Lyndhurst, in 1827.*

* Lord Eldon had declared his conviction that the measure would not give satisfaction. The result does not appear to have

Further Extract from the Report of the Lords' Committee.

" THERE now remains to be considered the most urgent " part of the matters referred to the Committee, namely, " the measures to be adopted for disposing of the present " arrears. None of those which have occurred to the " Committee can be adopted without many great incon- " veniences, but that must be resorted to which upon the " whole shall appear to be the most effectual and least " objectionable. Any such measure must necessarily have " something of novelty in its character, but being intended " for obviating a temporary difficulty, it may be hoped, " that it will be only of temporary duration; yet, even in " this view, it seems to be desirable that it should accord, " as much as possible, with established forms, and afford " to the suitor, as nearly as possible, the same tribunal as " that to which he considered himself to have brought his " appeal, or he may have just ground for complaint, that " the expectation on which he appealed has been defeated.

altered his opinion, as he took no steps to renew it after Lord Gifford's death. It should seem that the fresh experiment made last year, when, in the absence of the Chancellor, the present Lord Chief Baron and the present Master of the Rolls sat to hear Scotch appeals, was not more successful, as there is no talk of either of those learned personages again undertaking these duties. Indeed in a recent debate in the House of Commons, the country was congratulated on Lord Lyndhurst's having expressed his determination to hear all the appeals, and particularly the Scotch appeals, himself. It was said " the House could scarcely imagine how much satisfaction would be felt in Scotland, at the declaration of the present Chancellor, that he should sit in person on Scotch appeals."

"In forming any such arrangement, it seems also to be "desirable, that when it should become no longer necessary, the business so placed under it for the time may "revert with the least possible difficulty into the ancient "course of adjudication.

"The appeals from all parts of the United Kingdom, "since their respective dates of union, have been to England; and it seems, therefore, unadvisable to send "their adjudication to any tribunal constituted elsewhere; "and the appeals from Scotland, which are by far the "largest number, and give the principal occasion for any "new measure of this sort, would not, as the Committee "are informed, be decided anywhere so much to the satisfaction of the parties as in England, and in the House of "Lords.

"If in the House of Lords, the hearing must be either "in a Committee of the House or in the whole House. "To the proceeding on such matters in a Committee, it "has been considered as an insurmountable objection "that the Report of the Committee cannot bind the "House; and if the whole matter is still to be open to "the House upon the Report, no final adjudication is "obtained by this sort of tribunal, it remains that appeals must be heard in the whole House. The object, "therefore, of the Committee, has been to provide some "means of hearing appeals, by which the constant and "regular attendance of the Lord Chancellor may be dispensed with; and for this purpose it is submitted, that "it may be so arranged that a Speaker, appointed by "royal commission, should preside in the House, as according to the law of Parliament he occasionally does "preside now, in the Lord Chancellor's absence.

"In case this course should be adopted, it seems to be "highly expedient that such Speaker, although not a

"Lord of Parliament, should have liberty to declare his "opinion upon the case, and the reasons upon which it "is founded, before the question is put as to what the "judgment of the House shall be; respecting which it "may be important to remark, that according to the pre-"sent Standing Orders of the House of Lords, the judges, "and such of his Majesty's Privy Council as are called "by writ to attend, may speak and deliver their opinion "if required and admitted so to do by the House.

"It is expedient also, that provision be made for ob-"taining the opinion of the Court of Session in Scotland "upon any questions of law which it may be thought "proper to send for the opinion of that Court; such ques-"tions, and the answers thereto, to be entered on the "Journals of the House. The answer of the Court of "Session, if unanimous, to be given by the Lord Presi-"dent, with the reasons upon which the same is founded; "and in case of any difference of opinion amongst the "judges, the answers of each to be given separately, with "the reasons for the same, and transmitted through the "Lord President."

The following is a copy of the Resolutions:—

"*Resolutions respecting the Appellate Jurisdiction of the "House of Lords.*

"1st, Resolved, that until the number of appeals and "writs of error depending before this House shall be "sufficiently reduced, this House, in every future session "of Parliament, do sit to hear appeals and writs of error "on Monday, Tuesday, Wednesday, Thursday, and Fri-"day, in each week, unless the House shall think fit to "adjourn over any of such days.

"2d, Resolved, that the House do meet on each of

" the said days at the hour of ten o'clock in the forenoon, " and do continue sitting on the hearing of causes till the " hour of four.

" 3d, Resolved, that three Lords be required to attend " upon each of the said days of hearing appeals and writs " of error.

" 4th, Resolved, that for the better enforcing the " attendance of the Lords upon the hearing of appeals " and writs of error, the House be called over on the " Monday next after the meeting of each session of Par- " liament.

" 5th, Resolved, that the next day after the House is " called, the titles of such Lords as shall then be, and " as shall have been present in such session antecedent to " the said call, shall be written on separate slips of paper, " and put into balloting glasses at the table; and that " three of the said titles be drawn out by the clerks and " set down in rotation as the same are drawn, till all the " titles be so drawn out; and that days be appointed for " the attendance of each set of Lords whose titles have " been so drawn, after which the titles of the remainder of " the Lords (upon the roll), save as to those who it is here- " after provided shall be excused from the ballot, shall in " like manner be balloted for, and subsequent days ap- " pointed for their attendance; and that letters be written " to the said Lords, requiring their attendance on the " days so appointed for the same, and that a list of the " said Lords, and of the days on which their attendance " is so required in rotation, be printed and transmitted to " each of the said Lords.

" 6th, Resolved, that the three Lords so set down in " rotation do severally attend on the days respectively " fixed for such their attendance, during the time that the " House shall on such days sit on the hearing of causes,

" under a penalty of fifty pounds, to be incurred and paid " by any Lord who shall make default in that respect, un- " less he shall procure some other Lord to attend in his " stead. And that the said three Lords be, on the even- " ing preceding the day appointed for such their attend- " ance, duly summoned for that purpose.

" 7th, Resolved, that such Lords as are unable to serve " from age, being seventy years old and upwards, or from " permanent infirmity, do certify the same by letter to " the Lord Chancellor, or to the clerk of the Parliaments, " on or before the commencement of the session, and that " thereupon they be excused from the ballot.

" 8th, Resolved, that such Lords as are unable to " serve from ill health or domestic affliction, or for other " special cause to be admitted by the House, be excused " for their absence on the day appointed for such their " attendance.

" 9th, Resolved, that all Lords who shall take their " seats after the ballot by descent, or shall be introduced " upon a new creation or otherwise, shall be set down at " the bottom of the list in the order in which they respec- " tively take their seats, and days shall be appointed for " their attendance in rotation.

" 10th, Resolved, that a copy of such Standing Orders " as relate to the attendance of Lords on the hearing of " causes shall be transmitted to each peer, together with " the list according to the 5th Resolution."

CHAPTER XIII.

SHORT ACCOUNT OF THE PARLIAMENTARY DEBATES IN 1823 AND 1824, ON THE REPORT FROM THE LORDS' COMMITTEE, APPOINTED IN 1823 A SELECT COMMITTEE ON THE APPELLATE JURISDICTION OF THE HOUSE OF LORDS, AND ON A RENEWAL IN 1827 OF THE MEASURE RECOMMENDED BY THAT REPORT.

PARLIAMENTARY DEBATES.

Lord Liverpool.—Lord Carnarvon.—Lord Grosvenor.—Lord Erskine.—Lord Eldon.—Lord Aberdeen.—Lord Melville.—Lord Colchester.—Lord Ellenborough.—Lord King.—Lord Calthorpe.—Lord Holland.—Lord Harrowby.—Mr. Brougham.—Lord Lauderdale.—Lord Lyndhurst.

1823.

On the 26th of June, 1823, *Lord Liverpool,* in rising to move the order of the day for taking into consideration the Report of the Committee on the appellate jurisdiction, said, that in 1813 their Lordships had under their consideration the best mode of facilitating the administration of justice in that House, and they had then resolved to sit three days in the week during the session, for the purpose of hearing appeals. It was satisfactory to their Lordships, that whatever might be the difficulties either in that House or in the Courts, the House had nothing to reproach itself with, for it had most steadily adhered to the Standing Order then made; but on looking to the returns on the table, it appeared that the House had not been able (if he might use the expression) to overtake the business, and the grievance was as great now as it was in 1813. The Noble Earl here referred to the Report of the Committee for the present state of the appeals, from which it appeared, that the appeals from England were annually five, from Ireland eight or nine, and from Scotland forty. In addition to this numerical extent from Scotland, the time which the Scotch appeals occupied was much greater than those from any other part of the kingdom. The state of the case was this,—whatever might be the occasion of it, the whole of the grievance was the appellate jurisdiction from Scotland. If they came only in proportion to the judicial business from other parts of the empire, the business in that House could easily be kept within proper bounds, and the effect would be very great in the other Courts, particularly in the Court of Chancery, from which the distinguished individual who presided in that Court was withdrawn to attend to the duties which grew out of these appeals.

The first question, which naturally presented itself to every mind, was this,—would it be possible to remove the appellate jurisdiction of Scotch causes? If that were practicable, and conceived to be advisable, it would at once remove all the difficulties which they laboured under. And he had no hesitation in stating his opinion, (not meaning to say that it was the opinion of the Committee,) that with respect to removing the appeals from Scotland, he saw no objection to the principle, but very strong and forcible reasons in favour of it.—(Hear, hear). What were the cases in which the House was called upon to decide in the dernier resort? They were called upon to decide on the law, of which, as English lawyers, they knew nothing; the Scotch law being as different from the law of England as that of any foreign country. He knew that his noble and learned friend on the woolsack, with the accumulated experience of thirty years, had administered that law as much to the satisfaction of the people of Scotland, as he did the English law to the satisfaction of the people of England. But, with the exception of his noble and learned friend, and another noble and learned Lord not then present (Lord Redesdale), and two or three individuals at the bar who had made it their peculiar study, the whole of the bar and the bench of judges were entirely unacquainted with the law of Scotland; and looking then at this he would say, that the most simple remedy would be to relieve the House from the Scotch appeals, and appoint a special jurisdiction for the purpose. He was fully aware of the difficulties which would stand in the way of such a measure; and on the score of public opinion, (so far as the Committee could collect,) it appeared that the opinion of the people of Scotland leaned very strongly to the appeals to the House of Lords, and therefore it might be expected that they would look with disfavour on his suggestion. But there was another objection still more powerful. If their Lordships were of opinion that the Scotch appeals should be removed, still, before the House could adopt any such prospective measure, they must get rid of the arrears. It would, consequently, be a very considerable length of time before their Lordships could adopt any such measure, and the Committee had therefore looked to other remedies. There was another proposition suggested, it was, that the office of Lord Chancellor should be revised, and that it should be separated from that of Speaker of their Lordships' House. To this he had extremely strong objections; he was unwilling to see that high and ancient office frittered away by regulations for reducing or dividing its duties.

The *Earl of Carnarvon* said he had the strongest

objection to the measure proposed.* It would, he maintained, be derogating from their Lordships' dignity, and attended with inconvenience to the suitors. Three peers were to sit one day, and be succeeded by three others on the next. He would suppose an appeal commenced on one day; a part of it would be heard by the three peers who sat on that day, the next day three others of their Lordships would have to hear its continuation, who had not heard a word of the opening; three others would have to hear another part of the case on the ensuing day, and the three peers who might have to decide after the whole had been gone through, would have to give judgment on, perhaps, a most important matter, of which they had only heard the concluding part. How was it possible that strict justice could be done by such a mode of administering it? But it might be said, that the Speaker, or the individual to fill that office, would be acquainted with the whole of the circumstances of the case. That might be, but he not being a peer, could only give his opinion at the desire of the peers present; and then what would it amount to?—that the decision would not be that of their Lordships, but of the individual who had heard the case. This mode of proceeding would, he contended, be most

* The nature of this measure will appear from the Resolutions stated in the last Chapter.

unsatisfactory to the public, and highly derogatory from their Lordships' character, as constituting the highest Court of Appeal. It was said, that the attendance of their Lordships to these hearings should be compulsory. He could understand the justice of that principle; if the same lords were obliged to hear the whole of one case, but he could not understand it when three lords were to hear one part, and three other lords were to decide upon that which they had not heard. According to this new plan, three of their Lordships were to be brought by compulsion from distant parts of the kingdom, from their local duties, to act a part in the most ridiculous farce that ever was thought of. If he had not heard the very solemn manner in which this proposition was introduced by the noble Earl at the head of his Majesty's government, he should have believed that it was intended to satirize and ridicule their Lordships' privileges. As far as the appellants before their Lordships' were considered, it would, he thought, be doing them more injustice to oblige them to resort to this new tribunal, than if they had left them for their remedy to any other tribunal in the country. For his own part, nothing but compulsion should induce him to be present at any such proceeding.

On the 30th June, 1823, Earl *Grosvenor* said, in a debate on the Report of the Committee on the

Appellate Jurisdiction, that if the resolution were adopted, it would lead to a singular anomaly; part of a cause might be heard by three peers, another by three other peers, and the conclusion by three others, who had heard perhaps little or nothing of the case, and the Deputy Speaker could only give his opinion.

Lord *Erskine* said, in his opinion, the great arrear arose from their having brought before them points of facts, and not points of law.* It never was intended that appeals on facts should occupy their Lordships' time. For his own part, he was so well satisfied with the manner in which the judicial business of the House was conducted by his noble and learned friend on the woolsack (Lord Eldon,) assisted by another noble and learned friend (Lord Redesdale,) that he professed he could see no remedy for the evil, but impounding them in that House (a laugh.) It was very true they might lose the benefit of their services by death, but he believed they were too much men of honour, seeing their usefulness, to suffer any thing but death to cause the House a loss of their services. He might say, that he knew something of the law; but of Scotch law he was as ignorant as a native of Mexico, and yet he

* This subject is deserving of much more consideration than has ever been given to it. In France, the only ground of appeal in any case to the Court of Cassation is, when the decree of the inferior tribunal is on the face of it in contravention to the law.

was quite as learned in it as any one of their lordships, who could but bring to his office a legal apprehension.

The Lord Chancellor *(Lord Eldon)* said, he thought that in case of *any future Chancellor retiring, the minister should make his attendance a condition of his pension.* He believed that one noble Lord had suggested, that it might be expedient to take away from their Lordships all Scotch appeals. If that could be done constitutionally, it might be well; but he was afraid it could not. He believed that, if the Constitution would allow of it, the best thing that could be done would be to prevent the Scotch causes from coming into the House of Lords at all; but as, according to its constitution, that could not be done, the next best thing for their Lordships to do would be to try the present experiment. *For his own part he thought it would fail;* but still, on account of the great interests involved in it, it was only due to the country to try it. The learned Lord then alluded to the projects which had been started, one of which was to divide the duties of the Lord Chancellor and that of the Speaker of the House of Lords from being ever vested again in the same person; and another was to abstract from the Lord Chancellor part of the duty which he was now in the habit of performing. With regard to the first of these projects, he would assert now, at the close of his official life, that which he would not have ventured to assert so positively at its commencement, that he had never known any man in the profession who had not deprecated the separation of the two offices of Lord Chancellor and Speaker of the House of Lords; against that project, therefore, he opposed, not merely his own individual opinion, but the collective wisdom of an acute and intelligent profession. He had understood that it was the opinion of some distinguished characters, now no more, and for whom he felt the most profound respect, that the bankruptcy business, at least, ought to be abstracted from the Lord Chancellor, from that opinion he dissented most widely, and to any attempt to carry such a scheme into execution he would always say no.

Lord *Aberdeen* said, in the year 1784 a case had been tried by the Court of Session, and after it had been argued by the most able men at the bar, had been unanimously decided upon by the judges of that day. The judgment was not disturbed until the year 1818. The case was then reheard by the Court of Session, and again the judges came unanimously to the same decision as before. An appeal was presented to this House, and strange as it might appear, it was however not less true, that, by its authority, the unanimous decisions of the Court of Session on two different occasions were rescinded.

Lord *Melville* observed, that the people of

Scotland possessed the right of appeal to their Lordships' House, and that that right was essentially recognized by the Act of Union.

On the 1st of July, 1823, *Lord Colchester*, in the debate on the measures proposed for the better administration of justice in the House of Lords, said the prospective measures related separately to Scotland and to England. As to Scotland, from whence the large majority of appeals had flowed in, and such as created the whole of the present embarrassment, the Committee had entertained little or no difference of opinion upon the possible benefit to be derived from rendering the forms of proceeding in the Court of Session more concise and better adapted to separate matters of law from matters of fact, allowing perhaps in some cases an intermediate appeal in Scotland, and in other cases making the decision in Scotland final, but in no case bringing any questions but those of law to the House as the Supreme Court of Appeal in the last resort. As to England, prospective measures had also been suggested respecting the administration of justice in the Court of Chancery, from whence the English appeals chiefly proceed, and with a view to the same end, though by means somewhat different. Another measure, more directly bearing upon the object, was to make the decisions of the Court below final in certain cases to be limited and specified. He observed that the noble Earl (Lord Liverpool,) who moved originally for the Committee, and who had first brought the report under consideration, had stated, frankly and fairly, that his personal opinion would have been for sending all appeals upon Scotch questions of property to a tribunal of Scotch judges in Scotland; and his own high authority had the support of another authority greatly to be respected (Lord Aberdeen); but the noble Earl also fairly admitted, that the prevailing opinion of those most acquainted with Scotland had induced him to yield up that opinion, in deference to the alleged wishes of Scotland, that their appeals should be heard in England.

Lord Ellenborough said, if they were to have a commoner presiding over three peers, who might hear one part of a case, and then over three others who might hear the next, and then again over three more who might have to decide upon what they had partially heard, great inconvenience would arise to their Lordships, great dissatisfaction to the parties, and the character of the House of Peers as a Court of Judicature would be lost.

1824.

On the 2d of March, 1824, *Lord King* is reported to have inquired of the House what he was to do. He found that his attendance was required in that House for hearing appeal causes at the bar. Now he wished to learn from such of their Lordships as were better acquainted with the subject than he could pretend to be, whether he was in consequence of this order, which required him to hear causes, also bound to vote on them. If he must vote, he was also desirous of knowing whether, in the case of his happening to withdraw himself before the hearing of a cause should be concluded, he would still be obliged to give his vote upon it. Or might he vote, as was done in some cases, without hearing any thing on the subject, by proxy. Their lordships had in their wisdom determined, that each peer was to hear only fractions of causes; but how was this to be reconciled with the mode of voting by wholesale. Now, if vote he must on the above case, he hoped their Lordships would put him in possession of the means of voting rightly. He should, doubtless, be furnished with the notes which he supposed the peers who had already sat on the case must have taken; if, however, it should unfortunately happen that the peers who had heard the case had taken no notes, and that he would nevertheless be required to vote on it, then he would most humbly beg of their Lordships to amend their order, and direct that all peers sitting on appeals should keep notes of the cases they heard. Thus their Lordships would have before them the wisdom and information of their predecessors, and the labours of the sitting part of the peers would enable those who had to vote to perform their judicial functions properly.

On the 9th of March, 1824, *Lord Calthorpe*, in speaking of the new measures proposed for disposing of the appeals, said, the arrangement was, in his opinion, founded in a wrong principle, as far as regarded the presiding judge, and he thought it equally wrong as far as regarded the judicial colleagues of the learned Lord who was to preside. Noble Lords were not brought to attend to the whole of the pleadings, but, according to the regulations, came on certain days, and those regulations went upon the principle that noble Lords would attend only one day. It was optional for noble Lords to attend beyond that day or not. In fact, except on an extraordinary occasion, hardly any Peers attended but the two who were ordered.

Lord Holland said, in justice to himself and to the noble Lord who had first addressed them, he must say, that when he came to consider the plan proposed, it did appear to him the most unparliamentary resolution that had ever, within his recollection, passed that House. It was more directed against the honour and dignity of Parliament than any proceeding adopted in his time. This was the first instance in which the House, acting as the highest tribunal in the country, had declared to the public, that justice was administered there by one man. This was the first time the House had been laid prostrate at the feet of learned Lords, and the first time it had been announced, that all the other Peers were mere cyphers, attending to make up a House. This was the first time that individual Peers were to be regularly called on to discharge a duty which belonged to all. He did not object to the measure on account of any inconvenience to which it might subject noble Lords, but he protested against the principle of calling on individual members to discharge a duty which was common to all their lordships. It was true, that in coming to a decision they had the benefit of the learning of the Noble Lord on the woolsack, and it was true that the House would come to no decision without paying a due respect to the opinions of the other learned Lords in the House. But he knew of no distinction between learned and unlearned Lords; they were all peers in parliament, whether they sat on a woolsack or on a bench; but now, for the first time, this resolution, respecting the hearing of appeals, informed the public, that there were distinctions among them; that it was not the body of the Peers who gave judgment, but other persons who attended and decided for them. He knew it would be said, that it had always been so; that the decisions were formerly given by the law Lords who attended;* but the difference was

* This has been the case only since the beginning of the last century. When the House first acquired the jurisdiction, the other

very great when the fact was so distinctly exposed. Every man in the country was now informed of the manner in which this business was managed, and knew perfectly well that one noble Lord was summoned to hear an appeal on the Monday, and another noble Lord to hear the continuance of the same appeal on the Tuesday. He did not mean to say that any practical injustice was done to the appellants by this regulation; but what he objected to was the exposure which it created, which, as a member of that House, in which he had spent a considerable part of his time to make it useful to the country, he could not but deplore.

Lord Harrowby said, the only difference made by this regulation was, that the attendance of noble Lords was no longer voluntary, which, if it displeased those who were obliged to attend, saved the suitors who formerly came to the Bar and found no person to administer justice, a great deal of expense. The noble Lord said, it was absurd for a Peer to come during the middle of a cause; but this took place before, and would again

peers scrupled not to investigate the Appeals that came before them, and decide them according to their own notions of equity and justice. If I recollect right, it appears from more than one entry in the Journals towards the end of the seventeenth century, that when the Chancellor was obliged to leave the House by sudden indisposition, the House continued to hear and decide Appeals in his absence, without the assistance of any law Lord.

take place, whether their Lordships attended voluntarily or not. As to the observations made by the noble Lord who brought on this discussion, of judgments being pronounced by an inferior judge, it was not to be expected that placing a man on the woolsack would inspire him with knowledge: and though their Lordships were accustomed to place high and deserved confidence in the noble and learned Lord who had so long sat on the woolsack, it was not, therefore, a legitimate conclusion, that no other could be confided in.

1827.

In a debate in the House of Commons in the month of February, 1827, on the subject of the Court of Chancery, *Mr. Brougham* said, that with regard to making a Deputy Speaker, who might not be a member of the House of Lords, this, in his view of it, was one of the most unwise steps that could be taken. He could not express his condemnation of it too strongly. What had been the course of this practice? The Lord Chief Baron was first taken from the Exchequer in 1819. He fell ill, and the Lord Chief Justice of the Court of King's Bench was planted as his successor, under a royal commission. Still he was not a member of the House; he could not open his lips on the merits of the cases argued before him; all he could do was to put the question. That literally was the whole amount of his authority. Surely then, he (Mr. B.) was justified, without transgressing the bounds of propriety, in stigmatizing that practice as anomalous and absurd. Nothing could be more inconvenient—nothing more degrading, in appearance and in substance, to the dignity of the Upper House, than the situation of the Lord Chief Justice, under these circumstances, sitting with a Bishop and two Lords to hear causes, in the decision of which he had no more voice or vote than the door-keeper of the House or his own train-bearer. While he was on this part of the question, he would relate a fact that occurred while Chief Justice Abbott was sitting in that capacity in the House of Lords. A case was one day half heard before the Chief Justice, and appointed for further hearing on a day on which Lord Eldon, who had in the mean time recovered, came down to the House. The case was postponed till another day, when the Chief Justice heard the residue of it. The House then adjourned during pleasure, and other cases were heard by Lord Eldon. The Chief Justice went away to his own Court, and on another day judgment was given in this case. Did he say that judgment was given by the Lord Chancellor without knowing any thing of the case? No, he was perfectly well aware what was done. The Lord Chief Justice had communicated to some one or other what should be done; but was it not, he asked, a mockery on the sacred forms and attributes of justice, that in this manner we should make a puppet of the highest Judge in the kingdom, the next in rank to the Chancellor himself, the Lord Chief Justice of all England. Undoubtedly it was an insult upon his office; an unseemly mockery, he repeated it, on the administration of justice. [*Cheers.*] But the practice was under the new measure even still more absurd. The Lords were balloted for, to insure their attendance. Two of them came daily. Two one day heard one part of the case; on the next, two others heard the remainder; and the case thus proceeded, day by day, before a different set of Lords every day, until the Deputy Speaker, who, not being a member of the House, could not in fact speak at all, whispered the judgment to be passed by those who, perhaps, had not heard one word of the argument. He did trust, that the administration of justice would be spared this foul blot.

On the 7th of May, 1827, the *Earl of Lauderdale* stated, in the House of Lords, that he wished it should be explained by some member of the government, whether, by the Commission they had just heard read,* it was intended to make

* This Commission empowered Sir John Leach to sit as Deputy Speaker, in order that he might assist in hearing Scotch appeals.

the learned person therein mentioned the Chairman of the House, for the purpose of hearing and deciding appeal cases, without, at the same time, creating him a member of the House? If such was the object of the commission, he thought it involved a strange anomaly; since, after having heard the case, and drawn up the judgment, that learned person (for whose talents he entertained the sincerest respect) must put the judgment into the hands of a Peer, to move that it be received by their Lordships.

The *Lord Chancellor* (*Lord Lyndhurst*) said he would first recall to their Lordships the state of the business of the House on appeals. There were now before their Lordships seventy appeals from Scotland, and forty from the courts of England and Ireland. In the course of last session, the noble lord, to whom allusion had been made, (Lord Gifford) with all his talent for business, with all his quickness of perception and legal learning, and with all his perseverance and industry, (and he did not hesitate to affirm, that to his perseverance in the duties of his office he had fallen a victim,) could not get through more than forty of the Scotch appeals. In this state of things, what was the course pursued? It was proposed, and he again declared that it was proposed on his advice and responsibility, to dispose of the Scotch appeals by the assistance of the Chief Baron of the Court of Exchequer, who was intimately acquainted with the Scotch law, and who was to devote two days in the week for the hearing of the Scotch appeals. More than that time he could not devote to that object, without injury to the suitors of his own court. The assistance, therefore, of the learned individual named in the commission just read, would be required for one day, in furtherance of the same object. It was absolutely necessary that the Lord Chancellor should sit for two days in the week to decide English and Irish appeals. And he was quite sure, that if noble lords referred to the business of the Court of Chancery, they would be convinced, that the Lord Chancellor could not be spared from that court more than two days in the week, without prejudice to the public interest. By the system proposed, there would be five days in the week devoted to the hearing of appeals. The Scotch appeals would have three days employed upon them, by two individuals of great knowledge and talent, and both well conversant with the laws of Scotland; and the Lord Chancellor would sit for two days in each week, to dispose of the English and Irish appeals. This arrangement would give him four days for the Court of Chancery, a period which he trusted would be found sufficient to keep down the business of that court. He must say, that it would not have been just towards himself, to launch him at once into the hearing of all the appeals then before the House, and to require him, at the same time, to dispose of all the business then in arrear in the Court of Chancery. If their Lordships would grant him the indulgence, which he thought he might in justice require, he *would pledge himself, before the next session, to perfect a plan, with reference to the business of his court, that should secure its performance regularly, faithfully and accurately.* (*Hear, hear.*) The arrangement then proposed was merely temporary; and notwithstanding what had been said about Lord Liverpool's administration, he might observe, that it had had the good fortune to meet with that noble Earl's approbation.

Lord Holland said, that, as a member of that House, he must object to noble Lords using expressions which seemed to convey the idea, that the learned law Lords sat in the House to try and decide appeals. The right to try and decide appeals was not limited to any one noble Lord, or to any particular Peers, in preference to the rest; but resided in every member of that House equally. They were all "Peers," and that one word showed that they were all equal. It was the duty of every man in that House, as a Lord of Parliament, to sit and assist in the hearing of appeals. If the Deputy Speaker, or the Lord Keeper, was, as by the constitution of that House he might be, a commoner, should the King choose to appoint such a person to that office, he would only sit there to assist the House, and he would be bound to give the House such opinions as the House might exact from him. That there had been a change in the constitution of that House, with regard to the hearing of appeals, he was ready to acknowledge, but it was a change effected by no other power than a majority of that House; and not only so, but at the express recommendation of the noble Earl, (Lord Liverpool.) When that alteration was first introduced to the House, he (Lord Holland.) had warned them of the inconvenience of it, as it seemed to him it would introduce the practice of deciding appeals by some individual members, and not by the whole House. The Lord Keeper, the Speaker, and the Deputy Speaker, of that House might be commoners, and they could then only give their assistance to the House, and not decide the appeals brought before them. Even the Lord Chancellor himself, though a Peer, did not possess any additional power as Lord Chancellor in the decision of appeals; and when he spoke upon any subject under discussion he was obliged to quit his seat, and to speak only as a Peer, though he took, at the head of the Dukes' bench, that high rank to which he was entitled by the dignity of his office. If the Deputy Speaker was sitting, and the Lord Chancellor came in, he must also take that seat as the first Peer in rank. These were the rules of the

House, and he was sorry that they seemed to have been forgotten. It was not because they had the satisfaction of having some learned law Lords among them, that expressions were to be used, calculated to mislead the people, and to make them imagine that those learned Lords, and not the whole House, sat to decide appeals.

CHAPTER XVI.

APPEALS TO THE PRIVY COUNCIL.—LORD LANSDOWN'S MOTION IN THE HOUSE OF LORDS, IN MARCH, 1827, RESPECTING APPEALS FROM INDIA.

THE Chancery Letters, contained in the Appendix, propose that the jurisdiction at present exercised by the Privy Council over Colonial appeals should be transferred to a new supreme tribunal, some of the members of which should, like the French Court of Cassation, be acquainted with the laws of the countries from which these causes come. The persons for whose perusal these pages are principally intended, are probably not better acquainted with the defects of the Cockpit, as a court of last resort, than with those of some of our other tribunals: but it does not fall within the scope of this work to detail them, and I shall notice them only for the purpose of showing that the proposal above alluded to is made, not from any desire of innovation, but from the necessity of providing a tribunal more worthy of a great empire, and better fitted to judge the causes brought before it.

It appears from a preceding Chapter, respecting the Origin of the Appellate Jurisdiction of the House of Lords, that the Peers once claimed the privilege of judging colonial appeals; I believe, however, it will be found that the Privy Council has, from a very early period, exercised this jurisdiction. Appeals from the East and West Indies and America, are, indeed, all of a modern date. Barbadoes was the first of the West Indian islands of which we took possession, and no settlement was formed there until the year 1624. Jamaica was not captured by us from Spain, until 1655. Our settlements in America had not an earlier origin; and the East India Company did not lay the foundation of the three Presidencies until a still later epoch. But appeals from Guernsey and Jersey to the King in Council were so frequent and troublesome, even prior to the reign of James the First,* that it seems to have been the practice to send commissioners into those islands with authority to hear and determine them. One of the last instances of such a commission being issued is said to have been in the reign of James I.

* The Appellate Jurisdiction of the Privy Council must not be confounded with the right of his Majesty to determine, in Council, claims to a Province or an Island, granted by the King or his Ancestors. The well-known case respecting the Isle of Man, in 1597, was of this class. It was heard by order of Queen Elizabeth before Lord Keeper Ellesmere and others of the Council.

I apprehend, therefore, that it would turn out upon accurate research, that the House of Lords did not claim exclusive authority over appeals from the Colonies, but merely a concurrent jurisdiction with the Privy Council. And this seems more probable when it is recollected, that one of the Orders and Regulations of the Privy Council respecting Plantation appeals, is dated as early as the year 1664, before the great disputes between the two Houses of Parliament as to judicature had commenced; and that another is dated in 1689, at which period those disputes can hardly be considered as completely settled. In 1693, however, I find it asserted, in a reported case, as a matter no longer admitting of doubt, that on a judgment in Jamaica, an appeal lay to the King in Council; and now, under the authority of various charters, letters patent, acts of Parliament,* &c. the Privy Council alone has authority to judge all Plantation appeals.

I am not aware that there exists any account of the number of appeals to the Privy Council previous to the year 1815. In the infancy of our Colonies they must have been very rare, as few of the settlers could have been sufficiently rich to prosecute a suit, by far the most expensive of any known in this country. But few as the appeals

* It is very probable some charters and letters patent, which give the right of appeal from particular Colonial Courts to the King in Council, are of an earlier date than 1693.

formerly were, the government seems to have been careful that they should be decided in a satisfactory manner, as we always find, in the Plantation cases noticed in our old Reports, that the most eminent judges and lawyers were present, and concurred in the decree.* The Lords Chief Justice Raymond and Eyre, Sir Joseph Jekyll, Master of the Rolls, and Lord Trevor, who had been Chief Justice of the Common Pleas, all attended at the hearing of a case, in 1726, now lying before me. At this period, two or three days in the course of the year sufficed to enable the Council to dispose of all the appeals brought before it.

In 1774, the Lords of the Committee of Council made an Order, that for the better facilitating the dispatch of the Plantation and other causes depending before the Committee, the following days should be considered as standing days for hearing such causes, namely, the day before the first Seal preceding every term, at ten o'clock in the morning, and the day of the first Seal at twelve. And in case those days should not prove sufficient to dispatch the causes, their Lordships resolved to sit occasionally upon the day of the second Seal preceding Michaelmas, Hilary and Easter Terms. No days could be well found more inconvenient for the sitting of the Council than some

* The appeals of this period could rarely involve any intricate question of foreign law.

of the days fixed by this Order, and it has consequently long since ceased to be observed.

About this period, the King's Supreme Court of Judicature for Bengal was established, with the right of appeal to the King in Council, where the value of the matter in dispute exceeds 1000 pagodas.* I believe it was about the same time that the East India Company first established the Sudder Dewanny Adawlut (or chief Civil Court) at Calcutta, which hears appeals from the inferior Native Courts, and from whence an appeal lies to the King in Council, in cases where the property in litigation is of the value of £5000 and upwards.† A few years before the time of which I am speaking, France had ceded to this country Upper and Lower Canada, and by the constitution given to those provinces, an appeal lies from the Supreme Local Tribunal to the King in Council, where the matter in controversy exceeds the value of £500.

* The King's Supreme Courts at Madras and Bombay were erected at a later period. An appeal lies to the King in Council from the decision of the Supreme Court at Madras, where the value of the matter in contest exceeds 1000 pagodas. A similar appeal is allowed from the Supreme Court of Bombay, where the matter in dispute is worth more than 3000 rupees.

† The Company has also established Courts called Sudder Dewanny Adawlut at Madras and Bombay, from whence there is a similar right of appeal to the King in Council. Many appeals from these Supreme Courts of the three Presidencies are now lodged at the office of the Privy Council.

Most of the appeals which had hitherto been brought before the cockpit, depended upon questions of English law modified only by local acts and regulations;* but when the right of appeal from the decisions of Courts in the East Indies and the Canadas to the King in Council, was established, cases of Hindoo, Mahommedan, and French law, came under the cognizance of this tribunal. When we consider the indifference which the legislature has shown to the adaptation of our Equity tribunals to the increased demands of the suitors, we cannot be much surprised that when this right of appeal was given to the above-mentioned colonies, nothing was done to enable the Privy Council to discharge the important duties imposed upon it. It is true that the Master of the Rolls, about this period, began regularly to attend at the cockpit, but this advantage has been more than counterbalanced by the inconvenience arising from the absence of the other judges, who, for the last fifty years, have rarely assisted in the hearing of colonial appeals. The cases that since the middle of the last reign have been brought before the cockpit, are certainly of a nature to require for their due adjudication the collective wisdom of many judges. For how is it possible for any single

* The appeals from Guernsey, Jersey, and the Isle of Man, must be excepted.

judge, however splendid his abilities, however deep his research or extensive his knowledge, to acquire even a superficial acquaintance with the different systems of law which must govern the Council in their decisions?

Since the French Revolution, several foreign islands and settlements have been incorporated with the British empire; various conventions, charters, and Acts of Parliament, have confirmed to them the enjoyment, subject to certain modifications, of the laws and customs that prevailed at the time of their surrender to the British arms, and have given the right of appeal, in specified cases, from the supreme local tribunals to the King in Council. The appeals from these new possessions make it necessary that the Lords of the Committee of the Council should acquire a knowledge of other laws, besides those already alluded to, before they can venture to correct the errors of the colonial courts. Ceylon, Demarara, Essequibo, Berbice, Trinidad, Saint Lucie, the Cape of Good Hope, the Isle of France, &c. have all been added to the British crown. In Trinidad the Spanish law prevails. The Isle of France and Saint Lucie are governed by the ancient French law, under different modifications, introduced during the Revolution. In Demarara, Essequibo, Berbice, and at the Cape of Good Hope, the Roman Dutch law is in force, and in

Ceylon, besides the Roman Dutch law, the Mahommedan law, and the Hindoo law, the Buddhuist,* and the Mallealum and Malay maritime laws are observed.† If twenty years of study and practice be necessary to form an English judge, it must require many lives to qualify any man to decide, in the last resort, intricate points of French, Dutch, Spanish, Hindoo, Mahommedan, and Buddhuist law; and although much has been done by Government and the East India Company, and two or three individuals, to facilitate the acquisition of a knowledge of some of the least-known of the systems of law above enumerated, by the publication of some useful translations, yet as those works are, for the most part, elementary, or codes unexplained by any commentaries, there is as little probability of finding in them the solution of intricate legal questions, as of discovering in Blackstone's Commentaries the subtleties and refinements respecting contin-

* It is not immaterial to remark, that all these systems of law are observed with very different modifications amongst different nations. The Mahommedan and Hindoo, or Gentoo laws, in particular, undergo great changes, varying with the countries in which they prevail.

† This and some other information in this Chapter is derived from an excellent paper from the pen of Sir Alexander Johnston, late Chief Justice of Ceylon, containing a plan for the hearing and decision of Appeals from India. It is to be found in the *Oriental Herald*, for July, 1827.

gent remainders and executory devises that are contained in Mr. Butler's Fearne.*

The utter incompetency of the Privy Council, as at present constituted, for the due discharge of the important judicial functions with which it is invested, is not, however, the least hurtful part of the present system of colonial appeals. In 1827, a Return was made to the House of Commons, on the motion of Mr. Hume, of the Appeals lodged from the 1st of January, 1815, to the 31st of December, 1826, which then remained undisposed of, by which it appears that 234 of the appeals so lodged were then unheard.† What

* I believe the principal of the works here alluded to, are the *Code of Gentoo Laws*, translated by *Halhed*, and published by the East India Company in 1776; the *Hedaya*, a Commentary on the Mahommedan Law, translated by *Hamilton*, and published by the Governor General and Council of Bengal, in 1791; the *Commentaries on the Roman Dutch Law*, by *Van Leeuwen*, which Sir Alexander Johnston, whilst Chief Justice of Ceylon, caused to be translated by such translators as he could procure on the island, with an Appendix of the Malabar or Tamul Laws, and some special laws applicable to the Mahommedan inhabitants, published in 1820; the *Institutes of the Civil Law of Spain*, by *Doctors Asso* and *Manuel*, translated by *Mr. Johnston*, and published in 1825; and the *Institutes of the Law of Holland*, by *Van Der Linden*, translated by *Mr. Henry*, by order of Lord Bathurst, and just published.

† These appeals came from the following places—Jersey, Isle of Man, Demarara, Saint Vincent, Gibraltar, Lower Canada, Montserrat, Cape of Good Hope, Newfoundland, Isle of France, Guernsey, Trinidad, Bengal, Antigua, Prince Edward's Island, Berbice, Madras, Jamaica, Saint Lucie, Bombay, Tobago, and New South Wales.

was the number entered in the years prior to 1815, that was then depending, is not known, as the account only commences with that year. Notwithstanding this immense arrear of appeals, it appears by the same Return, that only 27 appeals were ready for hearing, of which five stood over at the request of the parties.

The cause of this appalling disproportion between the appeals lodged and those ready to be brought to a hearing, is to be found partly in the delay that has taken place from the Council not being at leisure to attend each case of appeal within a moderate time after it is lodged, and partly from the ignorance of the appellants and respondents as to the mode of proceeding requisite to bring their cases to a hearing in this country, and particularly from their ignorance of the necessity of having proper agents here to be answerable for the fees. Nothing can more strongly exemplify this than a comparison of the number of appeals disposed of during the years to which the Parliamentary Returns apply, with the number of days the Privy Council sat during those years. During twelve years, the Council sat only 120 days, and 319 appeals were disposed of. Now every gentleman in the profession of the law knows, that a much longer space of time would be requisite to hear even English appeals, and when we consider that the judges who presided at the cockpit were as ignorant of the laws to govern many of their decisions, as they probably were of the languages in which those laws are framed, it is obvious that a very few of those appeals were heard, but nearly the whole must have been struck out or disposed of upon the non-appearance of the appellant or respondent.* The number of appeals which the Council contrived to get rid of during this period was, nevertheless, much smaller than the numbers entered during the same space of time, and at the commencement of this period, there must have been a great arrear of appeals undisposed of, being the accumulation of perhaps nearly thirty years.

The reader may imagine that little hardship is experienced from these long depending cases; and if he does, it is probable his notion is not altogether incorrect. No hardship is *now* experienced from many of these appeals. Most of our fellow-

* The regulations that govern appeals vary according to the charters, &c. of the different colonies. In most of the West India islands, an appeal does not lie unless the property in litigation is of the value of £500. In general, it lies from an interlocutory as well as from a final order. It commonly stays all proceedings upon the appellant giving certain security. With such encouragement to a rich man, to harass his adversary by an appeal, can we wonder that many appeals are brought merely for delay, and abandoned when pressed to a hearing. It is much to be feared, that in numerous cases the poverty of the respondent prevents him from employing proper persons to force the appellant to bring forward his appeal, and then, according to the present practice, it may depend a century without any steps being taken.

subjects in various parts of the globe, who were interested in these suits, are probably long since dead, and the sufferings occasioned by an appeal to the justice of their monarch are at an end. If an order were made by the Committee of Lords of the Council, that all appeals should be dismissed in which no proceedings should be taken within eighteen months, and the lists were called over at the end of that time, it is probable that nearly the whole would be struck out. When the Imperial Chamber of Wetzlar was suppressed, the causes were in arrear upwards of fifty years. If the Roll had been read at that time, neither appellant or respondent would have been found to answer to his name.

There are, however, still some living victims of the delay and expense attending this system of Plantation Appeals. Many appeals are depending from the Courts of Bengal, Madras, and Bombay, called Sudder Dewanny Adawlut; and I observe, by the Return above alluded to, that in 1827 not one of these cases was ready for hearing, although one of them was lodged in 1818. When we recollect that these appeals from the supreme native courts cannot be brought where the matter in dispute is not of the value of £5,000, can any doubt be entertained as to the real causes of their not being prosecuted? The wretched parties are not acquainted with the steps which it is necessary to take to have their cases heard. They have transmitted them to be laid before their Sovereign, and they wait the result with resignation and patience, which are but ill requited.

The mode of prosecuting and determining appeals from decisions of the King's and Company's Courts in our India territories, was last year the subject of a motion made by Lord Lansdown in the House of Peers, and as his Lordship not only pointed out the prominent defects inherent in the present system, but suggested the best immediate remedies, I do not know that I can better conclude the present Chapter than by adopting the course pursued in other parts of this work, with regard to those tribunals which are the more peculiar subject of it. I shall therefore give a short account of what passed on that motion, and the reader will bear in mind that Lord Lansdown's observations in the East India Appeals are equally applicable to those from our colonies and settlements in America and the West Indies.

On the 30th of March, 1827, the *Marquis of Lansdowne,* in pursuance of the notice which he had given, called the attention of the House of Lords to the subject of appeals from India. He stated that he proposed, by his motion, to put their Lordships in possession, by the information it would cause to be laid on their table, of some circumstances which would show them that a great practical grievance was suffered by that portion of His Majesty's subjects who constituted that ancient part of the Empire. He hoped their Lordships would think no apology necessary from him, for bringing before them a question, concerning which he did not pretend to have any local information; but it must happen, while the government of countries of vast extent, and at a great distance, was under our sway, that such questions should come before their Lordships, and it was their duty to collect as much information as possible on all questions in which the welfare, the happiness, and, above all, the administration of justice in that distant country was concerned. He did not mean to say from what cause the difficulty had arisen, but the fact would be proved to their Lordships by the papers for which he meant to move, that ever since the year 1773, when, by the act of Parliament for regulating the judicature in India, the duty had been vested in the Privy Council of hearing and deciding appeals, a large number of them lay not merely not decided, but on which no proceedings had taken place at all. The number of these appeals from one court amounted to forty or fifty, on which no proceeding whatever had taken place. In one instance, there was an example of an appeal, in which the property of the whole Zemindary of Ramnad was concerned, which was an extensive district, containing many square miles, and many thousand inhabitants; and during the time the appeal was pending, on which no proceedings had taken place, no man could tell what were his rights in the district, and the people were ignorant to whom they ought to pay their rents. He did not mean to impute blame to any person, or to say that these causes had been put off or delayed by any one man's conduct, because he was induced to suppose that the machinery was defective by which appeals were sent from India to England, so that they were not brought under the consideration of the Privy Council.* No man who knew the zeal and ability of his noble friend, the President of the Privy Council, none of their Lordships who had acted with him on committees, and were aware of his manner of managing business in them, or in that House, could, for one moment, suspect that he was to blame for this delay. But it did appear that there existed a great practical grievance, a great delay in getting those appeals brought to a hearing, which defeated the intention of the Legislature, when it cast on the Privy Council the duty of hearing and determining these appeals. The consequences of these delays were most injurious. As long as litigious suitors in India knew that they had a power, by lodging an appeal, of keeping a cause suspended for years, it was a temptation to them to do so, as they were sure

* This statement is confirmed by Sir Alexander Johnston in the paper above alluded to.

of deriving a fraudulent benefit from their injustice, when, if they knew from authority that such appeals would be heard and decided, they would never bring them. As the number of those appeals increased which came from courts in distant parts of the country, their effects extended over more individuals, and produced greater mischief. He knew it would be said, that the delay was caused by no agents being appointed; and this was, he believed, the case; but, unless the machinery was provided for bringing these appeals before the Privy Council, it must be difficult for the native suitor, who employed Fakeels as his agents, to find the means of following up his suit. He did not know exactly what that machinery ought to be, whether there should be an officer appointed here to bring forward the appeals, or whether any other measure should be adopted. The Fakeels who conducted business before the Supreme Court might be competent to manage the business here; but many appeals came from provincial courts, and in them the suitors were destitute of all means of bringing their cause under the consideration of the Council. It was necessary to recollect that some of these appeals came from persons immediately connected with the Government of India. They were transmitted some to the India House, and some to the Board of Control; but in many cases, they came from persons who were accustomed to lay their statements before one or other of these bodies, and after sending in a roll of paper, to wait in silence and without impatience for a determination. From whatever cause the difficulty arose, it was due to the people of that country to endeavour to remedy it. If it arose from the constitution of the Privy Council, the members of which might find some difficulty in determining questions, arising from a dispute concerning rights which had to be determined by the laws of India, an obvious remedy might be found by calling to the assistance of the Privy Council some of those respectable individuals who had filled high judicial situations in India, who now enjoyed pensions for their services, and who might give this assistance for those purposes, and which he was sure they would be most willing to give. He did not say whether they should be employed as assessors, or whether his Majesty should be advised to place some of them in the Privy Council.* If the difficulty arose from counsel, there could be no difficulty in finding a remedy for it. If it began at the other

* Sir Alexander Johnston details the benefits that would result if the Council would avail themselves, as a court of appeal, of the assistance of the Colonial Judges, who retire upon pensions from their office. If any objections should occur to creating them Privy Councillors, he suggests they should be associated as legal assessors with the members of the Privy Council. See the paper above referred to.

end of the proceedings, if it arose from a difficulty of preparing and transmitting appeals and bringing them before the Privy Council, some provisions should be made to facilitate the bringing of them before the Council, so that they might be speedily decided. At present, from whatever cause it arose, the appeals could not be prosecuted to a conclusion and the delay amounted to a denial of judgement. Many of these appeals had been lying over ten, twelve, and twenty years. They came from different parts of India, and left numberless questions connected with property in an unsettled state. The noble Marquis concluded by moving for a return of all cases of appeal which had been transmitted from the various Courts in India since the year 1800, and from Ceylon, the Isle of France, and our other eastern dependencies, since they had been in our possession, stating how they had been disposed of. It had been his intention, he said, to have moved for the return from India since 1773, but on finding that, previous to 1800, the communications on this subject had not been made regular, he had extended his motion only to the year 1800.*

The *Earl of Harrowby* said, he did not rise to oppose the motion, to which he could have no

*The motion was agreed to, but upon inquiry lately made at the Parliament Office, I was informed that these returns had not yet been made.

objection under any circumstances. His noble friend, who had frequently called their Lordships' attention to many important subjects, had undoubtedly a right to call their attention to this; and had he even done it in a manner different from what he had, no feeling of soreness could have arisen in his mind. But the manner in which his noble friend had brought forward the subject was calculated to do away any unpleasant feeling, were it possible, which it was not, that any could exist. His principal object in rising was to make one or two explanations, that it might not be supposed that the Privy Council was the cause of the delay which existed. Their Lordships were aware that the Privy Council was a Court of justice, and, like other Courts, could take no cognizance of causes unless they were regularly brought before it. It could not hear those appeals unless the parties were present, or some agent for them. But when the appeals were entered and followed up by the agents, they were heard to an end and were not delayed. For what passed before the cause came before the Court, or before one of the parties made an application to it, the Privy Council could not be responsible. He believed his noble friend was misinformed, however, as to the number of the appeals which were undecided. Surely the counsel who advised the appeal from India should have sufficient experience to know, that unless there was an agent here to be answerable for the fees which went to the public, and to employ counsel, the appeal could not come before the Privy Council,—it could take no notice of it whatever. As far as the Privy Council was concerned he could say, that whenever causes were brought before it, there was no unnecessary delay. As to the Privy Council not being properly constituted as a Court, and as to his noble friend's suggestion to have assessors, the Council had questions to decide of Dutch law, of French law, of Spanish law, and of the law of every people from whom we had ever taken a colony; and he had not heard any complaints made by the learned and able persons who sat in the Privy Council that they could not understand those laws. He was persuaded that they did not find a greater difficulty in deciding such questions, than their Lordships had in deciding questions of Scotch law. He believed, also, that by the assistance of counsel, questions of Hindoo or Mahomedan law might be decided in the Privy Council. It appeared to him, therefore, premature to suggest an alteration in the constitution of the Court. He had not the least objection to produce the papers, though he must say that no *primâ facie* case had been made out for imputing delay to the Privy Council.

CHAPTER XV.

A SHORT ACCOUNT OF THE ORIGIN OF THE LORD CHANCELLOR'S JURISDICTION IN BANKRUPTCY.

As these pages are principally intended for the perusal of those who, it may be supposed, are not familiar with all the details of our judicial system, it may be useful to show, in a few words, in what way the business in bankruptcy, which anciently no more belonged to the Chancellor than to the common law judges, has become almost exclusively subject to the controul of the Great Seal.

The statute to which our bankrupt laws owe their origin was passed in the reign of Henry the Eighth, and gave the power of seizing the person and property of debtors "suddenly fleeing to parts unknown, or keeping their houses and not minding to pay their debts," to the Lord Chancellor or Keeper of the Great Seal, the Lord Treasurer, the Lord President, Lord Privy Seal, and other of the King's most honourable Privy Council, and the chief justices of either bench for the time being, or three of them at the least, whereof the Lord Chancellor or Lord Keeper of the Great Seal, Lord Treasurer, Lord President, or the Lord Privy Seal, should always be one. By this enactment, the above noble delegates had authority to proceed against every debtor who had committed either of the two specified acts of bankruptcy, although he were not a merchant or trader; and it is not unimportant to observe, that their power was not derived through the channel of a commission, but flowed immediately from the statute.

An act of the 13th of Elizabeth so greatly altered the act of Henry VIII., that the latter may be considered to have been substantially, although not in express terms, repealed.* Merchants and traders† only were made subject to its provisions; additional acts of bankrupt were introduced, and authority was given to the Lord Chancellor or Keeper of the Great Seal alone, *to name by commission such wise and honest discreet persons as to him should seem good,* in whom was vested the same great power over the person and property of the bankrupt, which was given by the

* The acts of Henry the Eighth, Elizabeth, James the First, Charles the Second, Anne, &c., mentioned in this Chapter, (which were not temporary acts,) were not expressly repealed until the Consolidating Bankrupt Act of 6th George IV.

† By a Parliamentary Ordinance during the Commonwealth, the operation of the Bankrupt Laws was again extended to every person committed to prison, and not paying his debts, although the debtor were not a trader.

statute of Henry VIII. only to the dignified, state, and judicial personages above enumerated,—a power possessed by no officer of any other civil Court in this kingdom.*

It is upon this statute that the bankrupt laws, as at present administered, are founded. Assignees chosen by the creditors, however, were not introduced until a later period. The Commissioners themselves possessed the bankrupt's property; part of it they not unfrequently sold to the creditors by appraisement, and other part they delivered to the creditors in satisfaction of their debts. When goods of the bankrupt were in the hands of parties who contested the right of the commissioners to seize them, they commonly sold the goods under the authority given them by the statute of Elizabeth, and the purchasers brought actions to recover the possession; and when they experienced any difficulty in getting in debts due to the bankrupt, they assigned the debts, under a power vested in them by an act of the first of James I., to persons who sued for them in their own names.

The Lord Chancellor, or Lord Keeper, is not named in the three acts relating to bankrupts that

* The messenger of the commissioners, for he is their officer although recommended by the Chancellor, may break open the bankrupts' houses, doors, chests, &c. He has, by the order of the commissioners, forcibly taken a paper out of the bankrupt's pocket.

followed the statute of Elizabeth; * and the Chancellor had, at this time, no more jurisdiction in bankruptcy than the Courts of King's Bench, Common Pleas, or Exchequer. From the first existence of the bankrupt laws, it was necessary that the person applying for a commission of bankrupt should present his petition, (which, after the statute of Elizabeth, was addressed to the Lord Chancellor,) showing that the bankrupt was indebted to him and others in a certain amount; and it seems to have been the practice of the Chancellor, in very ancient times, in order to prevent vexatious and frivolous commissions, to require the petitioner to verify his statement by an affidavit, and to execute a bond to the Great Seal, conditioned for the due proof of the debt and of the bankruptcy.† Upon these requisites being complied with the commission was issued, directed to persons nominated, it is true, by the Chancellor, but over whom, when this act of patronage was once exercised, the Chancellor had no controul. He might, of course, prevent them from being named in any future commis-

* The first James the First, twenty-first James the First, and thirteenth and fourteenth Charles the Second.

† The bond to the Chancellor existed in practice long before the statute of the fifth of Anne. An ordinance made by Lord Bacon, in 1618, required the petitioning creditor to enter into a bond, with good security in 200*l.* at least, to prove the bankruptcy.

sion; * but they were not amenable, for misconduct in their office, to him more than to any other judge of Westminster Hall.

The powers given to the commissioners of bankrupt were so large and important, that in ancient times they were often considerably embarrassed to know in what way to exercise them. In the early part of the seventeenth century, we find several instances of applications made by the Commissioners, not to the Lord Chancellor, but to the Common Law Courts, for their advice as to the conduct they ought to pursue; and it appears that the judges did not hesitate to give their opinions extra-judicially upon the questions proposed to them. There is no instance to be found in the books, of a similar application being made to the Lord Chancellor, before the year 1676, when a creditor, having offered proof of his debt to the commissioners, which they disallowed, Lord Nottingham was moved, upon the allegation that the proof was sufficient, that he might be attended by both sides, to hear and give order therein. The Lord Chancellor said, "Why should I not leave it to the course the statute hath provided? If it be granted in one, it will be asked on all cases." It appears, however, that his Lordship at last consented that the matter should be debated be-

* See the next Chapter on this subject, where the nature of the office of a commissioner of bankrupt is explained.

fore him, and, probably, recommended the commissioners to receive the proof.* From such a slight and recent beginning, has the Chancellor's present jurisdiction in bankruptcy arisen.

Lord Nottingham does not seem, after this time, to have hesitated about the exercise of this recommendatory jurisdiction; as we find that two years afterwards he directed, upon the petition of a Mrs. Rushworth, that she should be admitted into the distribution, she contributing to the expenses. This was not, however, the case of an appeal from the commissioners.

* There is a case reported, as decided by Lord Nottingham, in 1673, where he decreed that creditors should be let in to prove their debts, paying contribution money; but there a bill was filed, and the commissioners were made defendants. Two similar decrees were made by his Lordship; the one in 1676, in a suit to which the assignees of the commissioners were parties; the other in 1680, in a suit in which the commissioners were defendants. In 1682, we find Lord Keeper North adjudicating, but upon a bill filed, the rights of joint and separate creditors, under a commission issued against partners. From a case in Vernon's Reports, it appears that in 1690 the Lords Commissioners thought the Lord Chancellor might set aside a colourable distribution and sale, made by the commissioners, even upon petition; and they said it had been so done in Lord Clarendon's time. This may be very reasonably doubted, as at this period there certainly was nothing in the bankrupt statutes to give the Lord Chancellor any such jurisdiction. There is an instance in the books of a bill filed as far back as the year 1663, one of the principal objects of which was to be let in to prove and receive a dividend.

The act of the 4th and 5th of Anne* drew the link that connected the Chancellor with bankruptcy a little closer. It gave authority to the Lord Chancellor, or Lord Keeper, or Commissioners of the Great Seal, to enlarge the time for the bankrupt surrendering. This act too, for the first time, introduced the bankrupt's certificate of conformity, which was to be granted by the commissioners, and allowed and confirmed by the Lord Chancellor, Lord Keeper, or Commissioners of the Great Seal, or by such two of the judges of the Court of Queen's Bench, Common Pleas, and Exchequer, to whom the consideration of such certificate should be referred by the Lord Chancellor, Lord Keeper, or Commissioners of the Great Seal, for the time being; and it is remarkable, that so little did former Lord Chancellors consider the business in bankruptcy to be the province of the Great Seal, that before Lord Hardwicke's time they referred all certificates to the judges.

The act of the 5th of Anne first introduced assignees, chosen by the creditors, to whom the commissioners were required to assign the bankrupt's estate and effects. It also required the petitioning creditor to give a bond to the Great

* This act, and some of the acts subsequently noticed, were temporary, but most of their provisions were embodied in the act of the fifth of George the Second.

Seal as a security for proving his debt, and that the party had become a bankrupt at the time when the commission was taken out. The Lord Chancellor, as it has been before observed, was in the habit of requiring such a bond to be executed before the passing of this act.

Down to this period the Lord Chancellor possessed no more authority over the assignees, whether appointed by the commissioners or chosen by the creditors, than he had over the commissioners. It was only upon bill filed against them, in their characters of vendees or trustees, that they were amenable to his jurisdiction. The act of the 5th of George I. converted the assignees into officers of the Great Seal. It gave the Lord Chancellor, Lord Keeper, or Lords Commissioners power, upon the petition of any creditor, to remove the assignees, by directing that the assignment should be vacated, and a new assignment made to other persons. Authority was also given by this act to the Great Seal, to supersede the commission upon the petition of any creditor, and to award a new commission, in case of the bankrupt paying or giving to the person who sued out the commission against him money or goods, whereby such persons should receive more in the pound than the other creditors.

Thus the Chancellor had a clear jurisdiction given him by statute, in certain matters in bankruptcy, upon a summary application by petition, and without the intervention of a bill; and the Chancellors of the last century were not slower in enlarging that jurisdiction, than the ecclesiastical Chancellors of the fifteenth and sixteenth centuries had been in extending the operation of the subpœna, so that they soon began to adjudge upon petition, not only the cases over which authority was given them by the bankrupt acts, but every question arising between parties availing themselves of the benefit of the commission.*

The act of the 5th of George II., which incorporated in it all the material clauses in the preceding statutes, and the subsequent acts, throw no further light upon the mystery and obscurity in which the question, of the nature of the jurisdiction at present exercised by the Chancellor in bankruptcy is involved. Reported decisions, however, show, that twenty years after the passing of the act of the 5th of George II., Lord Hardwicke thought proper to adjudicate upon petition, without bill filed, almost every question that now comes under the cognizance of the Chancellor sitting in bankruptcy. But it is quite impossible

* The jurisdiction upon petition, in cases where the Chancellor had no statutory power, seems to have been pretty well established, even before the act of the fifth of George the First. We find Lord Cowper, in 1715, (three years before the passing of that act,) deciding on a petition in bankruptcy the right of joint and separate creditors under a joint commission against two partners.

to read the reasons given by Lord Hardwicke for the exercise of the jurisdiction, without perceiving them to be irreconcilable with the history of the rise and progress of the bankrupt laws. Down to the present day, whenever it is necessary to trace the Chancellor's authority in bankruptcy to its source, it is obvious to every one that it is for the most part founded in usurpation, although it has been used so long that it cannot now be called in question. Every attempt of Lord Eldon to explain the nature of the Chancellor's power, was evidently as unsatisfactory to himself as it must be to every one who attentively considers the subject. In one case, he intimated that the Chancellor had a specially delegated authority in bankruptcy as in lunacy,* which it is well known he has not; and his Lordship afterwards took occasion to explain, he meant only such special authority as the legislature has given to the Great Seal, and this of course must be sought for in the bankrupt statutes.

Such is the manner in which all the most important business in bankruptcy has been drawn within the circle of the Chancellor's power. How

* The Chancellor has no jurisdiction in lunacy as Keeper of the Great Seal. The King grants a warrant to the Chancellor, countersigned by two Secretaries of State, empowering him to take care of idiots and lunatics in right of the Crown. The warrant may, of course, be granted to any other person his Majesty may think it right to select.

far the immense patronage and emolument which bankruptcy produces may have induced former Chancellors to encourage its union with the Great Seal we have no means of knowing, but there can exist no doubt that these have been of late years the principal obstacles to a separation. Great men are not without their defects; and there is too much reason to believe that the fear of diminishing their immense and overgrown influence and revenue has tended more to the rejection by the Chancellors of the proposal to transfer the bankruptcy business to a new tribunal, in the place of the Chancellor and the commissioners, than the apprehension of any injury to arise to the bankrupts or their creditors.* Even the unprofessional reader must perceive, without advert-

* It will probably be found, whenever the question of creating a new bankruptcy court, to replace the Chancellor and the commissioners, is seriously agitated, that the income derived by the Chancellor from bankruptcy, even if it were as great as many persons, notwithstanding the returns, persist in believing it to be, will be given up with infinitely less reluctance than the patronage. The patronage belongs nominally, indeed, to the Chancellor; but it is an engine which the other Cabinet Ministers have been frequently permitted to use, and their consent to its destruction will, perhaps, be as difficult to be obtained as the Chancellor's. The emoluments might be supplied, without much difficulty, from a purer spring than the property of insolvents, but it would not be easy to find so prolific a source of patronage. The nation would not readily submit to the nomination, by the ministry of the day, of seventy new judges, with salaries amounting together to more than 20,000*l.* per annum.

ing to the recency of the connection, that it would be productive of no mischief to disunite bankruptcy from the Great Seal, when he is informed that, to this day, the Chancellor sitting in bankruptcy seldom, unless the parties desire it, decides any new and important question either of law or equity. There can be no appeal from the Chancellor in bankruptcy; and if there be any equity point of importance, he commonly gives leave to file a bill, in order that it may be carried, if the parties think fit, to the House of Lords. Upon some of the most difficult questions in bankruptcy the common law courts have a concurrent jurisdiction with the Chancellor, as upon the trading, the act of bankruptcy, the petitioning creditor's debt, the validity of the bankrupt's certificate, stoppage in transitu, lien, set-off, election, &c., and upon most of these points the decisions of those Courts are of greater authority than those of the Chancellor; * and when an important question of law occurs, the Chancellor generally directs an action to be brought, an issue to be tried, or a case for the opinion of a court of law to be stated, in order that it may be more solemnly decided.

---

* An appeal lies from the decision of these Courts to the Exchequer Chamber and the House of Lords.

After writing the above it occurred to me, that the Report of the Lords Commissioners, appointed to make a survey of our Courts of Justice, as to the Court of Chancery, dated in November, 1740, might, if it gave any account of the ancient officers employed by the Great Seal in bankruptcy, elucidate the origin of this branch of the Chancellor's power. I find that that Report takes notice of the Secretary of the Commissions of Bankrupts, and the Office of the Execution of the Laws and Statutes concerning Bankruptcy.* It does not mention the Commissioners of Bankrupt. From which circumstance it has been erroneously conjectured there were then no regular lists of London Commissioners, any more than there are now any regular lists of Country Commissioners. The Lords Commissioners of 1740, impannelled and swore juries under them, consisting of ancient Attornies and Solicitors in the Court, to present upon their oaths the matters directed to be inquired into. With respect to the Secretary for the commissions of bankrupt, the jury found that he was an officer appointed by the Lord Chancellor by parol, took no oath of office, and was removable at pleasure. But whether he was an officer that did, or of right ought

* The Report also mentions the Clerk of the Inrolments in Bankruptcy, an officer appointed by a then recent act of Parliament.

to belong to the Court of Chancery, they could not determine: and with respect to the Office of the Execution of the Law and Statutes concerning Bankrupts, the jury presented, that they could not determine whether this was an office that did, or of right ought to belong to the Court of Chancery.*

* This is a patent office, created under an act of Elizabeth.

CHAPTER XVI.

THE LONDON AND COUNTRY COMMISSIONERS OF BANKRUPT.

THE Commissioners of Bankrupt, like the Commissioners of Lunacy, the Commissioners for Examination of Witnesses, of Partition, for taking answers in Equity suits depending in the Courts of Chancery, Exchequer, Duchy Court of Lancaster, &c. derive their authority from each particular commission issued to them, and from no other source; and although it is usual to speak of the Court of the Commissioners of Bankrupt, and to name the Commissioners judges, yet it has been frequently decided, that the Commissioners have none of the requisites of a court of justice; that their authority, although nearly approaching to the judicial, is not judicial, but executory and ministerial; and that they are not judges, and they are consequently liable to an action, and may be compelled to make civil reparation for an illegal exercise of their power, although arising out of an error of judgment.*

The statutes of Elizabeth and James the First do not direct how many wise, honest, and discreet persons should be appointed in each bankruptcy. And it appears, from a book published by Serjeant Goodinge, in 1694, that the number varied according to the magnitude of the bankruptcy to be administered. The practice seems to have been, for the creditors taking out the commission to name seven commissioners at the least; and in order to insure a discreet and faithful discharge of the high and extraordinary powers with which the commissioners were invested, the Lord Chancellor required that two of the seven should be esquires of the quorum; and a clause was introduced into the ancient commissions disqualifying the other commissioners from acting, except in conjunction with one of the quorum commissioners; but this clause is, I believe, omitted in modern commissions.† In matters of great weight, there

* Such actions have been often successfully brought. It may be asked, is such a liability consistent with the independent exercise of the judiciary functions? The reader will find the system of the Bankrupt Laws to be equally at variance with just principles of legislation, in its minutest parts as in its more prominent features.

† In country commissions the practice seems always to have been, to designate two of the commissioners at least as esquires, under which title very improper persons were frequently named as commissioners. An Order of Lord Rosslyn, made in 1800,

were frequently nine, or more, commissioners, and three, or more, of the quorum.

Notwithstanding, however, these excellent regulations of the Great Seal, it does not appear that the manner in which the law was administered by the Commissioners of Bankrupt at that period gave greater satisfaction than at present. The Journals of both Houses of Parliament, at the early part of the last century, abound with notices of petitions of complaint of the City of London, and other corporate bodies, as well as of individuals, on the subject of the Bankrupt Laws.* It is true that most of the grievances enumerated in those petitions relate more to the defects in the system, than to the conduct of the commissioners; but enough is found to convince us, that the evils now reprobated, called, even at that period, loudly for correction.

I believe that little is to be found in the books as to the emoluments received by the commissioners, or the fund from which they were drawn,

requires that two of the commissioners in country commissions should be Barristers, residing at or near the place where the commission is to be executed.

* An Order made by Lord Nottingham, in 1680, notices that many complaints and petitions had been frequently made and presented to him, occasioned by the ill management of commissions of Bankrupt, in and about the city of London and Westminster, and the counties adjacent; but they seem to have mostly related to the losing and mislaying of the commissions, depositions, &c.

prior to the year 1718. It appears, however, from the well known case of Alderman Backwall, that Lord Chancellor Jefferys considered 20*s*. a day and 10*s*. half a day, &c. for each commissioner, an exorbitant charge. This was in 1687. But it is probable, from the severe enactments contained in some of the early statutes, beginning with the reign of Queen Anne, against the commissioners eating and drinking at the expense of the Bankrupt's estate, that the tavern bills of the commissioners formed much more formidable items in bills of costs in Bankruptcy, than the fees of the commissioners, as I believe it will be found they still continue to do in most country commissions. Lord Jefferys, in the case above alluded to, said he was no friend to Commissions of Bankrupt, they had occasioned much hurt, and he instanced a case lately before him, wherein the charge and expense of the commissioners and their attendance came to £400, and the distribution to the creditors was only 7*s*. in the pound.

That the commissioners should, in ancient times, have often misconducted themselves in the administration of the bankrupt's property, will scarcely seem matter of surprise to the reader, when he is informed that, until the year 1719, they acted only upon their honour, and without the obligation of an oath, for the true and faithful discharge of the high and excessive powers with which they were invested; that the only check upon them was the liability to make a true declaration to the bankrupt, at his request, of the manner in which they had employed and bestowed his property, and to pay over to him the overplus, if any such there should be; and that it was not till the year 1732, when the legislature gave to the Chancellor power to renew a commission *for any cause* whatever, that the commissioners came directly under the controul of the Lord Chancellor.*

* Although before that time there was no mode by which the Chancellor could remove the Commissioners, yet, as is stated in the former Chapter, he might of course order their names not to be inserted in any future commissions. The contradiction and obscurity that prevail in the books, as to the nature of the authority which the Great Seal has over the Commissioners, furnish further proof of the absurdities inseparable from the present system. We find great Chancellors expressing themselves, when speaking of their power over the Commissioners, as follows :—" I doubt the jurisdiction. Sitting here I have no more right to reverse an order of the Commissioners than the Court of King's Bench." Again, " There are many acts of the commissioners that the Great Seal cannot controul, the commissioners having the authority to do them given by the legislature." In another case, we find a commissioner of great experience expressing strong disapprobation at the Great Seal having *ordered* the commissioners to reverse one of their own decisions; he observes, the Chancellor ought to have *recommended* to the commissioners to reconsider the matter, and the commissioners ought not to have regarded the order otherwise than by remonstrating that obedience was incompatible with their oath of office.

In 1705, the expense occasioned to the estate of the bankrupt by the dinner bills of the commissioners engaged the attention of the legislature, and a clause was introduced into an act passed that year, directing that nothing should be paid or allowed for expenses in eating or drinking of the commissioners or creditors, or of any other persons, at the times of the meetings; and any commissioner permitting such payment or allowance was disabled for ever after from acting as a commissioner. It seems that this enactment only partially cured the mischief to which it was meant to apply, and the commissioners soon found other means of remunerating themselves for their time and trouble. From a Report of a Committee of the House of Commons, made in the following year, it appears that the merchants and traders of London were still loud in their complaints of the abuses and ill practices of the Commissioners of Bankrupt, the increase of charge occasioned to the disadvantage of the creditors by numerous and unnecessary sittings, the insolent manner in which they treated the creditors who desired any information as to the bankrupt's conduct and affairs, &c.

It was probably to prevent the appointment of improper persons as commissioners in the London commissions, that Lord Harcourt, about this time, established the London Lists of Commissioners, upon nearly the same footing as they exist at present.* These Commissioners are appointed by the Chancellor verbally, and without any other formality than a direction to the Secretary of Bankrupts to insert their names on the list; they take no oath on their appointment, and are of course removable at the Chancellor's or their own will or pleasure. Upon the death, surrender, or removal of any commissioner, the name of another gentleman is, by his Lordship's order, entered by the Secretary on the list. There are five commissioners in each list, and the London Commissions of Bankrupt are directed in rotation to the five gentlemen contained in the different lists. Three commissioners only attend and receive fees; a practice which is supposed to have had its origin in some order of the Great Seal, which is now lost.

These lists have never been in any manner recognized by the legislature. They are the creation of the Lord Chancellor, and may at any time be annihilated by him; and it is not at all improbable they would have long since disappeared, were it not for the vast and lucrative field of patronage which they present; for the reader, after perusing this and the subsequent Chapter, must be convinced it is not from any utility or advantage

* For some time previous, it had been the practice for the petitioning creditor to insert the names of commissioners at the foot of his petition, as is the custom now on applications for country commissions.

arising from them that they have been preserved to our time. What was the original number of lists I do not know. In 1739 and 1744, there were ten lists; in 1761, there were twelve; and in 1780, the number was thirteen. At present we have fourteen lists, but there is nothing to prevent the Chancellor from adding to or diminishing the numbers. Should he think that it will lead to a better administration of the Bankrupt Laws, he may direct the commissions in future to be addressed to all barristers willing to act as commissioners,* according to any cycle he may judge most convenient; and, on the other hand, should it appear to him more advantageous to bankrupts and their creditors, that their rights and interests should be entrusted to the superintendence and adjudication of a smaller number of

* The power exercised by the Chancellor of increasing the number of London commissioners has been thought to present an easy mode of obviating some difficulties which it has been said stand in the way of a suppression of this tribunal. "Revive Lord "Bacon's ordinance, which has fallen into desuetude, touching "town commissions—let not the same parties be too often used "in commissions—square the present number of lists—they will "then contain the names of every barrister in the country, and "in the following year abolish the system of the London Com-"missionerships of Bankrupt—continue the commissions, or at "least the fees payable upon them, during the lives of the present "patentee and the reversioner, and after their deaths, let both "the commissions and the fees cease."—*Letters of Eminent Lawyers*. The ordinance of Lord Bacon, alluded to in this extract, is mentioned in a subsequent note.

persons, he may order his Secretary to cancel as many of the lists as may appear to him to be unnecessary.*

Lord Chancellor Rosslyn nominated certain persons in Birmingham,† and, I believe, some other populous commercial towns, to whom only, like the gentlemen named in the London lists, commissions to be executed in those places and the neighbourhood should be addressed; but his successor, Lord Eldon, always declined to fill up the vacancies that occurred in these country lists, declaring he thought it would be injurious to young barristers, who might be induced to settle in the country, as they would be precluded from all share of that business till the death of their seniors. He said he thought it more fair and equitable to leave it open to the petitioning creditor, or his solicitor, to select any two barristers, on whose experience and abilities they wished to rely. His Lordship's reason seems just and con-

* If I recollect right, the Chancellors formerly either sanctioned or connived at the practice of inserting the most efficient lists in weighty and important commissions, and they have occasionally named persons as commissioners who were not in the lists, as was recently done in the analogous instance of lunacy. Gentlemen not in the lists of Commissioners of Lunacy, were commissioned to inquire whether Lord Portsmouth was of unsound mind.

† Four lists, of five each, were nominated in 1796, with directions for one of the four to be inserted in each of such commissions, as should be executed at or within twenty miles of Birmingham.

siderate. It may be permitted, however, to observe, that it is difficult to reconcile it with the principle upon which the London lists have been formed and continued.

But it is time to return from the digression into which the creation of the lists of the commissioners has led me. This measure of Lord Harcourt does not seem to have produced the advantage that was probably expected to flow from it.* In 1718, a petition of certain merchants and traders of London, for and on the behalf of themselves and others, was presented to the House of Commons, and read, setting forth that through the excessive charges of commissions of bankrupts, and proceedings thereupon, in most cases of bankruptcy, the estate and effects of bankrupts were swallowed up, and the creditors became losers; most commonly, very considerably. That the commissioners nominated in these commissions being commonly attorneys,† and persons of

* It is remarkable that Lord Bacon seems to have foreseen the evils which in such a system as the Bankrupt Laws permanent lists would produce. By his ordinance, mentioned in the preceding Chapter, he directed that the same parties should not be too often used in commissions.

† Of the fifty commissioners in Lord Hardwick's list, in 1739, twenty-seven appear to have been barristers and the remaining twenty-three attorneys. How the lists were constituted at an earlier period, I do not recollect to have read. The emoluments, until a recent period, were so trifling, that it is probable the quorum commissioners never attended the meetings oftener or

an inferior quality to those in commissions of the peace, and under no obligation of an oath for the true and faithful discharge of their trusts, were apt to be very partial and dilatory in their proceedings, out of sinister ends of gain to themselves, to the prejudice of both creditor and debtor, and praying that the commissioners might be obliged to take an oath for that purpose.

By an act passed in the same year, the legislature endeavoured to provide a remedy against the misconduct of the commissioners complained of by this petition. The statute of the fifth of George the First renewed the prohibition against any thing being allowed for the eating and drinking of the commissioners, and moreover declared, that any commissioner receiving more than twenty shillings for each meeting, or for executing any deed of assignment, dividend, or other deed, or more than ten shillings for executing any warrant of contribution or seizure, should be disabled for ever after to act as a commissioner in such or any other commission founded on the bankrupt statutes. The same statute also provided, that after

longer than they were obliged. Serjeant Goodinge tells us, that Serjeant Stone, a learned lawyer, who published, in 1654, a Reading on the Statute of Bankrupts, was the most considerable commissioner of his time. Except Stone, I am not aware that until our time any great lawyer was ever remarked as having devoted much of his attention to the duties of a Commissioner of Bankrupt.

April, 1719, no commissioner should be capable of acting until he should have taken an oath, faithfully, impartially, and honestly, to the best of his skill and knowledge, to execute the several powers and trusts reposed in him, without favour or affection, prejudice or malice; and commissioners were required and empowered to administer the oath to each other, and they were directed to sign a memorial thereof, to be entered and kept with the proceedings under the different commissions. The act of the 5th of George the 1st was temporary, and, after being twice continued by two subsequent acts, was suffered to expire; but the clauses as to the commissioners' fees, with some trifling alterations, and the administration of the oath, were introduced into the act of George the 2d, passed in 1732,* and the same clauses are to be found in the act of the 6th of George the 4th, consolidating the Bankrupt Laws.

These prohibitory enactments, whilst they were yet new, do not seem to have been more efficacious in suppressing the rapacity of the commissioners than they have been found to be in modern times. The commissioners soon discovered ways of augmenting their gains without subjecting themselves to the penalty of the act. They appointed a great number of meetings to take

* This statute may be considered the first that completely annexed the most important business in Bankruptcy to the Great Seal.

place at the same time, although they knew it would be impossible for them to dispatch more than a small part of the matters to be brought before them, and they adjourned from time to time the consideration of the different cases which the accumulation of business had prevented them from finishing. In this manner, meetings were multiplied without end, and upon all of them the commissioners received their fees. The letter of the act was observed, the spirit violated.* It must not be supposed, however, that the commissioners were always satisfied with this mode of increasing their emoluments, by multiplying the number of meetings. They occasionally bid defiance to the act, and not only ate and drank at the expense of the bankrupt's estate, but retained much larger fees than those which the legislature had assigned to them.† In 1739, a petition was

* Matters are arranged in much the same way now. Indeed, some of the commissioners plume themselves on possessing in greater perfection than their brethren the faculty of gaining a very large amount of fees in a very small space of time. One of them has boasted of having received thirty sovereigns one Saturday morning.—Thirty meetings in a few hours!!! I had this from an acting commissioner; and who did not scruple, five minutes afterwards, to assure me, that no branch of our law was better administered than that which falls under the superintendence of the London Commissioners of Bankrupt.

† The present commissioners are determined, in this respect, not to be outdone by their predecessors; for it should seem, from the statement of a gentleman who may be supposed to know

presented to the Chancellor against several of the commissioners, for taking more than 20*s.* a-piece at each meeting, and likewise ordering great sums of money to be charged for their eating and drinking; and the accusation being proved, they were removed from their office: and it is probable such occurrences were not uncommon, although no account of them has been preserved, except in some few instances, where, being connected with some point of law, they are incidentally noticed in some of our Reports.*

The Journals of the House of Commons in 1759 present us with a long Report from a Committee appointed to consider of the Laws relating to Bankrupts, but it affords no information as to the manner in which the commissioners of that day conducted themselves in their judicial capacity. It only appears that several of the London commissioners were examined before the Committee, and proposed different amendments in the bankrupt laws, in relation both to the creditors

something about the matter, that they receive fees when they never attend at all. Mr. Montague, in his evidence before the Select Committee of the House of Commons on the Bankrupt Laws, stated, he was not certain, but he believed that in general fees were paid when meetings were called, whether they were fully attended or not, the commissioners who were present receiving the fees for those who were absent.

* In more recent times, the complaints of country commissioners taking more than the fees allowed by the act have been very frequent.

and the bankrupt, and some also (as it is expressed in the Report) for the *ease of the commissioners.*

I am now approaching the times to which many persons now living can carry back their recollection. We have the following account of the manner in which business was conducted under London and country commissioners of bankrupt in the year 1783, given by a person intimately acquainted with the subject.

" From a desire of rendering the execution of these
" matters as commodious as possible to the merchants of
" London, all town commissions are transacted at Guild-
" hall. This is productive of great inconvenience. The
" apartments appropriated to this purpose are in general
" small. Two or three different lists are stationed at the
" same time in one of them, and not unfrequently each of
" these lists has at the same time before it two or three
" commissions in their different stages. When we con-
" sider the immense crowd which all this must necessarily
" occasion, and the noise, the heat, and the confusion
" which such a crowd must create, it will rather appear
" surprising that the commissioners should be able to
" breathe, than that they should hurry over an unpleasant
" business, and should be rejoiced to do it, at any rate, as
" expeditiously as possible. In such a chaos of papers
" and of clamour how can a due attention be preserved?
" It may, perhaps, be said, that such an accumulation of
" business at one time is improper, the commissioners
" ought to afford separate days to each commission. Such
" an appointment would, indeed, greatly obviate the force

"of our objection, yet such an appointment cannot, as "things now are circumstanced, reasonably be expected. "The distance is so great, the attendance at Guildhall "interferes so materially with the attendance upon the "Courts at Westminster and with chamber practice, the "fees of the commissioners are so disproportionate to "their labours, that this accumulation will never be pre-"vented, so long as the system of bankruptcy shall con-"tinue on its present footing.

"Another material objection likewise arises from the "above circumstances. Men of experience and of abilities "are unwilling to take upon themselves an employment "which must engage so much of their time, and which can "produce to them so little in return. It is a very common "thing for a commissioner, when he gets into business on "the circuit, or in Westminster Hall, to resign his com-"mission, as a thing which he is no longer at leisure to "execute. In other words, he retires from this business "at the moment when he becomes a proper person to ex-"ecute it. For, in transactions on which depend the "interests and the well-doing of the mercantile part of "this country, no small share of ability, of knowledge, "and of experience is surely necessary.

"Commissions which are executed in the country are "on a still worse footing. Compared with these, the "confusion and the imperfections of a town commission "are absolute regularity and precision. It were unne-"cessary to enlarge on this topic, of which many and "grievous complaints have frequently been made. One "circumstance alone will be sufficient to impress on the "mind of the reader an adequate idea of the manner in "which they probably must be conducted. A country "attorney, when he takes out a commission, inserts the "names of his own commissioners. If he is an honest "man, his choice will probably be judicious and respect- "able. If he is not, or if he should happen to have any "particular purpose to serve, it is not difficult to foresee "what are the probable consequences of such a nomina- "tion.*

In the ensuing Chapter, it will be more fully shown, that modern orders and regulations have wrought little, if any, amelioration in the administration of the bankrupt laws. The reader will find there collected much important information, but none more valuable than the observations of Lord Eldon and the late Mr. Cullen, first a commissioner of bankrupt and afterwards a king's counsel; and as those observations happen now to lie before me, I shall introduce them in this place as no inconvenient way of concluding this Chapter, notwithstanding, in point of arrangement, they should more properly be classed with the opinions of their cotemporaries in a subsequent page.

Lord *Eldon* is reported to have observed, as long since as the year 1801, *with warmth*, that the abuse of the bankrupt laws was a disgrace to the country, and that it would be better to repeal at once all the statutes, than to suffer them to be so misapplied; that there was no mercy to the estate. Nothing was less thought of than the objects of

* *Considerations on the Law of Insolvency, by James Bland Burgess, Esq. of Lincoln's Inn.*

the commission; as they were frequently conducted in the country, they were little more than stock in trade for the commissioners, the assignees, and the solicitor. Instead of the solicitors attending to their duty, as ministers of the Court, commissions of bankrupt were treated as matters of traffic. *A.* taking up the commission, *B.* and *C.* acted as commissioners. They were considered as stock in trade, and calculations were made how many commissions could be brought into the partnership.

Mr. Cullen, in the evidence given by him in the year 1818 before the Committee of the House of Commons on the Bankrupt Laws, described the tribunal of the commissioners of bankrupt as the worst constituted court of justice that could well be imagined. Each of the fourteen lists, he said, was perfectly unconnected with and independent of the rest. There was no uniformity, no consistency of determination; one law and one practice prevailed in one list, and another in another. Where there existed such a number of independent jurisdictions precedent had no binding force, and was very seldom listened to. As any three out of the five commissioners in each list might attend, the suitor was exposed, even in the same court, to a perpetual change of the judge, and this not from one meeting to another, but even in the course of the same meeting. The three commissioners assembled under a number, sometimes a great number, of different commissions at once. Their attention was solicited at one and the same moment by many suitors, all equally pressing and entitled to dispatch upon their respective cases; and these often involving many nice questions of fact and considerations of law. One party gained the attention of a commissioner; he was instantly broken in upon by another party, perhaps by another commissioner; the half-heard case must be repeated, and the second judge soon in like manner gave way to a third. The truth was, that the business was very generally done by one commissioner; the commissioners were apt to leave it to one, or by the distraction of other business in the same or another commission, they were forced to do so.*

* Those of the commissioners (it must be admitted they are few in number) who still venture to commend the system, of which they are appointed the organs, are singularly unfortunate; inasmuch as the strongest evidence of its defects has proceeded from the most wise, experienced, and liberal men of their own body.

CHAPTER XVII.

OPINIONS OF EMINENT LAWYERS AND OTHER INDIVIDUALS, AS TO THE SEPARATION OF BANKRUPTCY FROM THE OTHER BUSINESS OF THE GREAT SEAL, AND AS TO THE COMMISSIONERS OF BANKRUPT. REPORTS OF COMMITTEES OF THE HOUSE OF COMMONS, CHANCERY COMMISSIONERS, COMMON COUNCIL OF THE CITY OF LONDON, AND PARLIAMENTARY DEBATES, RELATIVE TO THE SAME SUBJECTS.

It has been said that all our eminent lawyers are adverse to the separation of the Bankrupt business from that of the Chancery. Very few of them, who can be considered unbiassed, have declared their sentiments in any public manner; but this chapter may suffice to convince the reader how little reliance is to be placed on such a bold and general assertion,

Sir Samuel Romilly, in the debate on the Vice Chancellor's bill, is reported to have said, he could not allow the justice of the conclusion, that as many of the bankrupt cases involved points of great difficulty and importance, and the decision was to be final and without appeal, it was absolutely necessary that the Lord Chancellor should determine them himself. If they were cases of difficulty and importance, it certainly required that they should be decided by a man of ability, but he saw no necessity why this man should be the Lord Chancellor. Men could be easily found of the highest professional eminence who would be perfectly competent to this part of the duty, and a sufficient compensation could be found out for them in the emoluments from those bankrupt cases.

Mr. William Courtenay, who was then a Commissioner of Bankrupt, and has since been a Master in Chancery, said, in the course of the debate on the same bill, that with regard to the separation of Bankruptcy causes from the other business of the Court, he was far from agreeing with those who thought that such a separation would yield no material relief. He was convinced it would, for the business in Bankruptcy constituted a very considerable proportion of the whole business of the Court.

Sir Lancelot Shadwell, in his evidence before the Chancery Commissioners, explicitly stated that the simplest and most efficacious mode of remedying the inconvenience occasioned by the insufficiency of the present number of judges to get through the business of the Court of Chancery with due expedition, would be to create a new

Court, which should dispose of and decide every thing in Bankruptcy.

Many of the other witnesses examined before the same commissioners expressed the same sentiments.

Mr. Cooke, one of his Majesty's Counsel and during many years a Commissioner of Bankrupt, said he was of opinion that the jurisdiction in Bankruptcy might be conveniently taken away from the Court of Chancery, and a new Court substituted, if a judge were appointed of eminence equal to those presiding in Chancery; and he thought such Court would be a very important advantage to the commercial world, and also to the Court of Chancery, as it would leave the time of the judges of that Court open to the proper business of the Court, and it would not be taken off with the Bankruptcy, which was a sort of extraneous business. Every practitioner in the Court of Chancery knows there is no opinion entitled to greater weight upon such a subject than that of Mr. Cooke.

Mr. Bickersteth stated, he thought the jurisdiction over Bankruptcy might easily be subtracted from the Court of Chancery.

The *Lord Chief Baron (Sir William Alexander),* in answer to the question whether a new satisfactory tribunal in Bankruptcy could be established, unless there was an appeal from that to some other tribunal, observed, it was a difficult question to answer. He could not say whether the public would be satisfied without going to the Chancellor. He could see himself no objection to it, as a measure to establish a tribunal for that purpose without appeal. He could not speak as to its being satisfactory to the public. He thought a choice might be made by which justice could be done.

There seems to have been a tenderness in examining the witnesses upon this subject; but it may be much doubted whether the Commissioners are quite correct in stating, that almost every witness who was examined was of opinion that the business in Bankruptcy could not be transferred to any other tribunal with equal satisfaction and advantage to the public. *Mr. Bell,* it is true, more than once stated it to be his opinion there should be in matters of Bankruptcy a final appeal to the Lord Chancellor; but then he assumed what may not always be the case, namely, that the Chancellor would possess the ablest judicial mind to be found in the Kingdom; and it is remarkable that the reason given by the Chancery Commissioners themselves for not separating Bankruptcy from the Chancery only applies when the Chancellor happens to be a great Equity lawyer. They observe, the supreme judge in Bankruptcy must not only be familiar with the general doctrines of equity but habitually practised in the whole range of equitable jurisdiction;* and they also admit in conclusion, that the jurisdiction in Bankruptcy ought to be withdrawn from the Lord Chancellor,† if it should appear that it cannot be retained consistently with the dispatch of the other business of the Court, which no one now can doubt to be the fact.‡

But whatever doubt may have existed amongst impartial persons as to the Court which should have the final jurisdiction in Bankruptcy, very little seems to have been entertained as to the

* If the supreme jurisdiction in Bankruptcy can only be satisfactorily exercised by a magistrate well versed in the principles of our equity courts, as some gentlemen contend, how is it that these same gentlemen convince themselves, that one who has never studied those principles, or practised as an advocate in the courts which found their decision upon them, may nevertheless be well qualified to discharge the functions of the principal Equity Judge of the kingdom? It is hardly necessary to say that the writer does not here allude to any of the Chancery Commissioners.

† A judge, than whom one of greater learning and talents and more inflexible virtue never sat in our Courts of Equity, nor indeed in any other court, has expressed his opinion, that the jurisdiction in Bankruptcy should be separated from the general business of the Court of Chancery.

‡ It was said in the last sessions of Parliament, that if Lord Lyndhurst found, at the end of twelve months, that three judges could not get through the business of the Court of Chancery, he would have no objection to sever the Bankruptcy from the Great Seal. See a former page.

bad constitution of the present Court of Commissioners, and that (to use the words of the Second Report of the Select Committee of the House of Commons on the Bankrupt Laws) its defects are such, that they never can be entirely removed, until a radical change shall take place in the nature of the tribunal.

In what the most substantial part of that change ought to consist it is impossible for any one to doubt who has read but a small portion of what has been published on this subject.

We have seen in the preceding chapter, that even in the last century the defective constitution of the Court of Commissioners of Bankrupt had engaged the public attention.

In 1783 Sir James Bland Burgess published his valuable work entitled, Considerations on the Law of Insolvency, with a proposal for a reform, already noticed, and as it is now but seldom to be met with, I shall not apologize for making some long extracts from it. It is generally more useful, in our endeavours to effect a reform, to revive in the recollection of the public ancient and forgotten opinions, than to introduce to the public our own notions, which are but too often hastily and imperfectly formed, and rather adapted to remedy the particular evil than to prevent the recurrence of similar mischief for the future.

The following is the plan suggested by Sir James Bland Burgess for the reform of the Court of Commissioners, which, in most of the leading features, coincides with several proposals, having a similar view, that have been made within the last ten years.

" The first object," he says, " which should engage our " attention must be the persons delegated to conduct these " commissions.

" There cannot be a more convincing proof of the in- " sufficiency of the present establishment than a com- " parison between the number of Commissioners of Bank- " rupt and the very little business they do, or the very " little advantage they produce. That this multitude of " Commissioners is unnecessary, that the business would " be done much more effectually by less than a seventh " part of their number, may not be difficult to prove. In " each of the three supreme courts of law there are only " four judges; in the Chancery there are only two. Yet, " what proportion can the business of insolvency bear to " the multifarious mass which is agitated and determined " before each of these tribunals? To a single branch of " the business of insolvency, are, however, now appointed " sixty-five judges. Whether any advantage has attended " upon so numerous a delegation is a matter to be deter- " mined by the public. A very contrary idea has, we " are afraid, prevailed, and it has pretty generally been " thought that, although the number of commissioners has " gradually increased, the interests of trade have not been " promoted, the iniquities of the fraudulent have not been " restrained.

" This insufficiency then is clearly owing to two imme- " diate causes—to the appointment of many persons in- " adequate to the discharge of so important a business, " and to the great difficulty, if not impossibility, of pro-

"curing others more qualified. And both these causes "are derived from a common source, the very inconsider- "able profits annexed to the employment, and the great "inconveniences which arise from its necessary inter- "ference with other and more profitable business. Men "of talents and of eminence will either not accept of so "barren and so troublesome an employment, or if they "find it convenient to take a small place rather than to "have none at all, they will convert it into a sinecure, and "prefer the receipt of 50*l.* a year without any trouble to "the receipt of 80*l.* obtained by numerous and vexatious "attendances at Guildhall. In consequence of this, the "majority of commissioners does and always must consist "of men neither of experience nor of knowledge. And to "such men are committed the great and important in- "terests of the credit and the commerce of this country.

"By a very easy arrangement all these difficulties may "be obviated. It may be made worth the while of eminent "and able men to undertake the task of superintending the "business of insolvency, to give up other views, and to "confine themselves to this one important pursuit. Nor "is this arrangement more simple in its nature than it "must certainly prove efficacious in its consequences. "Various and convincing instances of the possibility of "dispatching a great deal of business with a very few "hands present themselves to our consideration in all our "legal tribunals, in all the departments of state, and in all "the offices relating to the revenue. Let us then take them "for our model; let us adapt the experience of others to "the production of that reformation which can be sub- "stantially effected only by a similar institution.

"Pursuing therefore such a course, we submit to the "public consideration the propriety of abolishing the

" present phalanx of Commissioners, and of establishing
" in their place a regular Board of Insolvency.

" Such a constitution will comprehend every thing " which is at present diffused through sixty-five Commis- " sioners, and perhaps fifty times that number of other " persons mediately or immediately concerned in the con- " duct of Commissions of Bankruptcy, all of whom are " to be fed from the Estates of Bankrupts, and who con- " sequently all tend to diminish the dividend of the honest " creditor.

" The Board of Insolvency may consist of nine commis- " sioners, of a secretary, of a solicitor, of three assignees, " of an accountant, of a comptroller, of a cashier, of their " several clerks, and of a certain number of messengers. " With these few officers the whole business may be done " completely; for it is proposed that these officers shall be " competent men, that they shall have no other engage- " ments to call off their attention, and that a handsome " and proportionable reward shall be the consequence of " their abilities and good conduct.

" Of the Commissioners there is no necessity that the " whole should be lawyers, although for the proper dis- " charge of the business a great degree of legal knowledge " is absolutely essential, yet a knowledge of the interests " and of the different modes of commerce is not less so. " A Board, therefore, wholly composed of merchants, or " wholly of lawyers, would prove inadequate; if composed " of both, it probably will be as perfect as such a tribunal " can be made. These lawyers should really deserve that " denomination; they should possess a knowledge of the " principles of their profession, which seldom falls to the " lot of students or of attorneys; such persons, therefore, " we would exclude; we would even propose to confine " the selection to barristers of at least three years. Of

"five such barristers let the Chancellor have the nomi-
"nation.

"Professional reputation should also be the criterion "by which the choice of the four merchants necessary to "complete the number of Commissioners should be regu-"lated. Of this reputation not the Chancellor, but their "brother merchants, must be the most proper judges; to "them, therefore, the choice should be committed, sub-"ject to the approbation or the rejection of the Chan-"cellor.

"That able and proper persons should be induced to "accept of these employments, it will be necessary to "declare that their continuance in them shall not depend "on the arbitrary will of any man. Under such a check "integrity cannot freely take its course. Like the judges, "the Commissioners of Insolvency should hold their offices "'*quamdiu se bene gesserint,*' in other words, they should "be elected for life, subject only to a removal in conse-"quence of their own misbehaviour.

"The authority of these Commissioners will be two-fold, "general and special.

"By their general authority they will have a superin-"tending and corrective power over all the subordinate "departments of the office.

"Their special authority will be extended to various "matters; they will have the sole power of declaring in-"solvency, of issuing process, of directing a seizure of the "effects, or a personal imprisonment of an insolvent. "They will have the exclusive right of determining all "contested matters relative to debts and claims, and of "granting certificates. In all these matters the judgment "of the Commissioners should be final, subject only to "the future correction of the Chancellor, by the summary "process of petition.

"Expensive and tedious appeals ought as little as pos-
"sible to be cultivated. Some expedient should be de-
"vised by which contested matters may, without them,
"be brought to a termination. For this reason we pro-
"pose that out of these nine Commissioners five should
"constitute a quorum, who shall be competent to dis-
"charge the ordinary business of the Board. At the end
"of every month the senior Commissioner on duty shall
"retire, and the next in order shall succeed. By this
"method each commissioner will be engaged for five suc-
"cessive months. All points should be determinable by
"a majority, except in particular cases of superior intricacy,
"where either of the commissioners shall entertain a doubt,
"or where the parties shall conceive a proper cause to
"exist for an appeal from their adjudication. This
"ordinary Board shall meet on the Monday, Tuesday,
"Wednesday, and Thursday in every week, subject to no
"interruptions from holidays, other than those which are
"regarded by other courts of justice.

"All the appeals ought to be made to the General
"Board, which should be held on the first day in every
"month."

Such is the outline of Sir James Bland Burgess's scheme as to a new Court of London Commissioners of Bankrupt. His proposal as to a Board of Country Commissioners in each county has been often alluded to of late years. It is as follows:—

"So very defective is the present system, with regard
"to the Country Commissions, and so replete is it with
"every seed of irregularity and of fraud, that it cannot be
"very hazardous to propose some alteration; perhaps it

"may be far from difficult to suggest one in every way "preferable to that of which we complain.

"As in the several departments of the revenue there "is a regular subordination of officers who transact the "business committed to their charge in the different parts "of the kingdom, subject to the controul of their supe-"riors, so for the management of country Commis-"sions a system of the same sort may very properly be "adopted. There may be in each county a peculiar "Board, composed of more or fewer Commissioners, in "proportion to its size, of one or more assignees, and of "those other officers whom we have already described; "all dependent upon the superior Board and answerable "to it for their conduct. It may be deserving of con-"sideration, whether the receiver-general of the county "would not be the properest person for the cashier.

"For the due management of these country Commis-"sioners, another officer will be extremely necessary. To "each circuit there may be appointed a General Super-"visor, nominated by the superior Board, and totally de-"pendent upon it. It should be his business to superin-"tend the conduct of the inferior Boards within the juris-"diction, to inspect from time to time the different ac-"counts depending before them, to send up once in every "month an abstract of these accounts to be laid before "the General Board, to examine into the management of "the whole business, to develope every species of miscon-"duct and to exercise a kind of censorial power in all those "emergencies where the ministration of a superior and "disinterested person may be supposed to be particularly "necessary."

In 1809, *Mr. Abercrombie,* himself a Commissioner of Bankrupt, said, in a debate in the House of Commons on the Bankrupt Laws, that the Commissioners were generally young barristers, well qualified for that situation, but who connected with that object advancement in their profession, and to whom therefore the administration of the bankrupt laws was a secondary consideration. Pressed by their professional avocations, they were compelled to crowd into one day a number of cases which probably required great deliberation. In his opinion, the Commissioners of Bankrupt should be a distinct class, to whom sufficient emolument and advantages ought to be held out, to induce them to devote their exclusive attention to a subject, which, in a commercial country like Great Britain, was of such extreme importance. If, instead of seventy-five commissioners, the number was reduced to five, without any additional expense to the public, the object would be much more effectually accomplished.*

* It appears from the Journals of the House of Commons, that, on the 6th of June, 1811, leave was given to bring in a bill for the amendment of the bankrupt laws of Ireland, and Mr. Grattan, Mr. Ponsonby, and Sir John Newport were ordered to prepare it; and, Mr. Grattan presenting the bill, it was read the first time. On the 7th of June it was read a second time, and ordered to be printed, but it was not afterwards proceeded in.

The bill has been printed by Mr. Montague, in one of his numerous pamphlets on the bankrupt laws. It contained clauses for abolishing the present tribunal of Commissioners, and for erecting in its place a Court composed of five barristers, of twelve years standing, which should sit daily at ten o'clock, and should have jurisdiction to adjudicate, not only the matters which now

In 1818, on a bill for the Amendment of the Bankrupt Laws being read a second time, *Mr. Abercrombie* observed, that it was impossible to render the bankrupt law such as it ought to be, unless there was a total and radical change in those who have to administer it. He made such statement in the spirit of candour, and not with the view of impugning the conduct of the Commissioners, of whom he himself formed a part; on the contrary, he felt assured, that these gentlemen discharged their duties in the most creditable manner it was possible that they could be discharged, under the circumstances in which they were placed. The law could never be properly administered, until the Commissioners devoted their whole time to the administration of it, because it was too much to expect of any men that they should neglect their own private clients, in order to attend to a commission of bankruptcy, from which they derived inferior emoluments.

The late *Sir W. D. Evans*, (whose valuable works on several parts of our jurisprudence entitle his opinion to considerable weight,) in his Letter, addressed to Sir Samuel Romilly in the year 1810, on the Revision of the Bankrupt Law,

fall under the cognizance of the Commissioners, but all the questions now brought before the Chancellor, subject however to an appeal to the Great Seal. The members of the new Court were not to be permitted to practise any longer as counsel, and it was proposed to give them fixed salaries.

states, he conceived that the public would derive very great advantages from the institution of a tribunal appropriated to the particular jurisdiction of bankruptcy, with the liberty of appeal to the Great Seal, but under such restrictions as might prevent the recurring to it as a matter of course.

Mr. Montague, in his evidence before the Select Committee of the House of Commons on the Bankrupt Laws in February, 1818, stated, that in his attendance upon the different lists of commissioners, he saw a constant alteration, so that he was occasionally obliged to argue before new commissioners questions which were settled by the previous board, and which, before that previous board, he used to argue some years ago. Litigation attendant upon petitions to the Lord Chancellor was a consequence of this. That it was impossible, from the insufficiency of the emoluments, to insure the undivided attention, or the permanent continuance, of gentlemen of ability; that, as to the undivided attention of commissioners, gentlemen of attainment and considerable practice, who were commissioners, were, in proportion to their value, necessarily at different places, attendant upon the discharge of different duties, instead of being confined to the discharge of the duty of commissioners; and as to the permanent continuance, the appointment of commissioners was obviously more frequently a passage to other situations than a permanent situation;

that, from the difficulty of procuring the permanent attendance of commissioners, solicitors had considerable difficulty in occasionally assembling commissioners, either because the commissioners were in the country or on the circuit, or attending their duties in Court or in different places. Inconvenience too resulted from the nature of the board, as different commissioners attended sometimes at different parts of examinations of the same subject.

In his examination before the same Committee, *Mr. Montague* suggested the first specific measure to improve the mode of administering the bankrupt laws, that has, I believe, been brought forward since Sir James Bland Burgess's proposal in 1783. He observed that, with respect to remedies, should it appear that these evils called for remedy, it might be deserving consideration, whether the greater part of the business might not be better transacted by one commissioner, where the responsibility would be greater than it now is, or whether the commissions might not be directed to all the commissioners, so that the difficulty of procuring attendance might be annihilated, or, what perhaps might be the best of all modes, whether there should not be a standing board of some fixed number, say ten or twelve commissioners, with sufficient emolument to ensure their undivided and continual attendance, without there being a prospect of the situation of

Commissioner of Bankrupts being considered a passage for other more valuable situations. This would of course be attended with considerable difficulty. It had occurred to him, that should any mode of this sort appear expedient to be adopted, a board might be selected with the least inconvenience if it were formed from the present commissioners. If, for instance, there was a regular tribunal of twelve commissioners constantly sitting, to be supplied by the present commissioners in rotation, with an efficient chairman, a deputy chairman, and the places of the present commissioners, as they became vacant, not to be supplied until the whole was reduced to such number as might appear proper, the commissioners themselves would be benefited and not injured by this; and there would ultimately be a board of efficient commissioners, with a sufficient income to insure such attendance as would be beneficial to the mercantile interests: but he was by no means certain that this plan which had presented itself to him was practicable.*

In his evidence before the Chancery Commissioners *Mr. Montague* stated, that he thought the Court of the Commissioners of Bankrupt the worst constituted tribunal in this country. The defects were expense, delay, uncertainty, and

* An extract from the evidence of the late Mr. Cullen before this Committee has been given in the preceding chapter.

want of publicity, and of all the checks attendant upon publicity. In London, there were seventy commissioners in fourteen lists, each list unconnected and independent of the other, the practice in some respects varying in all of the lists, and the law in many of them, and, from the nature of the tribunal, in most of them, unless there was considerable professional exertion. With respect to their uncertainty in their judgments, when it was considered that in London there were fourteen different tribunals, and perhaps double their number in the country, and when each of these tribunals was composed of members who could not be constant in their attendance, and who were continually fluctuating, there must of course be occasionally opposite decisions, not only by different tribunals, but even by the same tribunals. He knew this to be so frequent, that, in questions submitted to his advice, he constantly inquired whether it was a country or London commission, and, when a London commission, what list of commissioners was to decide. The law, except in a few cases, was not publicly administered. All the evils attendant upon the want of publicity in the administration of justice, might be seen by the most common observer in the proceedings before the commissioners of bankrupt. First, the commissioners, counsel and parties did not always attend with sufficient punctuality at the times appointed for the sitting of the court. That gentlemen of attainment and considerable practice must (in proportion to their value) necessarily be at different places upon the discharge of different duties, instead of being confined for two hours for a fee of one pound, to discharge the duty of a commissioner of bankrupts, was in the theory obvious, and in practice familiar; the consequence was, great expense and delay to the suitor. Of this he saw daily instances, and, as he had mentioned before, he thought it his duty to observe all that passed since his last attendance. Only the preceding day a meeting was actually adjourned, and the parties were going out of the court, when one of the commissioners entered the hall, and the parties returned after having waited for an hour. He calculated so much upon this, that he always took cases in his pocket, that he might answer them while he was waiting. There was difficulty in fixing the attention of the commissioners; the judgment of the commissioners was often with great difficulty fixed upon the subject-matter of dispute. He had frequently to implore the undivided attention of the commissioners, but, at private meetings, the newspaper was sometimes a more powerful advocate than he was. The tribunal did not consist of permanent judges. The evil from this source, as far as related to experience, he had stated elsewhere. He then considered it merely as it related to uncertainty in the judgment, upon which he begged to refer to what he had already stated, and to add, that the evil of want of permanence was not, however, confined to the fluctuation in the judges, by the retirement of experienced and the admission of inexperienced men; but as any three of the five formed a quorum, the suitor was often exposed, even in the same court, to a change of the judge, and this not only from one meeting to another, but sometimes even in the course of the same meeting. He mentioned this the last time he had the honour of attending. Of this he saw daily instances. There was scarcely an adjournment of a bankrupt's examination, where the commissioners at the adjourned meeting were the same commissioners by whom the adjournment was ordered; in which case the business was, as it were, to begin again, to the vexation of the bankrupt, and the expense of the estate and of his friends. In case of disputed debts, where the question to be decided might relate to property to a considerable amount, this too frequently happened. There was an instance then pending, where the facts respecting the proof of a debt, to the amount of £36,000, attended with circumstances of the most deplorable distress, were partly investigated by some, and partly by other commissioners, and the decision was of course not found by all the commissioners who were present during the whole examination. Of the magnitude of this evil any man might form an estimate, by considering the case to be his own, and that the examination, after having been continued from time to time, was, at an adjourned meeting, resumed before one or two new commissioners, by whom, or by their predecessors, the judgment was to be pronounced. As a counsel he knew that it was his duty to argue and re-argue, to repeat and re-repeat what had occurred at former meetings, that he might insure to himself a consciousness that he had done his best that each member of the tribunal should know what the facts were. Having stated what appeared to him to be the uncertainty, with respect to the law, he then stated, in detail, the uncertainty in the practice before the different lists, and observed, there were, as there naturally must be, an almost infinity of other instances of discrepancies in the practices of so many independent tribunals, but without occupying more of the public time, he contented himself, unless called upon, with the instances which he had already stated. Speaking under the head of delay, he must repeat that the time of attendance was only two hours, and that the examination was taken down in writing, the consequence was, that a very small portion of business was done, and the delay was very great. As the fee was only one pound for each meeting, it appeared not very reasonable to require the attendance of the commissioners for more than two hours, the consequence was that the meetings, whether they were for the proof of debts, or for the examination of parties, or for passing the bankrupt's last examination, were frequently adjourned from day to day and from week to week, to the great inconvenience of the parties who were detained from their families and occupations. The expense also, from the nature of the tribunal, depended much upon the shortness of time appropriated to the investigation. Each meeting was of two hours, and the whole examination being taken in writing, the very simplest subject of inquiry might occupy many meetings; and every meeting, being attended by counsel on each side, cost at least about twelve pounds, which was about two shillings a minute. He then proceeded to the defects of the Chancellor's Court of Appeal, which appeared to be of three kinds, delay, expense and uncertainty. The delays appeared to be of two sorts, first in the hearing, and secondly in obtaining judgment; with respect to the delays in the hearing, the general truth that causes should be fully heard, deeply considered, and speedily decided, applied peculiarly to the case of Bankruptcy. The very nature of trade required that the decision should not be attended with delay, which, although perhaps of little relative importance in intricate questions respecting the settlement of real property, wholly frustrated the intention of this branch of commercial law, where contests were frequently between opulence and poverty, and where the ruin in which one house was involved was, without expedition, almost certain of entailing ruin upon others. In a case he mentioned as having occurred some time back, the ruin of two country banks, and all the consequent wretchedness attendant upon such failures, would have been inevitable, but for the immediate attention of the Lord Chancellor; an attention which, with every disposition to hear all complaints, would now be almost hopeless. Every species of exertion had, at different times, been made by the Court to meet the evil, but these exertions have been vain, the evil had increased and was increasing. Some years since there was a regular day appointed for hearing Bankrupt petitions, when the petitions were few in number, and the general business of the court not so extensive; but this practice was, after an attempt by the Vice Chancellor to renew it, wholly discontinued, and a Bankrupt petition was, instead of being *festinum remedium* (a saving of expense and a saving of time) a very dilatory, and, very often, a very expensive proceeding. Petitions unavoidably remained for a considerable time on the paper. He had, some years since, known the Lord Chancellor sit during the time appropriated to Bankrupt petitions from ten in the morning till eleven at night, with the daily interval of only two or three hours, for a fortnight together. But these exertions had been found vain, and of late years it had been found impracticable to hear all the petitions before the commencement of the long vacation, and for these last three or four years many of the petitions had been left as remanents. Since the appointment of the Vice Chancellor, these difficulties had much increased. Without inquiry into the causes, it might be perhaps most proper to inquire first into the fact, previous to the appointment of the Vice Chancellor. He thought he might venture to say, that the Chancellor, before that time, never suffered the vacation to commence until he had heard every Bankrupt petition. His labours to discharge those arduous duties could never be appreciated or conceived, except by those who had witnessed and remembered his exertions. Since the appointment of a Vice Chancellor, it was his belief, that the Lord Chancellor had generally, if not always, suffered the vacation to commence with an arrear, which had been increasing, of unheard petitions. And so he thought the Vice Chancellor had really, although perhaps not nominally, left Bankrupt petitions unheard, but he was sure the Lord Chancellor had. He anticipated the evil from delay some years ago, when he stated as follows to the House of Commons:—"With respect to the Court of Appeal, I do not mean to complain of any thing that is omitted, nor do I forget what is done, but from the great increase of business in the Court of Chancery, it appears to me that very serious inconvenience arises from the delay unavoidably attendant upon procuring ultimate decisions in Bankruptcy; and I am inclined to suspect that the intention of the legislature in this respect may, if business continue to increase, be frustrated." He was then speaking only of delays in hearing; he ought to add, that the number of petitions in bankrupcty had of course, since the Vice Chancellor's court was established, increased, because there was the usual number of petitions with the addition of the petitions of appeal.

Mr. Montague, in the course of his evidence before the Chancery Commissioners, further stated, he thought the whole business would be done infinitely better by a few commissioners giving their undivided and continued attention to the subject, and with a board of appeal, consisting of one or more commissioners, and by compelling all commissions which issued within a hundred miles of London to be directed to London commissioners; and he thought that one Barrister in each large provincial town or county, with the eyes of the public upon him, and the responsibility attached to the appointment, and one person with a similar appointment for two or three small counties, would insure an infinitely better administration of justice than now exists. He thought that if such intermediate board of appeal should be deemed expedient, it might instantly hear all appeals from London commissioners, upon the same evidence on which the commissioners from whose decision the appeal was instituted had decided; and that the board of appeal might, in the first instance, hear all the appeals from the country, although it was very probable that some or many better modes of determining the appeals from the country, in the first instance, might be adopted. So many important questions arose in Bankruptcy, and it appeared to him to be of so great moment that the commissioners should be under the inspection and controul of the highest authorities, that he ventured to suggest that there ought, subject to certain checks, always to be a right of ultimate appeal to the Lord Chancellor. He also suggested, that all the duties discharged by the seventy commissioners should be discharged by a smaller number, say six commissioners, to whom all the commissions might be directed (supposing there was any necessity for the direction of any commission* at all), and that any one should be a quorum, so that the business never would stand still; and of the evils attendant upon business

* Every body knows that commissions are no more necessary in Bankruptcy than in Insolvency. In 1826, a sum of £16,000 was taken from the property of bankrupts and insolvents for fees upon these commissions alone, and that not even for the purpose of paying the officers of justice, or of rewarding any faithful servant of the public, but, incredible as it will seem a century hence, for the benefit of a sinecure nobleman.

occasionally standing still, he observed, it was scarcely possible for any person not much conversant in Bankruptcy to conceive. He thought that if all the London commissions (supposing commissions necessary) were directed to six commissioners, to sit daily, with a fixed salary, of whom any one should be a quorum, and a court, consisting of one or more commissioners, by whom all the appeals should, in the first instance, be heard, and from whose decision there should be an appeal (under certain checks) to the Lord Chancellor, most of the defects which he had mentioned would be obviated; but he had not had an opportunity to consider whether, supposing a plan of this sort should appear expedient, the intermediate court of appeal should consist of part of the six commissioners, by which an union of decision might be procured, or of distinct persons, which might operate as a controul upon them all. He merely mentioned this as appearing to him to deserve consideration. As checks for unnecessary appeals, it appeared to him that an appeal might be preferred as a matter of right, whenever there was a difference of opinion between the court of appeal and the tribunal whose decision was reversed; or supposing the court of appeal to consist of more commissioners than one, if there were a dissenting voice in the court of appeal. He had thought, that upon a certificate by either of the commissioners of appeal, or the commissioners below, that the case was on account of its intricacy, or on account of its importance, deserving further consideration, an appeal should lie. He had thought, (although he was aware it was attended with great difficulty,) that upon some proper certificate, by one or two barristers, not as a mere matter of course, but that they really thought the decision was erroneous, an appeal should lie; of this, however, he had great doubt. He ought to state that there was a suggestion in a tract, published by Mr. Fonblanque, but he had much doubt as to the practicability of it, with respect to London commissioners going circuits.*

Mr. Bell, in his evidence before the same Commissioners, suggested that the bulk of the Bankruptcy business might be separated from the other business of the Court of Chancery, by making a

* *Mr. Montague*, in his evidence given before the Select Committee of the Common Council, stated his belief, that six or eight persons constantly sitting, from ten o'clock to four, with a court of appeal to be formed out of such persons, to meet once a week, would dispatch all the business at a very small expense, and with very great satisfaction. He further stated, he could not see any objection to nominating a barrister in each large town, or in each county, or for two or three small counties, for the administration of the Bankrupt Laws in the country, to whom responsibility would attach, and who, if properly selected, would prevent the improper proceedings which it was well known had existed under country commissions, and of which the Lord Chancellor had again and again complained.

perpetual commission of five persons, each acting alone in common matters, and a bench of three of them sitting once a week, or oftener, to hear matters any individual commissioner might adjourn to be heard before such bench, or an appeal from the decision of any individual, or from country commissioners, still reserving an ultimate appeal to the Lord Chancellor, but on the same evidence, with power to direct further inquiry, and subject to the usual guards against improper appeals.

Mr. Roupell stated, that the business in Bankruptcy would be one of the most convenient branches of the business to separate; that supposing another tribunal were instituted, to hear and decide the ordinary cases in Chancery, it did seem to him there would be a great convenience to the general Equity business of the Court of Chancery, and that the judges of that Court would be relieved from a great deal of business which occupied the time they might otherwise employ in getting through the general business of the Court.* He thought, however, that an appeal should still be reserved to the Lord Chancellor. In answer to the question whether he thought it would be de-

* *Mr. Leake, M.P.* stated, that if some means could be devised of relieving the Court from the load of Bankrupt Petitions, which then amounted, upon an average, to nearly 700 a year, and which then occupied, he believed, nearly one third of its time, a great benefit would be attained.

sirable that the present Commissioners of Bankrupt should be done away with, and a court consisting of five persons established, he stated, that as far as he could judge, he thought it would be exceedingly convenient and publicly useful, if there was an intermediate court between the commissioners and the Lord Chancellor, for the purpose of intercepting, hearing, and disposing of many of those questions and matters now brought by petition from the commissioners to the Lord Chancellor, and which must be heard by him or the Vice Chancellor.

Many of the other witnesses examined before the Chancery Commissioners expressed opinions not very unlike those already stated as to the imperfections of the Court of Commissioners.

Mr. Ellison, a Commissioner of Bankrupt, observed, that the bankrupt law was defective in not providing a better jurisdiction than the present tribunal of London commissioners, to administer the bankrupt law, and he suggested that the appointment of a board of commissioners; who should devote their time and attention exclusively to the administration of the bankrupt law, would be an improvement of the system, and a great benefit to the mercantile world, the board being composed of such a number of commissioners as would be necessary to dispatch the business with reasonable expedition.

Mr. Clayton, a Commissioner of Bankrupt,

stated, that although in his opinion any change must be attended with the inconveniences he pointed out, yet that delay, expense and uncertainty, might be materially obviated by limitation of number and selection of individuals as Commissioners of Bankrupt, without any other alteration of the law than what must by consequence follow that measure; and he gave it as his opinion, that six commissioners would be sufficient to transact the whole London business well and satisfactorily, allowing a liberal portion of relaxation to each.

The late *Mr. Glyn,* who was a Commissioner of Bankrupt, stated, the expense of the present system of commissioners, the want of uniformity both of practice and decision, and the fluctuations of the members of the court, by which the law was administered, to be the most prominent defects of the present bankrupt system. The judges consisted, for the most part, of judges who blended that duty with their professional practice; of course only a proportion of their time and attention could be expected to be applied to the business of bankruptcy. In almost every list of commissioners, a rota of attendance was established, the consequence of which necessarily was, that part of the proceedings under a commission was executed by one set of commissioners, and another part by another set; and even examinations upon the same subject-matter, when protracted from meeting to meeting, were sometimes commenced by one set, and concluded by another. This fluctuation of commissioners, which was not calculated to give efficacy, consistency, or authority, to their proceedings, necessarily resulted from the system, particularly when the commissioners, as most of them did, united private professional practice with their duty as commissioners. The number of commissioners too, to whom the execution of the bankrupt laws was committed, which might probably be better executed by fewer men entirely devoted to it, enhanced the expense and produced difference of practice and decisions.

Mr. Glyn also stated, that the suggestion which had been thrown out, of a permanent court of six or eight commissioners, if it was composed of persons devoting themselves altogether to the business of Bankruptcy, would probably go a good way to meet the defects complained of. If commissioners were selected, whose whole undivided attention was to be devoted to the administration of Bankruptcy, and who in some divisions would constitute a court of appeal, to which immediate and constant resort might be had, he should apprehend that the whole of the business now requiring three commissioners, (except, perhaps, the adjudication of bankruptcy,) might be safely entrusted to one of such commissioners, subject to the revision of the collected court. The importance and difficulty of many of the questions arising in Bankruptcy, the large interests involved in them, their intimate connection with points of equity and of common law, the established habit of resort to the highest judicial authority of the state, seemed to make it desirable, that, in the first instance at least, endeavour should be made to afford some relief to the Court above, and a more prompt and efficient remedy to the parties, by improving the character of the lower tribunals, confessedly open to objections as at present constituted. It might reasonably be hoped, that, in affording some remedy to the present defects of the tribunal of commissioners—by their improved character, the limitation of their number, their entire abstraction from other business, a tribunal might be constituted of such efficiency and experience, as would be likely to gain the confidence of the public, and would justify the committing to it, in the first instance, great part of the petitions in Bankruptcy, and that some relief would thus be given to the superior court. For the purpose (without separating Bankruptcy from the Lord Chancellor as the ulterior resort) of removing the defects necessarily incident to the present system of giving the means of prompt and efficient remedy, and of affording some relief to the Court above, through the improvement of the lower tribunal, two suggestions had been made; the one, a reduction of the number of commissioners by whom the business now executed by commissioners was to be performed, accompanied with the appointment of a single judge, whose duties would be limited to the determination of petitions in Bankruptcy; the other, the appointment of an adequate number of commissioners, devoted exclusively to Bankruptcy, who should not only execute the business now performed by commissioners, but should have, in the first instance, the determination of much of the business forming the subject of petition in Bankruptcy, with an appeal, nevertheless, to the Lord Chancellor, under any restriction that might be thought fit. The country commissioners should probably be permanent, but they could not well be detached from other business, and perhaps that arrangement would be most desirable which would combine the most direct and immediate controul by the London Courts, with the means of a prompt and efficient execution of the local business. If in all the districts beyond the proposed limits of London commissioners sufficient barristers could be found for the purpose, to them all the ordinary business might be committed, subject to an appeal to the London courts, which might also have the determination of such part of the petitions (not being matters of appeal) arising out of country commissions, as related to matters which in London commissions were to be within the jurisdiction of the London commissioners.

Mr. Glyn, in his examination before the Select Committee of the Common Council, stated, he thought the present tribunal of commissioners at Guildhall, in many respects, defective; the number of commissioners; the division into so many different courts or lists; the necessity of the joinder of three in every act, however formal; the difficulty of securing the undivided attention of the three same commissioners in protracted examinations; the holding three or more meetings in different commissions at the same hour; the encroachment of other business on the attention of the commissioners; the fluctuation of commissioners in the business of the same commission; the difficulty of obtaining a calm and undistracted consideration of points of law and equity, arising daily at the public meetings; the consequent necessity of the delay and expense of private meetings; were amongst the most prominent defects of the present tribunal of commissioners at Guildhall, and which seemed to him inherent in the system; and it appeared to him that a reduction of the commissioners to such a number of efficient persons, devoting their whole time singly to the execution of the business of commissioners, and also constituting a court of appeal collectively, as would be adequate to such duties, was the most unobjectionable, and yet most effective alteration that had been suggested. He should think that six or eight commissioners, each competent singly to transact the business then done by commissioners, and uniting in one or more courts, for the purpose of hearing bankrupt petitions, in order to afford an immediate decision of the subject of appeal, or of original application, would give a remedy to most of the defects of the present system. He was not prepared to say that any check or limitation could properly be placed on the right of appeal to the Lord Chancellor, which it seemed to him ought to be preserved. The best check upon appeals would be the public confidence in the more effective character of the lower tribunals. Certainly the tribunal should, in the first instance, be composed of individuals, each competent to the performance of the duty separately; in numbers sufficient to the due execution of the business, yet not so many but that they should feel themselves within the reach of the observation of the public. He did not think that the business of petitions in bankruptcy alone was sufficient for the occupation of a judge; but if the court of intermediate jurisdiction was composed of three or four commissioners, who also individually executed the business in the first instance, their time would be fully occupied in bankruptcy, and the public would have an efficient court, in the first instance, and a competent court of the intermediate appeal always sitting; a point of incalculable moment. He apprehended that the alteration suggested would be considerably less expensive than the present system. The delay in the decision of bankrupt petitions tended greatly to enhance the expense, and the more efficient the administration of the bankrupt laws was made from its inception, the less of subsequent dilatory and expensive examinations, re-hearings, appeals and petitions, would arise. Promptitude in the decision of questions in bankruptcy was essential to the mercantile world, and was one of the first objects to be aimed at in any alteration.

Mr. Fonblanque, one of the Commissioners of Bankruptcy, stated in his examination before the Select Committee of the Common Council, that when cases of bankruptcy were rare it might have been expedient to commit them to the jurisdiction of occasional commissioners, but since that class of business had become sufficiently considerable to furnish ample occupation to regular tribunals, he did not think the employment of temporary judges any longer reasonable. The same objection attached to many branches of our jurisprudence. We had commissioners of lunatics, commissioners for taking answers, commissioners for examining witnesses, and various other purposes, all which would be better executed by permanent and therefore more experienced and competent officers. He mentioned this because he believed the present time to be peculiarly fitted to the consolidation of the dispersed jurisdiction; the business of bankruptcy and insolvency, for instance, might be fairly united under one court. He wished to be understood, that in imputing great defects to the existing practice, his wonder was, that they were not more considerable. The system wanted connection, it was disjointed into parts, having no mutual relation or control. The Lord Chancellor had indeed a nominal superintendence over the whole, but it was merely nominal, for it was only in extreme cases the parties would be at the trouble and expense of applying to him. The commissioners, the solicitors, and the bankrupt office, were independent powers, without check upon each other. The messengers also were independent of the commissioners, and generally looked to the solicitors for their directions. He had considered the subject, and among many plans he thought that the constitution of regular local or provincial courts, which might combine the jurisdiction of bankruptcy and insolvency with other objects of jurisprudence, would be the most beneficial. Permanent courts at York, Manchester, Birmingham, Bristol, and Norwich, (perhaps, also at one or two other great trading towns) would be sufficient for the more important business, while detached and itinerant commissioners might take depositions and minor business in other places, so that if justice was not absolutely brought to every man's door, he might not have far to travel for it. In the first instance, the number of provincial

Courts might be small, and confined to the most important trading towns; but, if the system should work well, it might be extended, as the funds for its support would allow. He would produce to the committee a plan* which he had drawn out for the formation of Courts both in London and the Country. He was unwilling to be considered a legal projector, but it was necessary that some one should begin; and, therefore, after having waited some years for a leader, he must, however reluctantly, assume the character till it might be better filled. He proposed that the whole jurisdiction should be concentrated under one commission, that each Court should be auxiliary to the others, that the provincial Courts should be dependant on the central tribunal, and that such central tribunal should be under the ultimate control of the Lord Chancellor. He proposed this on the principle that progressive subordination and responsibility was essential to good government, whether legal or political, and under the impression that the want of it was a primary cause of the existing evils and abuses in the administration of the Bankrupt Laws. There was in Bankruptcy much important business of detail which no single judge could attend to. A board could subdivide

* This plan is too long for insertion here, the substance appears from that part of Mr. Fonblanque's evidence which I have extracted.

these labours; but under a single judge they would be committed to the clerks or accountants, and in a short time a new court, with a single judge, would have contracted (and from similar causes) all the abuses attributed to the offices of the Masters in Chancery.

It may appear extraordinary if the Report of the Chancery Commissioners be not here noticed. The Commissioners recommended, on account of the peculiar inconvenience which delay occasions in matters of Bankrupts, that the hearing of petitions should not, as was then generally the case, be postponed until the last sittings of the Lord Chancellor and Vice Chancellor before the long vacation,* and that the time allowed for the hearing of petitions after each term, except Easter term, should be extended. The Court is now acting upon this recommendation, three days in every week being allotted by the Vice Chancellor to Bankrupt petitions. The misfortune is that the commissioners, in their laudable zeal to expedite the decision of the causes in Bankruptcy, have forgotten that the legitimate suitors of the Court of Chancery, who by the constitution are entitled to have their rights adjudicated in that tribunal without delay, lose what those interested in the property of bankrupts gain, and that suits which

* Of late years the Court has risen for the long vacation, leaving a great part of the Bankrupt petitions unheard.

have been depending in the Court for ten, fifteen, or twenty years, are retarded in proportion as the bankrupt petitions are accelerated. *

The Commissioners further recommended, on the subject of bankruptcy, that ten or more persons should be selected by the Chancellor out of the Commissioners of Bankrupt to hear, in the first instance, all matters which are now the subject of appeal to the Chancellor from the decisions of the London Commissioners. That this measure would not relieve the Court of Chancery has been clearly shown by Mr. Montague. Out of 253 petitions that were in the Vice Chancellor's paper for hearing in July, 1826, only twenty-seven were appeals from the decisions of the commissioners. In the Lord Chancellor's paper for the same month of July there were sixty-seven petitions, and of these Mr. Montague has stated, he believed

* It may perhaps be supposed, from the great arrear of Bankruptcy business, and from the length of time the petitions have been set down, that Bankruptcy, being an excrescence on the equity jurisdiction, occupies but a small portion of the time of the Court. This, however, is not the case. It appears that in the years 1823, 1824 and 1825 the business in Bankruptcy occupied nearly one fourth of the time of the Court. What time was devoted to Bankruptcy in 1826 I do not know, and the impression upon my mind is, that in 1827 a smaller portion of time than usual was set apart for that business. A comparison, however, of the lists of the last and present year will show that few Bankrupt petitions were heard.

It had become then absolutely necessary, if the jurisdiction were retained, that the Court should set apart for the Bankrupt petitions a great portion of the present sittings.

there were not more than eight which were appeals from the commissioners. Considering how small a proportion the appeals from the Commissioners bear to the total number of petitions, it seems unaccountable that the Chancery Commissioners should have proposed the appointment of Commissioners of Appeal as a mode of relieving the Court of Chancery by correcting the errors of the general commissioners.

In the month of July, 1826, a special Committee of the Common Council of the city of London was appointed to take into consideration the state of the Bankrupt Laws as administered in this country, and also to take into consideration the propriety of presenting petitions to both Houses of Parliament for constituting a regular tribunal for the administration of the bankrupt laws.

The Committee, after procuring the written and oral testimony, as well of merchants, bankers and traders, as of barristers, solicitors and commissioners of bankrupts, (a portion of which is contained in the preceding part of this chapter,) made their Report, dated in March, 1827. The Committee, by their report, stated, that the present system of administration of the bankrupt laws fell far short of the necessities required by the commercial interests of this country; that the bankrupt laws required material and speedy alteration; and that, instead of the mode in which those laws were administered at present by seventy commissioners in London, a regular tribunal should be established for that purpose, having at its head a judge or judges of great experience and sound legal knowledge, and having proper officers; and the Committee recommended that petitions should be presented to both Houses of Parliament to constitute such a tribunal for the administration of those laws.

In a debate in the House of Commons last year on the Bankrupt Laws, *Mr. D. W. Harvey* said, if there ever was a sincere wish to purge the Chancery system of its gross abuses, the reconstruction of that part of it allotted to bankruptcy business should have been first thought of. It was ridiculous that young men of comparatively no experience in the law, or old men unfit for any business at all, should be commissioners of bankrupts, with salaries of 500*l*. a year each. Yet so it was, and what with the inexperience of youth, and the stultification of age, the House would judge what efficient men those Commissioners of Bankrupts were.

Mr. John Smith, in the course of the same debate, after making some observations on the way in which commissioners of bankrupt were paid, said, he had no wish to deprive the commissioners of all their emoluments, but he had a strong wish to see a code of law formed with regard to bankruptcy, on which the country could depend with as much certainty as it could on its law with regard to any other subject. Instead of seventy commissioners let there be six; let them receive a handsome remuneration for the services they might have to perform, and then private individuals would know what they are about, when they had any thing to do with matters of bankruptcy. He alluded to some recent decisions of the commissioners, which had created great surprise in the commercial world, and said, that such was the uncertainty prevailing in all questions in bankruptcy, that creditors daily acceded to the most disadvantageous compromise, rather than run the risk of losing every thing by suing out a commission.

In another debate in the House of Commons last year on the Court of Chancery, *Mr. D. W. Harvey* is reported to have said, that the whole mischief in the administration of the bankrupt laws was, as it was proposed now, to be got rid of, not by legislative enactments, but by a few regulations to be made by Lord Lyndhurst and the two learned personages who assisted him in that Court. He deemed it quite impossible that such a crying grievance could be so removed; and he corroborated his opinion by reference to that of Lord Eldon. He did not know that bankruptcy could be defined more simply than it was at present; nor was he certain that the principles of the law could be much better arranged. But with regard to the mode of its administration, nothing could be more injurious and absurd. He did not wish to speak with any personal disrespect of any one of the seventy-two gentlemen who now officiated as commissioners of bankrupt, but he must say this, that a more incompetent tribunal than that which they formed could not easily be imagined. The commissioners consisted of two classes of individuals; the first were young men of no experience, to whom the possession of £300 or £400 a year at the outset of life was a matter of importance; indeed it was a sort of apprenticeship-fee to experience, with this remarkable circumstance attached to it, that they received instead of paying it. The first, he repeated, were young men frequently of great promise, and generally backed by great parliamentary influence; the second were often men who had mistaken their talents, and after spending half a century in a briefless condition in the Court, received the appointment as a means of soothing their decline of life, and of saving them from distress and penury. It was his firm belief, that what between capacity with inexperience on the one hand, and experience with incapacity on the other, there were not more than five or six commissioners, out of the seventy-two, who were able to discharge their duty as they ought to do. He wished that any of the honourable gentlemen opposite would go down to Guildhall; because he was certain that they would see the necessity of supporting any measure which tended to the removal of such a nuisance as the existing tribunals in bankruptcy. There were fourteen petty courts, in each of which there were five commissioners, of whom three must necessarily attend to transact the business. He had no hesitation in saying, that this mode of administering the law was not more disgraceful to those who were engaged in it, than it was injurious to the suitors whose property was at stake. There were generally twelve or thirteen causes under each list, and scarcely any two of those causes arrived at the same stage. At one moment the commissioners had before them a creditor trying to prove a fraudulent debt; at another, a bankrupt undergoing his final examination; and at a third, another bankrupt claiming his certificate. All these cases, different and difficult as they were, were to be decided within two short hours, amid the clamour of a court where there was no presiding judge nor guiding rule. He did not know of any terms sufficiently strong to express his abhorrence of so disgraceful a system. He proposed, that instead of there being seventy-two judges, of whom one-half were inexperienced from youth, and the other imbecile from age, there should be five judges with liberal salaries, whose time should be exclusively given up to the adjudication of cases of bankruptcy. Instead of there being fourteen courts with five judges in each, there should be five courts with one judge in each. The bankrupt causes should be brought under his notice individually; and so well were the principles on which those cases were determined understood by commercial men, that he would venture to affirm, that there would very rarely be any appeal from the decision of that individual judge. In cases of appeal, however, he should suggest that the appeal instead of being made to the Lord Chancellor should be made to three out of five commissioners, and then if the parties were still dissatisfied, should be from the three commissioners to the Lord Chancellor.

In the course of the same debate, *Dr. Lushington* said, he was one of those who thought that the mechanism of seventy-two commissioners was one of the most absurd schemes that had ever entered into the brain of man. He knew that the existing system of bankrupt laws had produced evils in the metropolis to an extent which it was deplorable to describe. He knew that the honourable member for Colchester had not exaggerated the fact, that not merely hundreds but thousands of individuals had been reduced to ruin, not because there had not been property to divide among them, but because it had been wasted by the mal-administration of the law, which had been prostituted to the basest of purposes. He would not give up the opinion which he had formed upon this question. He could not, however, accede to what had fallen from the honourable member for Colchester, who had said that the commissioners protracted business at their different meetings in order to put money into their pockets. Such was the evil and such the iniquity of the present system, that he defied the Commissioners to do justice by all their exertions. It was true that no individual could hold a commissionership of bankrupt who was in great business. As soon as he became a Commissioner, he must either neglect his own business or that of the commissions on which he was placed. What could be so destructive of business as that the Commissioners should meet for an hour merely, on affairs of an intricate and complicated nature. He knew that another hour was sometimes given by them to business; but then at the conclusion of the second hour they must separate, on account of their different private avocations. He was of opinion that nothing could give to the merchants of the country proper security, except an entire revision of the subject, and the abolition of the existing lists of Commissioners. The honourable member for Colchester had suggested the erection of a Board of five Judges in their stead. Now the honourable member must not be allowed to take the credit of that suggestion to himself. He thought it proper that the country should have some statement as to the bankruptcy business, in order that it might undergo discussion at present, and be submitted to the House in the next session of parliament. He was convinced that nothing but legal enactments could remedy the evil; it was therefore absurd to expect that Lord Lyndhurst would devise a remedy for that which nothing but an act of parliament could remedy. He was of opinion that bankruptcy, in the last resort, ought not to be taken from the Lord Chancellor.

CHAPTER XVIII.

OF THE EXPENSE ATTENDING THE PRESENT MODE OF ADMINISTERING THE BANKRUPT LAWS.—UNCLAIMED DIVIDENDS.—EFFECTS OF THE SYSTEM OF LONDON COMMISSIONERSHIPS OF BANKRUPT UPON THE BAR.—A GREAT NUMBER OF JUDGES AGAINST THE POLICY OF OUR JUDICIAL ESTABLISHMENTS—MANNER IN WHICH THE FUNCTIONS OF JUDGE AND ADVOCATE ARE BLENDED IN THE COMMISSIONERS OF BANKRUPT.

Two or three evils arising out of the present manner of administering the bankrupt laws still remain to be noticed, and, although they are but remotely connected with each other, I shall make them all the subject of the present Chapter.

Of the Expense attending the present Mode of administering the Bankrupt Laws.

One of the most striking is the almost incredible sum which is yearly taken by the officers in bankruptcy from the property of the bankrupts and their creditors.* I shall purposely select a year prolific in commissions of bankrupt as the best suited to demonstrate the enormous injustice of the system.

The fees received in the office of Lord Thurlow, patentee for the execution of the laws and statutes concerning bankrupts, from the first of October, 1825, to the 1st of October, 1826, amounted to £16,176: 11*s.* 5*d.*

The fees received in the office of the Lord Chancellor's Secretary of Commissions of Bankrupts, from the first of October, 1825, to the 1st of October, 1826, amounted to the sum of £12,601 : 6*s.* 4*d.*†

The fees received in the office of the Patentee, as well as the fees received in the office of the Lord Chancellor's Secretary of Bankrupts, were liable to considerable deductions, for salaries and emoluments of secretaries, clerks, stationary, &c.; but this, although it may have diminished the net income of the Patentee or the Chancellor,

* None of those who think a law cannot be bad because it is three hundred years old have yet explained to us upon what rational principle of legislation, the judges, in cases of insolvency, should not be paid out of the public purse, as well as in cases of solvency.—See an observation in the evidence of Mr. Montague before the Chancery Commissioners.

† See *Returns, and Account of Receipts and Appropriation of Fees in Bankruptcy, from* 1811 *to* 1826, printed by order of the House of Commons in April, 1827.

did not lessen the charge paid in one year of commercial distress out of the estates of bankrupt traders and their creditors. And let it not be forgotten, that this money was paid to a sinecurist, and to a Chancellor, whose political and other services may have perhaps deserved more than his office ever produced to him, but who unquestionably ought not to have received five hundred pounds for the discharge of his judicial functions in bankruptcy.*

There are seventy London Commissioners of Bankrupt, and the amount of their fees in 1826 cannot be estimated at less than £28,000. The amount of such fees, in ordinary years, may be calculated at £21,000, it being admitted on all hands that the average emoluments of the commissioners, for some years past, have been £300 a year.†

* The only business in bankruptcy that the Lord Chancellor has done for some years past has been to hear a few petitions of appeal from orders made by the Vice Chancellor.

† Mr. Parry (a Commissioner of Bankrupt) stated, in his examination before the Select Committee of the Common Council, that, in 1811, a commissioner might have received, if he was constant in his attendance, £500. He thought that, in 1824, there was not a commissioner who received so much as £300. It appears from a passage in Sir James Bland Burgess's work, that the commissioners who attended constantly did not in his time get more than £80 a year. Mr. Montague informs us that the annual emoluments of a commissionership in his list, when he

The amount of the fees annually received by the country commissioners is calculated to be not less than that received by the London commissioners. Mr. Fonblanque, (a Commissioner of Bankrupt,) in his examination before the Committee of the Common Council, stated, he estimated the fees of the country commissioners at £10,000 a year more than those of the London commissioners. I will suppose, however, that the fees received by the country commissioners do not exceed those received by the London commissioners, this will give £28,000 for the amount of the fees paid to the country commissioners in 1826.

The following then will be the statement of the monies paid out of the bankrupt effects to the patentee, the Chancellor, and commissioners, in a year of great commercial misery.

	£.	s.	d.
Patentee	16,176	11	5
Lord Chancellor	12,601	6	4
London Commissioners . . .	28,000	0	0
Country Commissioners . . .	28,000	0	0
	84,777	17	9

The salaries of the twelve judges of the three great common law courts amount to £74,000

was first admitted, were about fifty pounds. This was twenty-three years after the period of which Sir James Bland Burgess speaks.

a year. The emoluments of the London and country Commissioners of Bankrupt, in ordinary years, amount to the sum of £42,000.

It has been most truly observed by Mr. Montague, in one of his numerous works on this branch of our laws, that the Court of Commissioners of Bankrupt administers the minimum of justice with the maximum of expense.

The reader must not imagine that the above sum, large as it is, comprises all that is yearly taken out of the property of bankrupts to remunerate the judges and officers under whose superintendence it is placed. It would be tedious to give the details; but the reader will find them in the evidence of Mr. Montague before the Chancery Commissioners and the Committee of the Common Council. In his evidence before the Chancery Commissioners he stated, he was satisfied that the expense was much underrated when he computed it at £242,000 a year; and in his evidence before the Committee of the Common Council, given at a later period, he stated the annual expense, before the late Bankrupt Act, to have been at least £250,000, and that, since the passing of that act, the expense had been much increased: and be it observed, that, in this calculation, Mr. Montague has not included the fees payable in the office of the patentee, or in the office of the Lord Chancellor's Secretary of Bankrupts.

Unclaimed Dividends.

Every body knows that, from various causes, it almost always happens that the final dividend on bankrupt's estates is not declared until a great number of. years after the issuing of the commission. In the mean time numbers of creditors die, the firm of partnerships is changed, and it is impossible to ascertain who is entitled to receive a large proportion of the dividends. Besides, the great majority of persons who prove debts do not see the Gazette, or any newspaper that gives any regular account of the dividends declared, and they cannot make continual inquiries respecting the proceedings in commissions under which they have proved debts; the consequence is, that large sums remain in the hands of the assignees, or their bankers, which are never claimed.*

I believe Mr. Montague was the first to call the attention of the legislature to this subject, in common with many other egregious defects in our commercial code. In his evidence before the

* I have somewhere seen it stated, that the amount of unclaimed dividends for the first fifteen years after the peace of 1802 must have been at least £500,000. It was probably much more. The annual loss arising to creditors from the maladministration of the property of bankrupts cannot be estimated at less than £200,000. I refer the reader to calculations made by Mr. Montague as to the different items of loss, and which are to be found in his evidence before the Chancery Commissioners.

Select Committee of the House of Commons on the Bankrupt Laws in 1818, he said, it appeared to be of considerable importance to ascertain the amount of unclaimed dividends under commissions, in order that it might be seen what a great disposable fund there might be, should it occur to the wisdom of the legislature that any plan ought to be adopted for appointing any permanent tribunal, or any permanent board of assignees or commissioners*; he conceived the magnitude of the unclaimed dividends to be quite unknown; there was, he conceived, scarcely a bankruptcy without some dividends being unclaimed.

It was not until the General Bankrupt Act passed in 1825, that any legislative measure was taken to ascertain the amount of these unclaimed dividends. By that Act, assignees under com-

* There is no want of the funds requisite for the establishment of an effective Bankruptcy Court and a new Chancery Judge. Besides the unclaimed dividends, the dead fund in Chancery, which belongs to nobody, inasmuch as it arises principally, if not wholly, from the interest and accumulation of interest of monies which the parties have never required to be laid out, yields a yearly surplus revenue of about £25,000, after paying the salaries of the Vice Chancellor and his officers, and the various other charges which the legislature has from time to time cast upon it. I have little doubt, it would turn out upon inquiry, that no inconsiderable portion of the other stock and cash (amounting to nearly forty millions) standing in the books of the Bank of England, in the name of the Accountant General of the Court, to the credit of different causes, can never, from lapse of time, and other reasons, be claimed.

missions of bankrupt are required to cause a certificate to be filed in the office of the Lord Chancellor's Secretary of Bankrupts, of all unclaimed dividends remaining in their hands fourteen months after the declaration and order of payment of such dividends, under the penalty of paying five per cent. interest on the amount, and such further sum, not exceeding twenty per cent. per annum, as the commissioners might think fit.

By a return made to the House of Commons, at the end of April, 1827, it appears that the amount of unclaimed dividends, of which certificates had then been filed with the Secretary of Bankrupts, in pursuance of the above-mentioned act, amounted, at that time, to the sum of £219,978: 9*s.* 10*d.*

This, and a multitude of other facts connected with the wretched system of the Bankrupt Laws, infinitely too numerous to be introduced in this work, require only to be stated. With those persons for whose perusal these pages are intended, it would be superfluous for me to make any comment upon them.*

* The new Bankrupt Act contains provisions to prevent the great loss arising to creditors from the immense amount of dividends retained by the assignees. Whether those provisions have been effective I do not know. The practice of many of the assignees is stated to have been to collect money and keep it in hand, as a capital to assist them in carrying on their business, until they were compelled to make a dividend; and when the

Effects of the System of the London Commissionerships of Bankrupts upon the Bar.—A great number of Judges against the policy of our Judicial Establishment.—Manner in which the functions of Judge and Advocate are blended by the Commissioners of Bankrupts.

There is nothing, in the writer's opinion, that has gone further to destroy the independence of the bar, than the patronage which the appointment of the London Commissioners of Bankrupt gives to the Great Seal.

Everybody knows that the office is usually held by a practising barrister. The young barrister seeks it as the best means of introducing him to business, whilst the barrister who has long since passed the threshold of the Court, but whose talents are not of a kind to overburthen him with

creditors became very clamorous, and the assignees had been summoned two or three times before the Commissioners, they would, at the end of two years, declare the first dividend: they would then take care to hold a considerable sum in hand, which they effected by entering claims against the estate to be proved at the next dividend, and they reserved the amount of the first dividend on such claims in hand. After the lapse of two or three years, they would declare a second dividend. The creditors being then wearied out, a third or final dividend was seldom obtained from assignees of this description.

clients, desires it as no contemptible addition to his professional income.*

Whatever may be the learning and talents necessary in a commissioner, it is quite clear that he at present is expected to possess but a moderate knowledge of law and equity. Fitness to fulfil the duties of the office is the last thing thought of in the selection that is made, and the public owes it to good fortune, and to no discernment of the Chancellor, that the commissioners are in general capable of discharging their judicial functions in a creditable manner. All important questions indeed are decided by the Lord Chancellor or the Vice Chancellor upon petition. The judicial functions of the commissioners too occupy but a small space of time, and the meetings are so arranged as to interfere as little as possible with

* It is said to be Lord Lyndhurst's intention to order the Secretary of Bankrupts to erase from the London lists those Commissioners who, from age or other infirmity, are incapable of acting. That he contemplates to remove a superannuated Commissioner I have the best authority for stating. It would be curious to know how many applications for commissionerships have been made in consequence of this rumour. Lord Lyndhurst has, I believe, ordered his Secretary of Bankrupts to erase from one of the lists the name of a Commissioner usually resident in the country. Both Lord Thurlow and Lord Rosslyn invariably removed those Commissioners who were elected to serve in Parliament. Who would not praise Lord Lyndhurst if he imitated so wise an example? Any measure that diminished the frequency of the union of the judicial and political characters would be decidedly popular.

their private practice; besides, there is nothing which compels them to attend, if they can occupy their time more to their satisfaction elsewhere. Sir Samuel Romilly, in his evidence before the Select Committee of the House of Commons on the Bankrupt Laws, objected to the appointment of fixed and permanent lists of commissioners in the country, to whom all commissions should be directed, on the ground that although the duty of the commissioners might be better discharged than at present; yet that that advantage would not sufficiently compensate for the mischief of extending the patronage of the Chancellor over the profession, by placing so many new offices in his gift. He justly observed, that the independence of lawyers was of great importance to the public, and that there was no more effectual mode of destroying that independence than by accustoming them to look up to the Chancellor for such an appointment.

It is apprehended that this evil, if there were no other arising out of the present system, ought to induce a government, desirous of adopting sound principles in the organization of its tribunals, to inquire whether some change may not be beneficially adopted in the Court of Commissioners of Bankrupt.

And here it may not be irrelevant to observe, that the number of judges in the Bankruptcy Court, when contrasted with their paucity in the other tribunals of the country, presents an anomaly in our jurisprudence. It has always been the great object of our government to uphold the character of our judges; and it is with that view, no doubt, that it has hitherto forborne to increase their number, although for some years past they have not been able to get through the business of the country in that time which a wholesome administration of the laws requires. Hence, in a great measure, no doubt, proceeds the veneration which the people in general entertain towards the judges, and which has so forcibly struck those intelligent foreigners who have of late years devoted their attention to our laws and the manner in which they are administered. In the Court of the London Commissioners of Bankrupt, however, there are five times the number of judges who are to be found in the three common law courts and the Court of Chancery together;* and if we only consider how much the multiplication of the number of tribunals and judges in a neighbouring nation has tended to degrade the magistracy, we may rest assured that were there not wanting other causes to lessen the public esteem for the London Court of the Commissioners, the host of judges would have that effect.

* In the newly-established Court for the relief of insolvent debtors, the whole judicial business is transacted by three or four Commissioners.

Another fault in the present organization of the Commissioners' Court, which cannot fail to strike every one who frequents them, is the manner in which the functions of the judge and advocate are there blended.* Without entering into the general question of the propriety of allowing those who sit as judges in one court to act as counsel in another, the writer can entertain very little doubt that the respect which it should be the policy of the law to create in the suitor towards the judge, must be greatly diminished by seeing that constant and sudden interchange of the characters of judge and counsel, which takes place in the courts of the commissioners. As for the respect which it is supposed the advocate should entertain towards the judge there can be none, unless it arise from some consideration very different from the mere circumstance of his being, for the moment, invested with the judicial office.

Notwithstanding these observations, I do not think, if the present system be continued, that

* "Dans les *Commissions de Banqueroutes*, qui sont divisées à Londres en quatorze chambres ou sections, j'ai vu tel des Commissaires siéger le matin comme juge, plaider un instant après devant un de ses confréres, devenu juge à son tour, et qu'il avait entendu une heure auparavant comme avocat, puis revenir l'après midi siéger encore comme juge, et entendre de nouveau son confrere qui venait d'être son juge à lui même."—*Rey*, *Institutions Judiciaires de l'Angleterre comparées avec celles de la France*, tom. ii.

the London Commissioners of Bankrupt ought to be prohibited to act as counsel before their brother commissioners,* as I believe it is found that the best commissioners are those who attend most as advocates before the other commissioners, and that the worst commissioners are those who have no professional business at all. Such an union of the two characters of judge and advocate, although it be at variance with those principles which ought to prevail in the formation of a tribunal of justice, ought to be tolerated, if it be clear that the separation of those functions would be productive of still greater mischief. The practice is here noticed only as affording an additional reason for the creation of a court, on the plan suggested by some of the gentlemen examined before the Committee of the House of Commons and the Chancery Commissioners, and the substance of whose evidence on this head has been given in the preceding Chapter.

* The Chancery Commissioners proposed that no London Commissioner of Bankrupt should be at liberty to act as counsel for any party, either before the general Commissioners, acting in execution of a commission, or before the Commissioners of Appeal, by whom, as they proposed, all matters upon subjects of appeal, from the decision of the London Commissioners to the Lord Chancellor, should be first heard.

CONCLUSION.

THE IDEAS OF THE AUTHOR RELATIVE TO THE MEASURES TO BE ADOPTED TO REMEDY THE PRINCIPAL DEFECTS EXISTING IN THE ADMINISTRATION OF JUSTICE IN THE COURT OF CHANCERY, THE HOUSE OF LORDS AS THE COURT OF LAST RESORT IN EQUITY CAUSES, AND THE COURTS OF THE COMMISSIONERS OF BANKRUPT.

WHEN I began, a month ago,* to collect the materials for these pages, my principal object was to place under the eye of the reader the most striking defects of the Court of Chancery, the House of Lords, as the Court of last resort, and the tribunal of the Commissioners of Bankrupt, as exhibited in various parliamentary debates and documents, and thus possibly incite those members of the legislature, whose little acquaintance with the subject may be the cause that they have hitherto regarded it with indifference, to

* Of the preceding chapters the first two or three were written in February and the remainder in March. I have been compelled, by more pressing demands upon my time, to defer the conclusion of the work to the Easter vacation.

concur in bringing forward effectual measures to cure evils under which the country has so long and so cruelly suffered. I never contemplated, that in the course of compilation so much of my own would be introduced as has already found its way into this work, much less that it would become necessary for me to propose any scheme for the better organization of the most important parts of our judicial establishment. I am told, however, by those of whose knowledge I am sure, and upon whose judgment I am willing to rely, that not to propound some system of my own as an improvement upon, or substitute for that which I would alter or destroy, would be not only to leave the task I have undertaken incomplete, but very much to diminish the utility of what I have done; and that, imperfect and mis-shapen as my notions may be, they may yet serve as materials for some more skilful artist to work upon.

It is with this last view only that I venture to publish them, premising, however, that they have not the merit (if merit indeed it be) of novelty.* Some of my propositions may at first appear new, but I trust it will be found they are all formed of those old unchanging principles which make the sinews of all well organized judi-

* The reader will find most of the reforms here proposed noticed in the Letters on the Court of Chancery, published last October.

cial bodies, and without which their movements must ever be defective for the purposes of justice.

The reader must not, however, suppose that I entertain the hope that the suggestions contained in this chapter will be adopted at the present moment. It is true, that within the last few years a disposition has been manifested no longer to legislate with a view only to the particular inconvenience to be removed, but to endeavour, by having recourse to first principles, to discover what enactment will prevent the recurrence of similar mischief for the future. But all attempts to remodel any part of our principal tribunals, with a view to the properties essentially necessary in establishments for the administration of justice, have hitherto failed, and although the time seems approaching when these endeavours will be no longer abortive, yet it comes with slow steps. The adversaries of improvement,* hoodwinked by prejudice or blinded by self-interest, are still too powerful for it to be effected, except after long and reiterated struggles. This persuasion has not a little contributed to the reluctance I have felt to develope my notions as to the reorganization of such of our civil courts as are the subject of this work.

It may appear to some persons premature and

* Nothing, perhaps, has more retarded the progress of a gradual and temperate reform, than the many wild and hasty schemes of innovation that have been formed within the last few years.

injudicious to reorganize the tribunals, whilst the laws themselves present a confusion and chaos surpassed by those of no nation, ancient or modern, except Rome in the time of the Emperors, and France at the epoch of the revolution. It has been urged, that if the laws be better administered, their inconveniences will be less felt, and the necessity for a change less apparent, and that general and effectual improvement is frequently prevented by a partial alteration. There is much truth and force in these observations, but they do not, in my apprehension, furnish any satisfactory reason why a reform of the tribunals of a country should not precede that of its laws; and a very little reflection must convince the reader, whether he be an admirer of *Codification* or one of the *Historic School*,* that nothing is more likely to cause the miscarriage of any considerable reform introduced into the jurisprudence of a great, wealthy, and commercial people, than the absence of courts sufficiently numerous and so organized as to be able to adjudicate, in a moderate space of time, all questions to be brought before them. The history of all the great innovations that have been made in the laws of every nation shows that they have been invariably accompanied by a great increase of litigation. The reason is obvious to any one who considers that there is hardly a statute or ordi-

* See the Appendix C.

nance, however carefully framed, which does not give rise to some doubt as to the meaning and construction of some of its parts, and that *that* doubt can only be resolved by a judicial decision. The numerous suits to which, it is well known, a new code of laws has given rise in France, was probably foreseen by the revolutionary government, and the career of legal reformation in that country was wisely begun by a multiplication (although perhaps excessive)* of the number of her tribunals. More judgment was certainly shown in this instance† than in the crude and hasty concoction of the code. Had not the number of courts been more than doubled, they would soon have been buried beneath the mass of causes produced by the new jurisprudence.

It follows then, that whether with the friends of Codes we plough up the ancient garden of the law, and root up every tree and shrub to be found there, and lay out and plant another according to some plan suggested by their fancy and contrived upon their taste; or whether with the disciples of the Historic School, instead of destroying all the labours of our ancestors, we set

* I allude to the *Cours d'Appel*, now the *Cours Royales*, that replaced the ancient Parliaments.

† It may be remarked too, that the defects in the quality of the laws are more easily discerned when the attention is no longer distracted by the vices existing in the manner of their administration.

ourselves to change the shape and order of certain alleys and parterres, to lop and prune decayed and redundant branches, and weed out noxious plants, we shall do well in providing ourselves with a sufficient number of skilful and industrious labourers to perform the additional work which must in either case arise.*

The changes which I suggest have, of course, relation only to the principal defects of the three great tribunals in question, which it has been the object of this work to bring into more prominent observation, and which can only be remedied by legislative enactments.†

* It may be observed, that in the natural order of things, judges and tribunals existed in nations long before the science of jurisprudence. St. Louis administered justice to his subjects in the Park of Vincennes, and Henry the First in his Palace at London, upon no settled rules or principles of law.

† There are a multitude of little flaws in all parts, which may be repaired by the hand of the judge.

THE COURT OF CHANCERY.

THERE SHOULD BE ANOTHER EFFICIENT JUDGE, IN ADDITION TO THE MASTER OF THE ROLLS AND VICE CHANCELLOR.

To give my reasons for thinking there should be an additional judge to hear original causes in Chancery, would be to repeat most of the facts stated in the preceding pages. The question whether it be expedient to retain the Lord Chancellor in the Court, to hear original or appellate business, will be considered in a subsequent part of this chapter.

THE THREE COURTS SHOULD SIT AT THE SAME TIME, FROM TEN UNTIL FOUR O'CLOCK.

At present the Vice Chancellor does not, in general, sit later than three o'clock, that is to say, no cause is called on after that time. I propose to add an hour to the time of his sittings, to which no objection can be made, if there are no evening sittings at the Rolls.

At the close of a work like the present, it cannot be necessary to say any thing on the uncertainty that exists as to the days and duration of the Chancellor's sittings. The new judge would replace the Chancellor; and as the Chancellor, when he does sit, sits at the same time with the Vice Chancellor, it would be no novelty that the Vice Chancellor and new judge should sit simultaneously.

The Master of the Rolls, at present, never sits in the morning, except for a very few days, during which the Lord Chancellor and Vice Chancellor hold no sitting. His ordinary sittings are in the evening, from six o'clock until ten. During term time he sits only three evenings in the week,* and out of term time he seldom sits oftener than four evenings in the week, as he never sits on seal days, or Saturdays, and there is seldom a week without a seal day. He never sits until the evening before the first day of term, although the other branches of the Court hold sittings for a week or ten days before the beginning of the term, and he never sits after the last seal after term, except one or two nights to dispose of cause petitions; and, in consequence, he generally rises for the long vacation, the first or second of August, although the other branches of the Court continue their sittings until the third week in that month.

Instead of the Master of the Rolls sitting four hours a day, I propose he should sit for six; and instead of his sitting three or four days in the week, I propose he should sit every day; and I

* The evenings he does not sit during term time are Wednesdays, Fridays and Saturdays.

also propose that he should not commence his sittings before term later, or finish his sittings after term sooner, than the other judges. In this way more than 100 days will, according to a calculation made by Sir John Leach, be added to the judicial year of the Master of the Rolls, which will be an immense gain to the public, and will not impose any greater burthen on the Master of the Rolls than rests on the shoulders of the other judges.

As, however, experience has shown us that the most reasonable propositions for the general good frequently meet with violent private opponents, it may be useful to anticipate the objection that may possibly be made to this measure by the individual who may happen to fill the office of Master of the Rolls, when it shall be propounded; and I do not know that this can be better done than by shortly tracing the origin of the present custom of the Master of the Rolls sitting in the evening, and only three or four times in the week.

The Lords Chancellors were in the habit, in very early times, of referring the consideration of causes to the Master of the Rolls and Masters in Chancery, who were authorized to adjudicate some finally, and upon others they were directed to report to the Chancellor. The regular sittings of the Master of the Rolls, as a judge of the Court, are not more ancient than the time of

Henry VIII. Before that time he seems to have been considered only as the principal Master.* Cardinal Wolsey, finding that his other avocations interfered with the discharge of his judicial functions as Chancellor, first devised the expedient of deputing the Master of the Rolls to hear causes when he himself was absent on state and ecclesiastical affairs; and, it is said, the Master of the Rolls sat for this purpose in the evening. It is probable, however, that these sittings did not take place at night. The Court of Chancery then sat at seven or eight o'clock in the morning, and it was usual to dine at twelve. It may be conjectured, that by evening sittings nothing more is meant than that the Master of the Rolls sat on the business of the Court after dinner. In later times the Chancellor sat on Wednesday and Friday mornings at the Star Chamber, and on

* We find one melancholy point of resemblance between a Master of the Rolls of the sixteenth century and the Masters of the beginning of the last century. King Edward the Sixth has recorded in his Journal, that Beaumont, his Master of the Rolls, being judge in Chancery between the Duke of Suffolk and the Lady Powis, took her title into his hands, paying her a sum of money, and letting her have one of his own farms. He then caused an indenture to be made with the old Duke's counterfeit hand to it, by which he gave the lands in dispute to Lady Powis. It is well known that the office of Accountant General was created at the beginning of the last century, in consequence of the Masters embezzling the property of the suitors entrusted to their care.

those days the Master of the Rolls presided, during his absence, in the Court of Chancery.* In the evening, after the business of the Star Chamber was over, the Chancellor took his seat in his own Court, and the Master of the Rolls was released; and this seems to be the origin of the custom of the Master of the Rolls not sitting on Wednesday and Friday evenings during term. The regular sittings of the Court of Chancery out of term are of a much more recent date. The Chancellor, after the commencement of these sittings out of term, never appears to have sat in the evenings, except on seal days, when the Court frequently sat to dispose of all the motions, until one or two o'clock of the following morning. The Master of the Rolls, therefore, as an officer whose duty it was to preside in the Court in the absence of the Chancellor, sat every evening out of term, except on seal days, (Saturday and Sunday of course excluded.)

* This was not the only part of the Chancellor's duties, which he was, even in those ancient times, obliged to perform by deputy. The House of Lords seldom sat on Wednesdays and Fridays when the Chancellor was absent in the Star Chamber, but so much inconvenience was experienced by the suspension of Parliamentary business on those days, that it was at one period of the reign of James the First resolved by the House, not to discontinue their sittings, but to appoint a temporary Speaker, whilst the Chancellor was away. The following passage from *D'Ewe's Journal of the Parliament during the Reign of Queen Elizabeth*, page 67, will show this, and will serve to illustrate one or two

Until the beginning of the last century, the Master of the Rolls continued to be considered as merely the deputy of the Chancellor, empowered by him to sit only during his absence from the Court, to aid him in the dispatch of business; and it was even doubted whether any of his decrees and orders were valid until the Chancellor had confirmed them; and certain disputes having arisen on this subject, it was thought advisable to put an end to them by an Act of Parliament, declaring all the decrees and orders of the Master of the Rolls valid decrees and orders of the Court of Chancery, except such only as by the course of the Court ought to be made by the Chancellor only. By force of this statute* and of ancient

other observations made in the course of this work. "Upon a motion unto the House, that there was a great cause in the midst of hearing to be heard in the Star Chamber, the day following being Wednesday, the Lords were content to forbear sitting that day, but withal it was provided that it should not be drawn into a precedent, but that the House (being the Supreme Court) may sit upon any Star Chamber day, notwithstanding the absence of such Lords as do use to attend that Court; and accordingly the House was adjourned unto the next day, being Wednesday, in the afternoon, and the next Star Chamber day being Friday, the House did sit both in the forenoon and in the afternoon."

* The reasons of the doubt entertained as to the validity of the decrees and orders made at the Rolls may be found in three works, published at the time, which also contain much valuable historical information with regard to the Court of Chancery. The first was written by a Mr. Burrough, and is entitled

usage, the Masters of the Rolls have become much more independent of the Chancellor than the Vice Chancellor now is; but notwithstanding the great augmentation in the business of the Court within the last 150 years, and the appalling arrears that have sometimes loaded their lists, it has never occurred to any of them to multiply their sittings. The sittings of the Master of the Rolls still continue to be regulated upon the old notion of his having no authority to hear causes, except in the Chancellor's absence and as his deputy, and this, extraordinary as it may appear, is the only reason that can be assigned for the

"*History of the Chancery, relating to the Judicial Power of that Court, and the Rights of the Masters.*" Lord King was so much pleased with the work, that he rewarded the author with a Mastership in Chancery. This performance called forth the "*Discourse of the Judicial Authority of the Master of the Rolls,*" in answer to which, Mr. Burrough published "*The Legal Judicature in Chancery stated, &c.*" "The Discourse" has been sometimes attributed to Lord Hardwicke, and sometimes to Sir Joseph Jekyll. I am inclined to think it was the joint production of both. There is still at the Rolls House some part of the work as corrected for the press by Sir Joseph Jekyll, and I have a copy of a letter (the original of which is at the Rolls) consulting him as to the price at which the book should be sold, calling it his "Honor's Book." Mr. Burrough, it appears, was asssisted by Mr. (afterwards Bishop) Warburton, in composing the Legal Judicature. Upon its appearance, the Discourse was republished, with great additions; Lord Hardwicke, who was then Attorney General, probably assisted Sir Joseph Jekyll in this second edition.

Master of the Rolls not sitting on Wednesday and Friday evenings, during Term, and at other times when the Chancellor was anciently in the habit of holding his sittings.

That it is desirable in the present state of the Court of Chancery, that the Master of the Rolls should sit longer and more frequently, it is impossible to deny, and the above sketch of the origin of the present whimsical arrangement of his sittings (unexampled, be it observed, in any other tribunal in the country,) must convince every dispassionate mind, that there is nothing in the history of the rise and progress of the office that would make such a measure impracticable or inexpedient. But it may be said that the Master of the Rolls has other public duties to perform. The House of Lords having declined to entertain colonial appeals, the jurisdiction has reverted to the Privy Council, and the Master of the Rolls is the only judicial personage in that august body, who has leisure to adjudicate them. This objection, however, and some others of less importance, have been fully answered by Sir John Leach, in his speech in the House of Commons, on the Vice Chancellor's bill, an extract from which will be found in the Appendix to this Chapter.* It would be presumption in me to attempt to add any thing to the arguments there

* See the Appendix, A.

used. Those who are not convinced by Sir John Leach would never listen to me; I will therefore only observe, that as the measure of hearing colonial appeals before so badly constituted a tribunal as the cockpit has not even the recommendation of antiquity, I hope it will not be of long duration, and that England will soon give to her colonies a court of last resort more worthy of a great and powerful empire.*

THE SAME CAUSES SHOULD NOT, IN THEIR DIFFERENT PARTS OR STAGES, BE HEARD BEFORE DIFFERENT JUDGES.

THE CAUSES SHOULD BE DIVIDED AMONGST THE THREE COURTS, AT THE COMMENCEMENT OF EACH SITTING, IN SUCH A MANNER, THAT THE CAUSES FIRST SET DOWN MIGHT HAVE PRECEDENCE ON THE DIFFERENT LISTS.

THE JUDGES THEMSELVES SHOULD DISTRIBUTE THE CAUSES BETWEEN THE SEVERAL COURTS, AND SHOULD MEET TOGETHER A CONVENIENT TIME BEFORE THE SITTINGS FOR THAT PURPOSE.

AT present, a cause is frequently discussed upon motion before one judge, argued on the original

* It is not impossible, if the Bankruptcy were immediately separated from the general business of the Court of Chancery, and a new judge appointed, to replace the Chancellor, with talents for the dispatch of business, and, above all, if Sir John Leach

decree before another, and finally disposed of upon further directions by a third. It is not necessary to point out the particular inconveniences of such a practice. It is enough to say, it often occasions needless repetition, and therefore wastes the time of the public, and it still oftener causes fruitless dissatisfaction or an abortive appeal. The judge before whom the cause was first brought, has, perhaps, upon a partial view of the case, expressed a different opinion from that of the judge who has finally disposed of it; the effect of which is, that the vanquished party is confirmed in the notion, which, without such a corroborative circumstance, he is apt enough to entertain, that the last decision is erroneous. If the litigated matter be of sufficient value to bear the additional expense and delay, he forthwith appeals, and has the mortification to find the order appealed from affirmed; but if the subject of dispute will not bear any additional expenditure of money or time, he cites his suit as another instance of the law's

were to sit every day and in the morning, that the Court of Chancery might, like the Court of Exchequer, occasionally experience a dearth of employ; but for the reasons fully stated in the preceding part of this work, I do not think this would be the case, except when the new machinery should be first put in movement. As soon as it came to be known that equity suits could be speedily and effectually heard, their number would rapidly increase, and would shortly bear the same proportion to our augmented population, riches and commerce, that our other legal business does.

uncertainty, and as long as he lives is persuaded that the judge who determined against him was mistaken, and the decree, which was adverse to his interests, unjust.* I think, therefore, the same causes should, in their entire progress, be discussed before that judge only,† who first obtained cognizance of them.

The next part of my proposal is the most important, namely, that the causes should be divided amongst the courts according to some fixed mode.‡

The unequal distribution of the business between our three principal common law courts must be well known to every reader. By the

* Another inconvenience, or rather injustice, arising out of the present practice, should also be mentioned, as not being likely to occur to the unprofessional reader. It is this—a plaintiff has the privilege of choosing the judge before whom his cause is to be set down. If then any intimation of an opinion favourable to his case has, upon any interlocutory application before the hearing, escaped from a judge, he of course carries the cause to his court; but if that opinion has sounded adverse to his claim, he takes care to set his suit down for hearing before the other judge.

† This, like all other general regulations, must bend to particular circumstances. The illness or unavoidable absence of the judge, who first became possessed of a cause, may make it necessary that it should be heard before a different judge, where the delay would be productive of irremediable mischief.

‡ The scheme here suggested is that adopted in the organization of the French tribunals. See the Letters on the Court of Chancery.

ancient mode, in which, after the dissolution of the *Aula Regia*, its jurisdiction was parcelled out amongst the principal courts of Westminster, the Common Pleas was to adjudicate all causes between subject and subject, whilst the King's Bench had cognizance only of criminal pleas, and the Exchequer took those cases that related to the King's revenue; but this line of demarcation was not long observed. The desire of the judges and officers of the other courts to extend their authority* and augment their emoluments, the inadequacy of the Court of Common Pleas to dispose of the increased business produced by the growing wealth and commerce of the country, and some other causes, probably conspired to favour the invention of those legal fictions which continue to this day to give to the Courts of King's Bench and Exchequer the power to hold pleas of civil actions. But whatever may have given rise to this device, there can be little doubt the principal reason for conniving at and tolerating it was the necessity of producing a more equal distribution of business amongst the different courts. Experience, however, has taught us that this scheme, beneficial, useful and ingenious, as it has been called, has for centuries past failed of attaining the object in view. Causes, which it

* "Boni judicis est ampliare jurisdictionem," was formerly considered by our judges a maxim of duty.

would be superfluous here to enumerate, have at different times turned the stream of civil actions into one particular court, until it has overflowed, whilst the others have frequently been left without a suit. At the present moment, the Court of Exchequer can seldom find means to occupy itself during a short hour, whilst, on the other hand, the Court of King's Bench, notwithstanding the immense exertions of the great judge who presides there, is unable to subdue the mass of business brought before it.

It is this inconvenience, this prodigal waste of the public time and money, this possibility of having judges with large salaries and no causes to try, against which I would guard in the reorganization of our equity tribunals, and which can only be done by regulating the practice as to setting down causes; and the simplest regulation would be, that all the causes remaining unheard at the end of the preceding sittings, and all those set down since, should, previously to each sitting, be distributed in the lists of the three judges, the oldest cause being placed first. A fresh division would be necessary at the commencement of each sittings, to correct the inequalities that would otherwise constantly arise, as well from the different capability of different judges for the dispatch of business, as also from the circumstance that as causes always vary in intricacy and importance, a given number of causes on one list would rarely or ever occupy the same time as an equal number on the other.*

It has been said, that such a mode of cantoning out the suits would create dissatisfaction amongst the suitors, who would not be able to obtain the judges and counsel they wish.† But, in answer to this, it may be observed, that according to the present system, the plaintiff is the only party who has this privilege. An equity suit may be carried before the Court of Chancery or the Court of Exchequer, as the plaintiff chooses, and if it be carried before the Court of Chancery, the plaintiff may set it down for hearing before the Vice Chancellor or Master of the Rolls, as he pleases. He may also forestall the defendant of the most able counsel, by previously retaining those practising in the particular tribunal where he chooses to have his cause heard.

* It would be necessary also to provide for the transfer of causes from one list to another, in the event of one judge dispatching the whole of the business allotted to him whilst there were arrears before the other two.

† I have heard that objections have been made to this scheme of distributing judicial business as injurious to the interests of counsel.

"As well might one object to a law which was calculated to check the progress of infectious disease, because it would diminish the profits of physicians, as oppose a regulation which was to expedite the decision of causes, because it might diminish the emoluments of advocates."—See *A Letter to a Noble Lord, &c.*

Now it may be permitted to ask, upon what principle, ever recognized or known in the wise formation of judicial establishments, ought such an advantage to be given to a plaintiff over his adversary. I have known repeated instances of a particular judge having been chosen because the plaintiff was acquainted with him in private life. We are all aware such a circumstance could not have the slightest influence upon the judge's determination, but it is not always so easy to produce the same conviction in the minds of the parties whose interests it affects. The appearance, therefore, the suspicion, the possibility of partiality, should be removed.*

THERE SHOULD BE NO APPEAL FROM EITHER OF THE THREE COURTS, EXCEPT TO THE COURT OF LAST RESORT.

At present a party may appeal from the interlocutory order, and also from the definitive decree,

* It may seem surprising that I have not noticed the project entertained of creating out of that amphibious Court the Exchequer an effective equity tribunal. It is well known that an attempt of this kind was made some years since, which has failed of producing any thing, except the usual result of all similar measures, in which the philosophy of legislation is disregarded and even experience is set at defiance. The reader will find the reasons against such a patchwork scheme stated shortly, but perhaps sufficiently, in the Chancery Letters.

upon matters of fact as well as questions of law, from the Vice Chancellor or Master of the Rolls to the Lord Chancellor, and from thence to the House of Lords, so that a double appeal is allowed upon almost every possible point that can arise in a cause.* I shall say nothing here of the palpable absurdity of an appeal from the Lord Chancellor sitting in Lincoln's Inn Hall to the same noble and learned person seated on the woolsack; nor shall I here consider the propriety of an appeal upon mere matters of fact. The expediency of a double appeal is my only subject of inquiry, and a very few words will suffice to resolve this question.

The reader must be informed that, according to the existing practice, parties who conceive a decree or an order to be erroneous may, in general, obtain a rehearing, upon the certificate of counsel that there is good reason for having the matter reheard. So that wherever there has been any error or undue precipitation, any material evidence has not been read, any argument has been omitted, or any parallel decision not cited, the cause may be again brought under the consideration of the judge; and it is obvious, therefore, that a rehearing must, in most cases, answer the purpose of an appeal; but it will not in all. The

* If the matter come before the Master of the Rolls or Vice Chancellor, upon exceptions to the Master's Report, there are three ranks of appeals.

most learned and acute judges may decide differently difficult and intricate legal questions, and in process of time we should have numerous conflicting judgments of the courts upon the same points, if there were not some supreme tribunal, whose definitive decree controuled them all and preserved the necessary evenness and uniformity in the laws. A Court of Appeal is necessary for another reason. No good legislator ever takes it for granted that men will do their duty because they ought to do it, and least of all should this be assumed in the formation of tribunals of justice. In spite of the publicity attending judicial proceedings, and the responsibility attaching itself to the magisterial office, judges have been, and may again be, guilty of misconduct; and it is necessary, in order to prevent the mischief and injustice that would be occasioned by a bad or weak judge under no restraint, that his orders should be subject to the revision of a superior court.

These are the two principal motives for the establishment of a Court of Appeal, but what reason can be suggested for an intermediate appeal? The delay and expense inseparable from appeals so frequently produce a failure of justice, that nothing less than the certainty of their being indispensable can justify such an institution; and if more than one gradation be instituted, of course these inconveniencies are greatly increased. Let those then who are advocates for a plurality of appeals indicate some advantage that outweighs the prejudice they produce, and if none can be pointed out, let the present practice of a double appeal be abolished.*

According to the above proposal, we should have three courts, each composed of a single judge.†

It is one of those anomalies not uncommon in our jurisprudence that four judges sit together in the common law courts, where the questions to be decided are of comparative simplicity, the property litigated generally of small value, and the rights to be adjudicated those only of the plaintiffs and of defendants, having the same identical interests to support, whilst a single judge only presides in the different branches of the Court of Chancery, where the questions, both of law and equity, to be determined, are of the most entangled and complicated nature, and those raised not between the plaintiffs and defendants only,

* Much has been said about the additional expense that will be occasioned by taking away the intermediate appeal. The costs on an appeal to the supreme tribunal ought perhaps to be moderated, but it must be remembered, that there is hardly a case in which a rehearing may not be had, at a very trifling expense, before the same judge, and, formed as the English Bench and Bar now are, that mode appears to me infinitely more satisfactory.

† Some persons think the equity business of the country would not furnish occupation for three courts independently of the bankruptcy business. Some remarks on this subject will be found in another part of the present chapter.

but frequently between different defendants having hostile and conflicting interests, and where the property contested must, from the great delay and expense inseparable from the proceedings of the tribunal, be of large amount.*

It may seem surprising, after these remarks, that the writer should not be an advocate for a plurality of judges in the Court of Chancery, but after an attentive consideration of the arguments brought forward by the most able writers, as to the expediency of placing one or more judges in civil tribunals, they appear to him so equally poised, as to afford no justification for disturbing an established usage. Besides, as it has been justly observed, it ought not to be forgotten, that economy and simplicity are on the side of a single judge, and therefore the *onus probandi* lies entirely on the other side.

* The great majority of actions are brought for sums less than £20. A man had better lose £500 than recover it through the ordeal of a Chancery suit, in the manner in which it may be, and often is, carried on.

THE THREE COURTS SHOULD HOLD THEIR SITTINGS UNDER THE SAME ROOF, IN SOME PLACE NEAR THE MASTERS' OFFICES.

The Courts should sit near the Masters' offices, for the convenience of the solicitors. The solicitors are required, either by themselves or competent clerks, to attend in Court at the hearing of all causes, petitions, and motions, in which they are concerned, and are severely mulcted if absent. The necessity for the attendance of themselves or their clerks before the Masters in Chancery is not less urgent, as their neglect of this duty would occasion great pecuniary and other losses to their clients, which they would be compelled to make good by the verdict of a court of law or the decree of a court of equity. The majority of solicitors have not more than one or two clerks to assist them in carrying on their business, nor can they afford to increase the number. The present practice seems to assume, that during the sittings at Westminster these gentlemen have the faculty of legal ubiquity.*

* I have said nothing here as to the mischief and inconvenience arising to the junior part of the Chancery Bar from the custom of the Court sitting at Westminster during Term time (which had been many years discontinued) having been lately revived. On this subject the reader will find some observations in the Letters on the Court of Chancery.

The three courts should sit under the same roof, for the convenience both of the barristers and solicitors.

The practice of one Court would never yield sufficient emolument to barristers or solicitors to induce men of character and education to devote themselves to it, unless a few had the monopoly of the whole business, and experience has taught us that this remedy would be worse than the disease. Justice can never be well administered if the advocates and attorneys be not in general men of knowledge and respectability. It is rather, therefore, to promote the ends of justice, than for the accommodation of the bar or of the solicitors, that I propose the three courts should sit under the same roof.

THE HOUSE OF LORDS.

THE House of Lords should abandon a jurisdiction which they have been incompetent to exercise ever since its first acquisition.

The motives for such a measure are to be found scattered in different parts of this work, and it would extend this chapter to a very inconvenient length were I to collect them in this place. My notions of a Supreme Tribunal, to replace the House of Peers, do not differ from those of the author of the Letters on the Court of Chancery, and I have therefore annexed a translation of those letters that relate to this subject, by way of Appendix to this Chapter.*

The reader will also observe, that it is proposed to give to the new Court of last resort the cognizance of colonial appeals.

I have no doubt the charge of newfangleness will be urged more violently against this part of my scheme for reorganizing our Courts than against any other, although the origin of the appellate jurisdiction of the Lords, the recency of its acquisition, the incompetency of the peers to discharge the duties they have assumed, the union of the legislative and judicial characters, and many other defects and absurdities in the constitution of this august tribunal, concur to show there is no part of the present system that calls more loudly for an entire reform. I shall not attempt to anticipate all the objections that will probably be levied against such an innovation as the establishment of a permanent Court of Appeal in this country, upon a plan in some respects similar to that of the Court of Cassation in France. There are, however, one or two points connected with the proposed alteration, that it is impossible to pass by without notice.

Those who take the trouble to peruse these pages will probably ask the following questions,

* See the Appendix, B.

some of which have immediate relation to the topic now under consideration, whilst others are more connected with former heads of this Chapter, although I have thought it more convenient to introduce them in this place.

Is it proposed to separate the office of Chancellor from that of Speaker of the House of Lords?

Is it proposed that the Chancellor should be one of the Judges of the Court of Appeal?

Is it meant that the Lord Chancellor should no longer preside in the Court of Chancery?

SEPARATION OF THE OFFICE OF CHANCELLOR FROM THE OFFICE OF SPEAKER OF THE HOUSE OF LORDS.

It has been said, I think, by Lord Ellesmere, that the Chancellor is the Prolocutor of the House of Lords by prescription. It is certain that the Chancellor presided in Parliament long before the famous John de Waltham invented the writ of subpœna, to enrich the sinecurists and secretaries of the present day, or an equity cause had been created out of the chaos of the law; and, zealous reformer as I am, I cannot discover sufficient reason for the separation of offices which appear to have been united since the infancy of our monarchy.

OUGHT THE CHANCELLOR TO BE A MEMBER OF THE SUPREME COURT OF APPEAL?

THE Lord Chancellor, the head of the judicature of this country, is always raised to that high dignity from the walks of Westminster Hall. Although a very humble barrister, I have too much of the *esprit de corps* not to think it would be a hazardous innovation if the person at the head of the judicature of the country were not a principal member of the government and a lawyer.*

The preservation of this character in the Chancellor cannot be better insured than by placing him at the head of the Supreme Court of Appeal; but it must not be understood that I would have him preside in that tribunal, except upon extraordinary occasions. If it is asked, in what cases

* It may be observed, however, that the Chief Justiciar, who originally presided over all the tribunals of justice, and was a principal minister of the Crown, and the second man in the kingdom, was seldom educated as a lawyer.

The Chancellor, although he was, like the Lord High Constable, Lord Marshal, Lord High Steward, Lord Great Chamberlain, Steward of the Household, &c. a member of the *Aula Regia*, was not at this period a lawyer; and, it is well known, that after the Courts became stationary at Westminster, and the office of Chief Justiciary fell into disuse, and his functions had devolved upon the Chancellor, several centuries elapsed before it was considered necessary that the person holding the Great Seal should have a practical knowledge of the laws.

the Lord Chancellor ought to take his seat in the Court of last resort, I say, on occasions similar to those in which, in France, the Chancellor, or Keeper of the Seals, presides in the Court of Cassation, as where the appeal has been once heard, and the opinions of the judges have been equally divided, &c.

OUGHT THE CHANCELLOR TO CONTINUE TO SIT IN THE COURT OF CHANCERY?

THESE pages furnish abundance of reasons why he should not, and one only reason why he should; this one reason, however, requires some reflection, and as it is more logical to discuss the affirmative before the negative, I will consider it first.

From the peculiar nature of the doctrines governing Equity cases, which are not to be collected from statutes, but from a series of decisions of judges frequently applying to particular combinations of circumstances, the rules of which they themselves were the authors, it has been urged that it is essential that the appellate judge should, at the same time, be in the constant habit of hearing original Equity causes, in order that the principles regulating them may be kept constantly alive and present to his mind. It has been contended, that the occasionally looking back into reports and precedents on particular heads will never alone enable him satisfactorily to decide cases in the last resort, and that if the duties of the Chancellor, as an Equity judge, are to be limited to his adjudicating a few appeals in the course of the year, whilst the inferior judges, by the uninterrupted exercise of their functions, are kept constantly familiar with the law of the Court in all its branches, the appeal will soon lie from judges, masters of the law, to one but imperfectly acquainted with it, and their number will probably be diminished, but an evil of another character and much greater magnitude will arise.*

The first remark that it occurs to me to offer upon these objections is, that the persons urging

* What is here stated comprises, I believe, the substance of the principal objections urged by Sir Samuel Romilly and Sir John Leach, as to the diminution of the original business done by the Chancellor that must necessarily take place if a Vice Chancellor were appointed. It must be recollected, however, that the learned persons using these arguments were active members of a political party, opposed to the creation of an additional judge, as a measure introduced by their adversaries.

It is not a little remarkable that Sir Samuel Romilly had himself been a few years before Solicitor General under a Chancellor notoriously deficient in the knowledge and practice of Equity and the doctrines of real property, which in his speeches and pamphlets he described as indispensable in that high judge; and Sir John Leach shortly afterwards accepted the very office, the establishment of which he had condemned, and, by his zeal and talent, rendered it by far the most useful and effective branch of the Court of Chancery.

them must assume that original jurisdiction may be united to appellate, a proposition which every one acquainted with the philosophical writers on this branch of legislation knows cannot be maintained consistently with any of those principles to be adopted in the organization of tribunals of justice.

But as few English lawyers ever think of illuminating the dark chambers of our jurisprudence with the lamp of philosophy,* I shall not detain the reader by demonstrating how fallacious such objections are when theoretically considered, but shall proceed according to the usage of the last quarter of a century, and which, it must be admitted, can never be too much commended, when a cautious regard for the public weal and not self-interest presides over the research, to inquire, in a more practical manner, what mischief can be the result if the Lord Chancellor be taken from the Court of Chancery.

Nothing will, perhaps, better contribute to enable us to arrive at a safe conclusion upon this subject, than to take a short review of the quantity of judicial business which the Lord Chancellor, as a judge of first instance, disposes of in the course of a year; and when we consider the pe-

* "Innutritus Philosophiæ, cum ad prudentiam juris animum appulissem, resiliebam, quoties occasio dabatur, ad priora; et quod vel ex ipsis, vel affine ipsis erat, curiosè annotabam."—*Leibnitii Specimen Difficultatis in Jure.*

culiar circumstances which attended Lord Lyndhurst's accession to office, I do not know that I can select a period more favourable to the arguments which I presume to combat than Lord Lyndhurst's first judicial year. The language of his Lordship's panegyrists is yet fresh in our memories. We were told, that, with such a Chancellor, it was no longer necessary to remodel the Court of Chancery; that we had at length a Chancellor who had the benefit of youth, health, and activity; and who, although not educated in the Equity Courts, would more than compensate that disadvantage by the remarkable power he possessed of simplifying and dealing with the most complicated cases, and who, in short, was *judex à judicando*, and not *judex à non judicando*;* that with a few simple regulations, the Chancellor and the two assistant judges would be more than equal to do all the business, without the occurrence of the least delay, and that those regulations would be made without the aid of a cumbersome bill in Parliament.

The reader, who has attentively read the foregoing pages, will nevertheless, perhaps, be sur-

* Those who have read the former part of this work must know how fully the author concurs in the justness of the above encomium with one exception, and that exception implies no censure of Lord Lyndhurst. The *judex à judicando* is not applicable to Lord Lyndhurst, and it never will be applicable to any Chancellor as long as the present system remains.

prised at the statement, that it is probable Lord Lyndhurst, since his appointment to office, has not made more special orders on original business in Chancery than would occupy a judge who had no other duties, either political or judicial, more than a few days. He had, at the beginning of Hilary Term, heard six original causes and five causes on exceptions, and I believe it will be found he has heard none since. How many original motions of a special nature he has disposed of, it would be difficult to ascertain with accuracy, unless a return of the number were made to Parliament. The number, however, must be extremely small. He has also, since he received the seals, made orders upon between seventy and eighty cause petitions, some small proportion of which were of a special description.*

Now every practitioner knows, that the present Master of the Rolls, during his morning sittings, between the last day of term and the Seal, disposes of a much greater mass of original business than the Chancellor appears to have disposed

* I have not been able to obtain any information, upon which I can sufficiently rely, as to the number or description of bankrupt petitions disposed of by Lord Lyndhurst. His Lordship in general will hear none but appeal petitions. There are some few however, of a different nature, which he is occasionally compelled to entertain. Those counsel in the court, who have the best means of knowing, assure me the total number disposed of by his Lordship, including even appeal petitions, is small.

of in twelve months.* In the space of a week, 200 cause petitions, of every description, 40 or 50 short causes, and as many causes on the general list are frequently heard and decided.

But it will be said, that the Chancellor's time is, as appears from preceding chapters, almost exclusively occupied by the appellate business; and if, as I propose, the intermediate appeal were abolished, the Chancellor would be at liberty to employ himself upon original causes.

Let us see, then, what would be the probable result of such a change in the nature of the Chancellor's occupations. He has succeeded, by the means and exertions pointed out in former parts of this work, in hearing as many as between 50 and 60 appeals, although his other duties have not yet permitted him to give judgment in more than two-thirds of the number.

Could the Lord Chancellor have disposed of a greater quantity of original business in the same time? Before I answer this question another must be put.

If the 50 or 60 appeals had been heard by his Lordship, sitting as a judge of first instance, and

* If the quantity of lunacy business, and the original business in bankruptcy, disposed of by the Lord Chancellor, were added to the fruits of his twelvemonth's labours, I think it would be still found that a week's labours of Sir John Leach are more productive.

not as an appellate judge, could he have disposed of them in a shorter space of time?

The obvious answer is, that he could not. An appeal is infinitely more simple than an original cause; it comes before the Court stripped of a multitude of petty facts and circumstances which are necessary ingredients in an original cause, and require a considerable time to be adjusted and understood, but when adjusted and understood, admit of no further discussion. An appeal may be compared to an army at the end of a campaign. In the collision of the first hearing, the greater part of the litigated points are generally placed at rest; and although it happens that in the second conflict the combatants are often as numerous as in the first, the *materiel*, at least, is always much less, and the fight is seldom so warm or so protracted.

But it will be objected, that I am forming an estimate of the quantity of original business that the Chancellor could dispose of from very erroneous data, inasmuch as I suppose him to hear not the ordinary causes, but those only which are made the subject of an appeal and involve matters of considerable doubt and difficulty. But I would ask, ought the Lord Chancellor, ought the Speaker of the House of Lords, a principal member of the Cabinet, the first Temporal Peer, and the Keeper of his Majesty's Conscience, with lay and ecclesiastical patronage equalled by that of few sovereign princes, and an income more than double that of any other judge in Europe, to have his time occupied in hearing trifling legacy and foreclosure suits, and other matters of that sort, that may be as well or better disposed of by any barrister of three years' standing who pleads before him. It is clear he ought not. Hercules ought not to hold the distaff. It is not incorrect, then, to estimate the Chancellor's services by the quantity of business he would dispose of, which it would require a judge of the dignity of a Chancellor and with the salary of a Chancellor to perform.

The answer to this second question being now obvious, it furnishes me with a satisfactory answer to the first. If the Lord Chancellor had been occupied in hearing original business, the quantity of valuable original business that he could have disposed of could not have exceeded the quantity of appellate business he has disposed of.

The conclusion, then, is, that the Lord Chancellor would not make more than three or four score Special Orders in matters of any importance, if he devoted his time to the hearing of original instead of appellate Chancery suits; and I apprehend the adjudication of that quantity of business can never be deemed of sufficient importance to retain the Lord Chancellor in the Court of Chancery. It can never furnish that constant exercise in the business of the Court which would give to the Chancellor as familiar an acquaintance with its principles and doctrines as the subordinate judges or even the leading advocates possess; and that being the case, one of the principal reasons for his continuance in the Court of Chancery fails.

But I am not inclined altogether to admit the hypothesis of the adversaries of a removal, that it is necessary an appellate equity judge should be habitually practised in the adjudication of original causes.*

It is true that a knowledge of the doctrines and practice of our Courts of Equity is not to be acquired in a few months or in a few years; and no man, however great his talents and accomplishments, or however deeply versed he may be in the common law of the country, can, perhaps, now preside in any branch of the Court of Chancery to the advantage of the public, who has not, during a long series of years, practised there as an advocate, and thus rendered himself familiar with the principles governing its decisions; the shades and gradations of Equity, as of every other science which has received a high degree of cultivation, being too delicate and numerous to be dis-

* The reader will recollect, it has been also stated to be a principle adopted by the best philosophical writers on legislation, that appellate and immediate jurisdiction should not be united; the proposition here combated is, of course, irreconcilable with this principle.

tinguished by any but a practised eye. If the case were otherwise, then would our system of jurisprudence be a fraud and a deception. All that has been done by the Bacons, the Nottinghams, and the Somers to perfect it, would be worse than useless, and the years of study and experience, without which, it is supposed, no one can safely practise in the Court of Chancery, would be thrown away.*

But just and well-founded as these remarks undoubtedly are, we must not conclude that those who dispense equity in the Court of last resort must serve a perpetual apprenticeship. Like other crafts, it can only be thoroughly learnt at the dawn of life, when impressions are most easily received and most strongly stamped on the

* It must be admitted, there are not wanting in the history of our courts examples of common law advocates making good equity judges; but it should be recollected how narrow formerly was the field of our jurisprudence in comparison with its present extent. The whole of it was familiar to every barrister in good practice; the serjeants pleaded in Chancery, and the predecessors of the present race of equity draftsmen went the circuit. Our system of equity had its birth only towards the middle of the seventeenth century, and our commercial and bankrupt law were in their infancy at the commencement of the late reign. Since the beginning of the present century, the number of reports has more than doubled, and the number of treatises on different branches of our laws has increased in a greater proportion. The number of volumes containing our statutes at the same period was 42, whilst at present they amount to 67. Our law

mind. The same change, it is true, takes place in the doctrines of our equity tribunals as in all other human institutions, but its progress, during the ordinary period of a professional career, is almost imperceptible. He who in the spring and summer of his days has well stored his memory with its maxims and decisions, will find them authoritative and current at the end. The old procedure may be destroyed by new rules and orders, but the great principles upon which the system is built must remain unaltered. He who migrates from and afterwards returns to his Court may find himself a stranger to some parts of its practice, but its doctrines will be still familiar to him; and everybody knows it is with the latter, and not with the former, that the appellate judge has to deal. It should be remembered too that if the judge of appeal has a less extensive range of experience than the subordinate judge, yet that he brings to the performance of his judicial functions advantages which the latter does not possess. The case is stripped of all extrinsic and irrelevant circumstances, the whole reasoning

has thus become spread over too wide a surface to permit us to do more than acquire a cursory knowledge of it as a whole. Subdivision of labour has operated in it, as in other branches of learning, so to refine and multiply the different parts, that an advocate, to render his talents useful, must devote himself to the study of some of them, and be content with a general survey of the rest.

and argument are brought to the illustration of the particular points on which he is required to exercise his judgment; and, above all, he is not compelled to give a hasty nisi prius decision, but has ample time for deliberation.

It appears to me then that a judge, whose education early placed him on the vantage ground of history and of science, who, before he began his career as an advocate, drank at the pure fountain-head of the law, who has industry to look into the authorities and precedents applicable to the questions he is called to decide, acuteness to distinguish their differences, and a sound logical head to guide him in his conclusions, may be safely entrusted with the adjudication of causes in the last resort, without having his legal knowledge constantly kept alive by the exercise of original jurisdiction.*

* It appears, from the former part of this work, that some objections have been brought forward against any project that may diminish the quantity of the Chancellor's original business, independently of those I have noticed in the text.

It has been said, that if such a scheme be carried into effect, the office of Chancellor will soon become political instead of judicial, the reward of political intrigue and connection and not of legal eminence. But it may be asked at what period of our history has the Chancellor been selected for the abilities he has evinced as a counsel in any court of Westminster Hall, unless they were of a kind to dazzle in a public assembly of a far different description. It is notorious that nothing less has been thought of than the choice of the man who was most versed in

The final result then of this branch of my enquiry is, that no practical mischief can arise if

the laws of his country, far less of him who had the most intimate knowledge of that part of our system of jurisprudence known under the name of equity. And, in despite of my prejudices as a lawyer, when I reflect on the preponderating weight and importance of the Chancellor's public duties, which partake more of the political than judicial character, I cannot avoid entertaining an opinion that the Sovereign has been generally well advised in elevating to the giddy height of the Chancellorship an individual whose accomplishments and talents fitted him to shine rather in the senate than at the bar. The taking the Chancellor from the Court of Chancery, together with the creation of a permanent Court of Appeal, in the place of the House of Lords, as suggested in the Chancery Letters, would, in my apprehension, entirely remove the insurmountable objection at present existing to the appointment of a common law advocate to that high office. Everybody knows it is a farce and a mockery for a judge, with even Lord Lyndhurst's quickness and talents, to sit in appeal on the decrees of a Grant or a Leach, and rehear the decisions of an Eldon.

It has, also, been objected, that if the Chancellor's original jurisdiction be taken from him he will be withdrawn from his Court, and will no longer have an opportunity of becoming acquainted with the individual merits of advocates, and exercising his patronage in the manner most advantageous to the public, by appointing to situations in the law men of the greatest aptitude. One cannot, to be sure, sufficiently admire the self-possession of those who, when they urged this topic, were able to preserve their gravity, as if it were not notorious, that for years past the fitness of the individual to fulfil the duties of the office to which he was appointed was not one of the last things that decided the choice of the Chancellor or those who have had the controul of his patronage. It reflects no great credit on the discernment of those who have held the Great Seal, that the persons who are the Chancellor be taken from the Court of Chancery; and it does not appear that any benefit at all commensurate with the inconveniences consequent upon the immense consumption of the Chancellor's time would accrue from a continuance of the services he at present performs there.

The Chancellor, therefore, ought not to continue to sit in the Court of Chancery.*

---

supposed to have owed their elevation solely to the Chancellor, have been in general infinitely more incompetent than those whose advancement is said to have been occasioned by political connection and influence.

* Some persons think, that when the business of the Court of Chancery shall be subtracted from the Chancellor's other occupations, he will be left without sufficient employment; but, I apprehend, those persons form their judgment upon a very erroneous conception of the multifarious duties attaching themselves to the Keeper of the Great Seal. It should be recollected, that during the sitting of the House of Lords, the Chancellor's time must be fully occupied with his parliamentary duties, and the House sits from six to eight months in the year. The numerous claims to peerages, claims to vote on elections of peers for Ireland and Scotland, divorce and other private bills, besides the other general business of the session, afford an ample field for his labours. When Parliament does not sit, the ordinary business of the Chancellor, if duly attended to, cannot be less than that of most of the other cabinet ministers. He is required to advise his Majesty on almost all great and important questions, whether they concern our domestic affairs or our relations with foreign powers. Few days can elapse, in a country like this, that it does not become necessary for the Crown to consult its first law officer, to

BANKRUPTCY.

SEPARATION OF BANKRUPTCY FROM THE GENERAL BUSINESS OF THE COURT OF CHANCERY.—ABOLITION OF COMMISSIONERSHIPS OF BANKRUPT.

THE reasons for the separation of the bankruptcy business from the general business of the Court of Chancery are detailed in some of the preceding chapters. The principal reason, undoubtedly, is,

say nothing of the inordinate portion of the Chancellor's time that within the last half century has been consumed by state trials and the proceedings attending them. The Chancellor has the appointment of all the justices of the peace throughout the kingdom. He has the superintendence of all charitable uses. He is visitor, in right of his Majesty, of all colleges and hospitals of Royal foundation; he is the guardian of all lunatics, idiots, and infants. It is his anxious and melancholy duty to examine the different cases in the Recorder's report, previous to its being received by the King. The exercise of his ecclesiastical patronage does, or ought at times to engage no small part of his attention. He has jurisdiction to remove coroners for misconduct. He grants and repeals patents and charters, grants writs of supplicavit, commissions of review, &c. In fine, it would require more space than can be allotted to this note merely to enumerate the judicial or ministerial duties of the Chancellor which are extrinsic to the ordinary business of the Court of Chancery, and all of which, as our books of reports show, occasionally occupy considerable time. Besides these numerous and discordant duties, (some of which it would be advisable to detach from the Great Seal,) it must be recollected that, in this country, there is no standing commission appointed to superintend our system of jurisprudence, and that that care is the peculiar province of the Chancellor, and is alone too extensive for any individual.

the delay arising from the inadequacy of our great equity tribunal, for the dispatch even of those suits which lie more peculiarly within its province. But it may be urged, that as it is proposed to create a new judge, such an increased power would be given to the machinery of the Court as to enable it to render the Bankrupt Laws, by a speedy hearing and decision of all the cases to which they give birth, that *festinum remedium* which the legislature intended them to be, and that there would no longer exist any cause for disuniting two systems which time has so closely interwoven.

The possibility of three judges, who should constantly devote themselves to the hearing of equity suits, succeeding at first in disposing of all the business on the roll, has been already admitted; and from the facts stated in the former parts of this work, I have ventured to predict that this ebb would be succeeded by a regular and perpetual flow of causes into the Court. But supposing this conjecture should prove to be incorrect, supposing that our equity judges should occasionally find themselves in the situation of those venerable magistrates of our common law courts of ancient days, who, when the harvest of litigation was less plentiful, were able, after disposing of the business of their courts, to attend the House of Lords, early as it then met, and advise that assembly on the wisdom and expediency of the different laws propounded, as well as on the form in which they should be couched; supposing, I say, this should be the case, I cannot persuade myself that such a result would prove detrimental to the public. Of late years the judges, who by the extent of their knowledge, the liberality of their minds, and the correctness of their judgment, have been most capable of improving our laws, have been so overwhelmed by the more urgent work of executing them, that although their defects in some parts, and their severities in others, have almost daily called forth expressions of their deepest regret, they have rarely found leisure to supply the former or mitigate the latter. It should, in accordance with the maxims adopted in the formation of all well-organized judicial establishments, be an imperative part of the duty of the judges to point out to the legislature those evils in our laws, of which they must have daily examples, as well as to suggest fitting remedies, and no statute should be enacted affecting that portion of our legislation which commonly comes under the consideration of our courts of justice, in civil and criminal cases, and forms the nucleus or code of the law in many other nations, without being previously submitted to their scrutiny and observation. But, to enable the judges duly to perform this task, almost as important as the execution of the existing laws, they must have more leisure than is now enjoyed either by the Lord Chancellor or the Vice Chancellor.*

It may be said, perhaps, that some of the judges are, during a large portion of the year, almost without employ, and it may be urged as an argument against my proposal, that their freedom from business has seldom been productive of any hints for the improvement of the law. But we should recollect, that these judges have often been placed on the bench, as the only expedient of getting rid of men who have in other offices disappointed the expectations raised of them, or have fulfilled the temporary purpose which was the cause of their first elevation.

There is perhaps another and more powerful motive for a disjunction of Bankruptcy and the general business of the Court of Chancery. The bankrupt law and commercial law, in all countries, so intertwine, that they can never long be administered under distinct systems, and no one will dispute that it is of the utmost consequence to a great trading people, that simplicity should be a leading feature

* Nothing would tend more to the improvement of our laws than the appointment of a perpetual commission to receive communications from the judges and other individuals, as to the alterations and additions which they require. The shadow of such an institution has existed two centuries in the grand committee for courts of justice.

in the laws regulating its commerce. Now that our present bankrupt and commercial code is of the most complicated and entangled nature, and in many respects wholly unfit for mercantile purposes, has long been the subject of loud and just complaint, and I cannot help thinking, that the evil has been considerably augmented by the administration of the Bankrupt laws by Equity judges. Equity has, by a succession of decisions upon the ever varying transactions of men, become a most subtle and abstruse science, which is thoroughly understood but by a very few even of its professors, and the Chancellors, having many motives for making bankruptcy the adopted child of the great seal, have not been backward in applying equitable rules and principles to the cases to which it has given rise. The consequence has been that every great question in Bankruptcy has been drawn within the vortex of our court, and the niceties and distinctions of a science, already too refined, have been multiplied, until the perception and comprehension of them require the deepest thought and meditation, and the speedy and immediate decision of questions connected with them is become altogether impossible.

The time perhaps is not remote when our laws will successively pass through the alembick of a philosophical legislator, and no part will then be found so mixed with impurities as that which governs the relation of debtor and creditor.* It will require no common skill to introduce principle and order into such a mass of confused and heterogeneous elements, as compose this branch of our law, but much greater address will be necessary to prevent them from relapsing into their ancient state of chaos, if so considerable a portion as Bankruptcy be placed under the superintendence of a court, whose judges, from Lord Nottingham to Lord Eldon, have been

* There is no part of our law to which the attention of Parliament has been more frequently called than that which regulates the relation of debtor and creditor. Some amendment has been made, but the evils had been felt and complained of for centuries before any remedy was applied. In 1653, a pamphlet was published entitled "*The Laws Discovery or a brief Delation of sundry notorious Errors and Abuses contained in our English Laws, whereby thousands are annually stripped of their Estates, and some of their Lives.—By a Well Wisher to his Country.*" The following extract from the Introduction to it will serve to illustrate the observation just made :—" The author was a gentleman born to a fair estate, by degree a barrister, who, partly through sickness and partly for conscience, deserted the profession of our laws, as epidemically evil. He spent divers of his last years in supervising the defects thereof. Amongst many grievances wherein he desired redress, personal imprisonment for debt was one, and the insufficiency of our laws for charging the debtor's estate another. Therefore several of these subsequent proposals tend chiefly for securing of creditors out of the debtor's estate, whereby the debtor's person may go free." The pamphlet is in 4to. and contains five pages ; it is reprinted in the Harleian Miscellany.

characterised for subtilising into niceties all matters that have come before them. The necessity of preserving that character of simplicity which it ought to be the object of any change to impress upon our commercial law, appears to me to furnish a sufficient motive for disuniting Bankruptcy from the other business of the Court of Chancery.*

All the principal objections that have been brought forward against the proposed separation of the bankrupt business from the Great Seal have

* Many persons think that a judicious reform might give us such a bankrupt system that a considerable part of it might, as in other countries, be administered by a tribunal of intelligent merchants. We have seen that Sir J. B. Burgess suggested, that the Bankruptcy Court should be in part composed of merchants. The idea is not new. The anonymous writer of a pamphlet published in 1659, entitled "*A Rod for the Lawyers*," quoted in the first chapter of this work, proposed the establishment of merchant courts, to decide all controversies arising in commerce. "What a ridiculous thing is it," he observes, "that the judges in Chancery must determine of merchants' negotiations transacted in foreign parts, which they understand no better than do the seats they sit on, and so they are as capable to do equity therein as a blind man to shoot a hare." The project of having a Bankruptcy Court, some of whose members should be merchants, has been revived within these few years. In the present state of our laws such a scheme would be quite impracticable, and, it should be remembered that some eminent philosophical writers upon jurisprudence have expressed themselves adverse to the measure of placing merchants, under any circumstances, on the judicial seat, to try questions of commercial law. The subject, however, deserves further consideration.

been perhaps sufficiently noticed in the preceding chapters. There is one, however, which has been so often urged that I cannot forbear making some further observations upon it in this place. It is said, that questions in bankruptcy involve such difficult and intricate points, that they should be submitted to that judge only who possesses the greatest learning and talents. But what is to be done, if that judge be already overwhelmed with other duties equally important, and which more peculiarly belong to him than the bankruptcy business, so that years must pass away before he can find leisure to adjudicate questions, which, from the very nature of the commercial transactions out of which they arise, ought to receive an immediate decision? Where is the utility of an elaborate judgment, not pronounced until the occasion which first called for it has ceased to exist, and great part of the property which it is intended to bind has, in the progress of litigation, been lost or destroyed? We live in no island of Utopia. We have not only a great many laws, but a great many suits arising out of them; and these suits, although of a different nature, are frequently of equal importance. The same reason that is urged for the administration of Bankruptcy by that individual only who is most deeply versed in our jurisprudence equally applies to the other principal branches of the law. But it is obviously impossible to give that degree of perfection and excellence to our tribunals, that every important legal problem shall be solved by the ablest judicial mind in the Kingdom. Besides, this objection against separating the adjudication of bankrupt cases from the duties of the Chancellor, is founded on the supposition that the Chancellor unites the greatest knowledge of all parts of our jurisprudence to the talents and accomplishments which he must of course possess as a statesman; and although this has sometimes been the case, it may be safely predicted it is not likely to occur again, until at least our laws are condensed into the comparatively small space occupied by them a century ago. *

ABOLITION OF COMMISSIONERSHIPS OF BANKRUPT.

All persons seem agreed as to the necessity of putting an end to the present system of the commissionerships of bankrupt,† and it is greatly

* It is obvious that those gentlemen who have urged the necessity of the judge, in the last resort in bankruptcy, possessing the greatest legal attainments, imagine that the judicial qualities increase in proportion to the rank of the tribunal; to be consistent in their arguments, they should propose to give the ultimate jurisdiction in bankruptcy to the House of Lords.

† "It (*the Court of Commissioners of Bankrupt*) is the most "baneful and poisonous plant that, from want of care and weed-"ing, has been allowed to run to rankness in the garden of the "law. All living that alights upon it languishes and dies. Every "honest lawyer must desire to see it utterly rooted out."—*Letters of Eminent Lawyers.*

to the honour of the London commissioners that the most zealous advocates for the abolition of the Court are to be found amongst them.

I would replace the commissioners by a court modelled upon a plan resembling that suggested by Mr. Montague, in his evidence before the Select Committee of the Common Council, the prototype of which is to be found in a scheme for a new bankrupt court for Ireland, proposed by Mr. Grattan, for the adoption of the legislature, as far back as the year 1811.*

The court should be composed of four or five barristers, of twelve years standing, who should have fixed salaries, and should, upon their appointment, become disqualified from acting as advocates. Any one should be a quorum for the transaction of that business which now falls within the province of the commissioners, but not fewer than three should sit to adjudicate those matters which are now brought before the Chancellor upon petition.

The court should be composed of judges as efficient as those of our other principal tribunals, as regards that part of the law which would come under their administration; and I think it ought not to be subordinate to any branch of the Court of Chancery, and consequently that the appeal should lie at once from the new bankruptcy tribunal to the court of last resort.

* See a Note to Chapter XVII.

The great expense that must attend the proceedings before the supreme tribunal of the country, will, perhaps, be urged as a reason against transferring to it the appellate jurisdiction in bankruptcy, and it may be said, that it is to avoid this expense that the legislature continues to the Lord Chancellor the final decision of bankrupt cases. But those who shall venture to use such arguments must be altogether unacquainted with our Bankrupt Laws, or must presume upon the ignorance of the persons they address. As if a legislature, which allows the Chancellor and the holder of a patent office, to receive out of bankrupt property, in a single year, the sum of £28,000, and notwithstanding the reiterated complaints of the people and their representatives, persists in administering that property under a system which yearly takes from it not less than £200,000 more than would be necessary upon a more simple and more effective plan, can, in maintaining the present scheme, have in view an economical distribution of bankrupt estates.*

* It is not irrelevant to observe, that the great value of property administered under the Bankrupt Laws has always been used as an argument why the jurisdiction should be vested in a judge of a rank not inferior to the Lord Chancellor. I have before remarked, that if this argument be of any value, it is in favour of giving the ultimate adjudication of bankrupt cases to the House of Lords. The reader should also be informed, that the appeal from the decision of the Scotch courts, in matters of

But I have been led to make the foregoing observations for the purpose only of showing the fallacy and inconsistency of such arguments. The objection may be best removed by diminishing the expense of an appeal to the court of last resort, as regards bankruptcy cases, supposing it should not be thought advisable to lessen it with reference to the general mass of appeals; and even if this be not effected, little inconvenience will ensue, provided proper judges be selected to preside in the court of first instance, and the privilege of a rehearing be allowed.

I have now only a few words to say as to the mode of administering the Bankrupt Laws under country commissions. And here again I would adopt the plan suggested by Mr. Montague, in his evidence before the Chancery Commissioners and before the Select Committee of the Common Council. All commissions which issue within one hundred miles of London should be directed to the London commissioners,* and a barrister should

bankruptcy, lies to the House of Lords, and certainly the expense and inconvenience of such an appeal from Scotland cannot be less than would attend an English appeal.

* According to the present practice, a country commission cannot be executed within forty miles of London, and it must be executed within ten miles of the place to which it is issued. Subject to those rules, the petitioning creditor may sue out the commission to be executed either in town or in the country, so that every petitioning creditor may, if he pleases, have his commission executed in town.

be named in different provincial towns, at a more remote distance from the metropolis, to whom all the commissions to be executed in that town, and within a certain district around it, should be addressed.*

I would not, however, give these barristers a more extensive jurisdiction than that which the commissioners at present possess. The new bankruptcy tribunal should have the decision of the petitions arising out of country commissions, in like manner as the Lord Chancellor and Vice Chancellor have at present.

The part of the arrangement proposed which presents the most difficulty, is the mode of remunerating these commissioners. It is a subject upon which I feel very unwilling to express any

* This scheme is open, but in a much less degree, to some of the objections made in a former Chapter to the present system of the London Commissionerships of Bankrupt. Unless other judicial functions be superadded to the bankruptcy duties, the new country commissioners must necessarily be allowed to practise as advocates. A valuable patronage too must be vested in the Chancellor. As the country commissionerships, however, would not, for obvious reasons, be so eagerly sought as the London commissionerships now are, this patronage would be infinitely less injurious to the independence of the bar, than that at present possessed by the Great Seal. If such a plan as is suggested with regard to country commissions were ever put in execution, and the London tribunal of commissioners were also abolished, such of them as may desire it, and shall not be incapable of performing the duties of the office, should be appointed to the country commissionerships.

opinion, without possessing further information than I have as yet been able to acquire. I shall merely remark that it is not improbable, if a proper choice were made, that barristers appointed to permanent situations, with the publicity and the responsibility attending all their proceedings, would give so great satisfaction in the administration of bankrupt cases, that they would be found useful for the transaction of other judicial business, and possibly make the foundation of regular and efficient local tribunals, the want of which has been long so grievously felt.* Whenever

* The reader must not suppose me to be ignorant of the swarm of petty courts already spread over the country. I have now before me an abstract of more than seventy Acts of Parliament, establishing Courts of Requests in England and Wales, which have various and often conflicting powers and jurisdiction, and each giving rise to a series of judicial decisions, forming its own peculiar code; and in a large proportion of these acts, there is to be found a provision, that nothing therein contained shall extend to prejudice the rights of various Courts Baron, Courts Leet, Courts of Wapentake, Hundreds, Liberties, Manors, Boroughs, &c. But it should be remembered, that from the notoriously defective formation of these tribunals, they are, for the most part, unavailable for the distribution of justice, and the most trifling cases are in consequence tried at the assizes, at an expense which, when we look at the value of the matter in dispute, it is more appalling to contemplate than even the costs of a Chancery suit. The inefficiency of these courts has compelled the legislature to give to the Court of General Quarter Sessions, a variety of civil business, which by its constitution it is very ill adapted to transact. I am persuaded that nothing would give greater satisfaction to the country, than district courts, organized in a respect-

such a measure is carried into effect, they should receive salaries out of the public treasury, suitable to the importance of their new duties; and in the mean time, I can suggest no better scheme to compensate them for their labours as Commissioners of Bankrupt, than that the fees payable on the different commissions should be collected into a common fund, out of which they should receive fixed yearly sums. The total amount of adequate salaries for the requisite number of permanent commissioners would fall short of the fees paid to country commissioners under the present system.*

---

able and efficient manner, so as really to take justice to the poor man's door; and I cannot but think they might be established without imposing any additional burthen on the public. Whoever will take the trouble to ascertain the immense sums of money that are yearly expended in executing commissions of bankrupt, commissions of lunacy, and partition, commissions for the examination of witnesses, and for taking the answers and examinations of parties in equity causes, and in a variety of other matters, too numerous to be here detailed, will soon find that a fund might be raised much more than adequate to form the courts in question. For who can doubt, if such courts existed, that all judicial business of the description just mentioned, would be much better performed there; and fortunately there would exist no barrier to its immediate removal within the jurisdiction of any courts so organized as to be able to transact it. But this subject is much too important to be discussed in a note.

* I cannot conclude this important subject of bankruptcy without observing, that whenever the legislature shall undertake

Such is the outline of the change I would introduce in those tribunals which are the subject of this work. My principal aim has been to approximate to the principles which, according to the most esteemed writers, ought to be adopted in the formation of the judicial establishments of a great and wealthy people, without, however, losing sight of the favourite maxim of our own legislators, that all our reformations ought to be made with reference to antiquity. It is respect for this principle which has induced me to unfold the origin of the appellate jurisdiction of the House of Lords over equity causes, and of the present mode of administering the Bankrupt Laws, in order that the unprejudiced and impartial reader may convince himself, that an alteration might be effected in those systems, without doing any violence to our ancient institutions, upon which they are only modern excrescences.

I have stated in the commencement of this Chapter that I do not entertain the hope, that the suggestions it contains will be adopted at the

the task of revising our law of debtor and creditor, the necessity of which has been more than once alluded to in these pages, it is not improbable that the distinction between bankrupt and insolvent will cease to exist, and that bankruptcy and insolvency will be administered in the same tribunal. Upon what rational principle is insolvency administered by three or four individuals, without appeal, whilst bankruptcy occupies an army of judges under the controul of the Lord Chancellor and the Vice Chancellor?

present time, and some persons may doubt the expediency of detailing a plan which it is not probable will be now carried into effect, and they may be disposed to think it would have been more useful to circumscribe my scheme within narrower and more practicable limits. But, besides that I could never have conscientiously presented to the notice of the public any plan which was not traced upon the principles alone capable of insuring to the tribunals to be constructed upon it, the possession of the properties requisite for a cheap, speedy and safe distribution of justice, I have two objections to pursuing the course here suggested.

My first objection is, that I cannot reconcile to myself those imperfect measures projected to stave off an evil to a distance, but which are not capable of preventing its return; whose object seems to be rather to adapt our laws to our tribunals, than our tribunals to our laws, and which treat the unhappy suitors as if they were made for the courts, and not the courts for them.

My other objection is, that I cannot think that we ought altogether to despair of a speedy reform in our equity tribunals, merely because the strong interests and brilliant talents which are for some reason arrayed against it, seem to render the present moment rather favourable to perpetuate than to correct the abuses of the existing system. There is no power, wit, or eloquence, which, when thrown into the scale, can counterbalance the native sterling sense of the English people, assisted as it now is by education, and above all by a free and cheap press;* and reforms, which are regarded as practicable only at some remote period, may in a few years be carried into effect.

The necessity of classing and abridging the statutes, and introducing greater plainness and simplicity into the language of them, was felt as long since as the reign of Edward the Sixth. In the reigns of Elizabeth and James the First, several plans were formed for revising and simplifying this part of our laws, which were revived again both in the time of the Commonwealth and after the Restoration; but they were all blossom that produced no fruit:† and it was reserved for a

* "There are machines which may be used for purposes very different from those for which they were intended by their inventors." "The light which was meant to make visible the defects of others may show greater faults in ourselves." "Instruction opens the eyes of the scholar, even to the failings of those who teach him."—*Letters of Eminent Lawyers.*

† The plans that have been formed for the improvement of the statute law, since the reign of Elizabeth, are generally known. But it has escaped the attention of many of our most eminent writers on jurisprudence, that a similar project was entertained at the commencement of the reign of Edward the Sixth. The following passage is extracted from the Historian of the Reformation:—"There was also (*in* 1549) put into the House of Commons a bill for reforming of process at common law, which was

Statesman* of our times, to commence the execution of a work projected nearly three centuries

sent up by the Commons to the Lords, but it fell in that House. I have seen a large discourse, written then upon that argument, in which it was set forth, that the law of England was a barbarous kind of study, and did not lead men into a finer sort of learning, which made the common lawyers to be generally so ignorant of foreign matters, and so unable to negotiate in them. Therefore it was proposed, that the common and statute laws should be, in imitation of the Roman laws, digested into a body, under titles and heads, and put in good Latin. But this was too great a design to be set on, or finished under an infant king. If it was then necessary, it will be readily acknowledged to be much more so now, the volume of our statutes being so much swelled since that time, besides the vast number of reports and cases, and the pleadings growing much longer than formerly. Yet whether this is a thing to be much expected or desired, I refer it to the learned and wise men of that robe."—See *Burnett's History of the Reformation*, v. ii. p. 96. folio edit.

The following extract from the *Remains* of our amiable Edward VI, published in the volume just cited, will not perhaps be unacceptable to the reader. It is to be found in the work entitled "*A Discourse about the Reformation of my Abuses.*"—"Devising of good laws, I have showed my opinion heretofore what statutes I think most necessary to be enacted this session. Nevertheless I would wish that besides them, hereafter when time shall serve, the superfluous and tedious statutes were brought into one sum together, and made more plain and short, to the intent that men might the better understand them, which thing shall much help to advance the profit of the Commonwealth."

* So much has been written and said respecting Mr. Peel's excellent labours, that I shall merely here express a wish that he will, in the progress of his undertaking, keep in view those

ago; and which, from the immense increase in the number of the statutes, had become so appalling as almost to preclude the hope of any man being found possessed of the judgment, talent, and perseverance requisite for such an undertaking.

These pages show, that the project of reforming our great equity tribunal is almost as ancient as that of digesting the statutes; and if we look at the comparative difficulty of the two measures, we shall find much more reason to expect a re-organization of the Court of Chancery, than to see the bulk of the statute law condensed in a moderate number of volumes.

I am inclined then to hail the partial consolidation of the statutes as the harbinger of some improvement in those Courts which are the subject of this work; and the more so, as if there be any part of our judicial system for whose reformation the country most loudly calls, it is the Court of Chancery. A government that knows the advantages of a timely over a late, of a volun-

maxims and principles which, however modified and changed to suit the difference in the government and situation of nations, are the basis upon which every wise legislator should raise his system. There is no danger of a disciple of Bacon casting our whole law into a new mould; but there are some parts of it which ought to be re-modelled, and a form and shape given to them more worthy of an enlightened age, and better adapted to the wants of a rich commercial people.

tary over a forced reform, and that has for years past admitted that *no intellectual, no physical strength can cope with the duties imposed on the Chancellor, or prevent the ruinous delays suffered by the suitors of his Court under the present system,** cannot long be deaf to the public voice.

After these observations I cannot, perhaps, better conclude this work, than with the words of one of the most accomplished statesmen of modern times, and than whom none ever showed himself more attached to our ancient institutions, or more opposed to rash innovation. "The ground," says Mr. Burke, "for a legislative alteration of a legal establishment is this, and this only, that you find the inclinations of the majority of the people, concurring with your own sense of the intolerable nature of the abuse, are in favour of a change.†

* See Mr. Peel's speeches in the House of Commons on the subject of the Court of Chancery, *passim.*

† See *Burke's Speech on the Acts of Uniformity.*

APPENDIX A.

SIR JOHN LEACH'S PROPOSAL, THAT THE ROLLS' COURT SHOULD SIT IN THE MORNING.

In the course of his speech in the House of Commons on the debate respecting the Vice Chancellor's bill, on the 13th of February, 1813, *Mr.* (now *Sir John*) *Leach* said, that, without assuming more than belonged to the circumstances that attended the examination of the question before the House, he should suggest a remedy, which he was satisfied would be found fully equal to meet the evil in its broadest extent. There was an office created for no other purpose but to assist the Lord Chancellor, and when that judge wanted more assistance, was not their attention naturally directed to the office so created? The office of the Master of the Rolls was such office, and the question was, could the House, by a different distribution of the business, make him more effective for the end for which he was constituted? As he had only 20 effectual judicial days, and only 100 fractions of days, at present occupied, so it followed that he had one half of his time unappropriated. But an honourable and learned friend of his had said, that, though the Master of the Rolls had less of his time occupied in Court, he had many other important duties attached to his office to discharge. For his part, he did not understand what was meant by the words attached to the office. He did not understand any duty to be attached to an office unless it entered into its constitution, and specially belonged to it. Those duties described to be attached to the office of Master of the Rolls were prize and plantation appeals. He, however, contended, that the Master of the Rolls had no more to do with those causes than any other privy councillor. He had his (the Master of the Rolls*) own words for saying so, for he, five years ago, withdrew from them for fifteen months. Could any man conceive that this great and excellent officer would have withdrawn himself from those causes if it had been his duty to have attended to them? What censure would he not have subjected himself to, if, for the gratification of his private feelings, he had withdrawn himself from the duties of his office? Such, however, was not the case, but it was a mere voluntary occupation of his unemployed time. And should the House not rather call on this great officer to do that for which he was created, rather than suffer him, because he was not sufficiently occupied in that, to employ his time in what was not his duty? It became the House not to appoint two assistants to the Chancellor, when the business of Equity could be done with one. On the supposition then that the Master of the Rolls were withdrawn from the cockpit, the question was, could he give the assistance required to the Lord Chancellor, and meet the evil of the accumulation they were desirous of removing? If he were to assert at random, that he knew the Master of the Rolls had time enough for the purpose, he might not get credit, and might be met by an assertion of an opposite tendency; but he professed to state, with actual and positive precision, the grounds on which his opinion was founded. To decide

* Sir William Grant.

this question, let it be seen how much of his Honour's juridical time was employed in matters of Equity. With this in view, he must go into a pretty minute detail. The juridical year, deducting for the long vacation, Christmas, Easter, and Whitsuntide, consisted of 206 juridical days, from which six holidays were to be subtracted, leaving a total of 200 days in the juridical year, during which the Chancellor sat for the administration of justice. Then, on how many of those days did the Master of the Rolls sit for the purpose of assisting the Chancellor? To show this, he should state when he did not sit. During term time he sat three evenings in the week, and on the other three days he did not sit at all. There were three terms in the year of three weeks each, so that there were nine days in each of these terms in which he did not sit; this made, for the three terms, twenty-seven days on which he did not discharge any business. The fourth term consisted of four weeks, producing twelve days, on which his Honour did not at all sit, making a result on the whole of thirty-nine days on which he was unoccupied. He never sat on Saturdays out of term, except on the first Saturday after each term; this gave nineteen Saturdays out of term on which he did not sit at all; this, added to the former thirty-nine, made fifty-eight days on which his Honour did not at all sit in Equity. He did not mean to say that the learned judge did not sit elsewhere, but he now went upon the assumption that he was withdrawn from those other functions. His Honour never did sit on seal days, and that for a reason which did not now exist, namely, because it was formerly no unusual matter for the Chancellor to sit on seal days, probably till two o'clock on the following morning, and the counsel being the same in both Courts, they, of course, would be engaged before his Lordship. These seal days amounted to twenty, making, with the former fifty-eight days, a total of seventy-eight days wholly unemployed by the Master of the Rolls in equitable jurisdiction. It remained to be inquired, whether those would meet the evil complained of according to the statement of the noble lord (Lord Castlereagh) who introduced the bill. It was intended that the Chancellor should sit three days in the House of Lords. Now, the Chancellor's days, though he ought regularly to sit from ten o'clock till four, would be overrated if stated to be on an average four hours. The days of the Master of the Rolls would consist of six hours; so sixty of the Master of the Roll's days would be equal to ninety of the Chancellor's: to this add twenty seal days, which would be equal to 110 days which the Master of the Rolls would be able to add to the 200 juridical days of the Lord Chancellor. Here then was an adequate relief on the supposition of any imaginable increase, the whole juridical year consisting, as he had stated, of 200 days, distributed in the proportion he had described. Suppose the increase of business to be equal to one half of the whole; here it was all provided for and more. He asked of his honourable and learned friends to consider this, and to answer it if they could. Let them swell the phantom to any size they pleased, and let them say if these 110 days would not only afford ample assistance to the Chancellor, but were out of all measure above the evil. Assuming then, as facts, what he had endeavoured to lay down, with what shadow of reason could that House venture on a measure, which appeared pregnant with so much danger, when they found in the constitution of the office already created for that purpose, ample means to meet and remedy the evil complained of. He was aware that there could be no objection to what he had now suggested, except what was personal to that great judge to whom he had so often alluded; and it might be urged, that if he were to sit 200 juridical days, a much larger proportion of his time would be occupied, though surely not more than that of the other judges, or than the Chancellor himself, who united the offices of Speaker of the House of Lords and Cabinet Minister. With respect to the compensation which this additional labour would demand, there could be but one feeling; but he felt confident, that, if an encroachment on the ease of that extraordinary and excellent person would be productive of public benefit, he would feel that to be an ample compensation. He was sure that it would not require more than two years to subdue the existing arrear, and when that was done the leisure afforded to the Master of the Rolls, by withdrawing him from prize and plantation appeals, would be more than equal to the increase of business in Chancery. The business which he proposed to withdraw from the Master of Rolls, to be sure, was not so great as that which he had suggested the propriety of imposing on him. But, he asked, would this truly meritorious person, in that case, have more to do than the other judges? The Chancellor had as much to do at present; and why should not the situation of Master of the Rolls be rendered as efficient? If any magistrate in this country was entitled to call for a sacrifice to be made to his private feelings, he confessed that the present Master of the Rolls was exactly the person. But no magistrate whatever had a right to call on the public to make any sacrifice to his private feelings. There must, in consequence of the increased labour, be an increase of emolument, not adequate indeed to the encroachment made on the ease of this most excellent and valuable judge; but he was certain that highly respectable character would submit to the additional labour, feeling, as he must do, that the good of the country called for it. The encroachment on the ease of his Honour too, he was certain, would not be for more than two years, as then the arrear would have been made up; and he would have the satisfaction of having so eminently served the country, while the alteration would, in the result, be a relief to himself rather than a burden.

APPENDIX B.

TRANSLATION OF FIVE OF THE "LETTERS ON THE COURT OF CHANCERY."*

LETTER XVIII.

THE greatest part of the English appeals carried to the House of Lords come from the Court of Chancery, and are appeals from the judgment pronounced by the Lord Chancellor.

You will doubtless be surprised at learning that Lord Eldon and Lord Redesdale * * * * are in fact the only Peers usually present who are familiarly acquainted with the laws of the country. Since jurisprudence has become a science so complicated from its subtleties, and so difficult to be fathomed, the other members of the House have had the good sense not to give their votes. It is indeed with reluctance that they attend the adjudication of appeals. Never more than two or three Peers are to be seen, and even they would not be there if they were not obliged to make their appearance, each in his turn. But as this obligation assigns them but one day, which is never repeated, except at a considerable distance of time, without, however, being fixed, it follows that the same Peers are not to be met with two days together; so that with the exception of Lord Eldon, who presides in the House constantly, a cause (for it often lasts several days) may be opened, argued, and decided before different Lords. It therefore happens very frequently, that after years have elapsed since judgment was given in the first instance, the

* See Appendix C.

suitors in Chancery, or rather their descendants, (it being a certain fact that the original parties hardly ever see the end of their suit,) have the agreeable pleasure of seeing their appeals from the judgment of the Lord Chancellor, given in Lincoln's Inn Hall, decided by him again in the last resort, assisted, it is true, by Lord Redesdale. But it would be regarded as a miracle, if Lord Redesdale's opinion differed in the slightest degree from Lord Eldon's; and this circumstance is really fortunate, for if difference of opinion should take place between these two dignitaries, the other Lords (hereditary judges in the last resort as they are) would nevertheless be much embarrassed how to decide them.

The other appeals to the House of Lords come, in general, from the Scotch courts, and are very numerous in consequence of the litigious spirit of the people of that country. I cannot apply the same observations to these appeals as to those of the Court of Chancery, that they are appeals from the Chancellor, of Lincoln's Inn, to the Chancellor, of Westminster. But I must add, that there are not wanting other subjects to censure. At present, to avoid entering into details, I shall mention but one circumstance relative to the Scotch appeals. It is, that the laws of that country are as different from the English laws as these last from our code; and more than that, that no one in the House of Lords is versed in the knowledge of Scotch jurisprudence.

After this description of the organization of the House of Lords, as a tribunal of dernier resort, it seems to me that it is in vain to say, that nothing is more imposing and solemn than the decrees that are pronounced there; and that the spectacle that is presented you, of judges utterly ignorant of the science of which they should be masters, and who are forced to be present at audiences where they have the right of voting without venturing to obtrude their opinions upon the decisions, and who, to pass the time, amuse themselves by reading the newspapers, or some new pamphlet; it seems to me, I say, that this scene is little calculated to inspire sentiments of respect and veneration. And assuredly, in the infancy of our monarchy, at the time when causes were debated before the great Barons,* that spectacle would not present an exposition more revolting to common sense, than the appeals heard in our days before the House of Lords of England.

Besides the inconveniences of which I have been speaking, it is proper to observe, that the House of Lords only hears appeals during the session of Parliament; that the Parliament itself sits only at the King's pleasure; and that though it would be impossible for the King to dispense with Parliament for a year, persons of reflection cannot avoid censuring the dependance which exists between the Court of dernier resort and the Parliament, particularly when it is considered that the session is not sufficient for the House of Lords to dispose of the numerous appeals which are carried there, and that, consequently, the most ruinous delays result from it in the administration of justice.

It is to be regretted that the English, always so ready to criticise the institutions of other nations, do not pay more attention to the shocking defects of their own. Such advocates for reform ought, it appears to me, to begin with themselves.

* The Author probably speaks of the time when the *Chevaliers Clercs* (one of the titles of the Lawyers introduced into the Parliament, to explain the laws to the Barons, even in the reign of St. Louis) had not as yet any deliberative voice. It was not until after Philip le Bel had made the Parliament stationary, that they acquired this right; and we know that soon after that event, the great Lords, disgusted with their judicial functions, deserted the Parliament, and the Lawyers remained the only judges. No tribunal ever existed more deserving of the respect and consideration of a nation than the Parliament of Paris, such as it was in the sixteenth century.—*Note by the Editor.*

LETTER XIX.

You have put two questions to me, first, whether M. Meyer* is correct when he alleges that, in England thirty years may elapse between the commencement of a suit in an inferior court and its conclusion by a decree in the House of Lords? Secondly, what are the measures recently adopted to get through the cloud of appeals accumulated in this Court, and whether those measures have been successful?

I will at once then answer both your inquiries, and will tell you that in 1812 appeals were to be found in the House of Lords which had been depending since 1793.† It would be impossible for me to inform you the precise period at which those suits were instituted in the inferior tribunals, but there is no doubt that they were instituted before the judges, counsel, and solicitors who are now engaged in them, had entered upon their professional career. After this account, "non ci sarebbe bisogno, ch'io mi mettissi a provare la lunghezza, per non dire l'eternità delle liti praticata ne' nostri tempi."‡

Certainly if Chancellor Fortescue were now alive, he would be surprised to see his country, which boasts that it is not only the richest and freest, but also the most civilized and best governed country in the world, nevertheless behind ours in one of the most essential points which a wise and enlightened government can arrive at, and that it

* "Il n'est pas râre de voir des causes se prolonger trente ans et plus, avant que d'arriver au plus haut degré de jurisdiction."—*Meyer, Institutions Judiciares des principaux pays de l'Europe*, vol. ii. in the chapter intituled *Défauts des Lois Anglaises.—Note by the Editor.*

† Vide *First Report of Commons' Committee, on Delays in Suits in Chancery*, Appendix, No. 2.—*Note by the Editor.*

‡ *Muratori, Dei difetti della Giurisprudenza.—Note by the Editor.*

is to England and not to France that the description* may be now applied which this magistrate has left us of the culpable delays which took place in France 400 years ago in the administration of justice.

In 1825 these delays had so increased the number of appeals, that Lord Eldon found it indispensable to have a Vice President created to assist him by hearing Scotch appeals in his absence. For this purpose he made choice of Lord Gifford, the late Master of the Rolls. * * * * * * *

Lord Gifford found no difficulty in disposing of a considerable part of the Scotch appeals, by confirming the decrees of the original tribunals, conduct very prudent in a judge who, like him, knew no more of Scotch jurisprudence than he had learnt the preceding vacation at the sea side, where he was staying with his family. But joking apart, I still mean to applaud this magistrate who, under these circumstances, displayed more wisdom than * * *

I should have thought, that in a country where the laws are well administered, the principal tribunal should not endeavour to reverse the decrees of the inferior courts, and thus diminish their influence and credit, that being a sure way to encourage parties to appeal; but, on the contrary, should presume their decisions to be just, unless it is proved as clear as the light that they are otherwise. It is by thus increasing the consideration of those inferior tribu-

* "Sunt quippe in Regno Franciæ in curiâ ibidem supremâ, quæ curia parliamenti vocitatur, processus quidam qui in eâ plusquam triginta annis perpenderunt. Et novi ego appellationis causam unam quæ in curiâ illâ agitata fuit, jam per decem annos suspensam fuisse, et adhuc verisimile non est eam infra annos decem alios posse decidi. Ostendit et mihi dudum, dum Parisiis morabar, hospes meus processum suum in scriptis, qui in curiâ parliamenti ibidem ipse tunc octo annos pro 4s. redditus, qui de pecuniâ nostrâ 8d. non excedunt, prosecutus est, nec speravit se in octo annis aliis judicium inde obtenturum," —Vide *Fortescue, De Laudibus Legum Angliæ.* * * * * * * * * *
—*Note by the Editor.*

nals, that the parties litigant would remain satisfied with the judgments given there.

This nomination of a Vice President to hear, in the Chancellor's absence, the appeals carried to the House of Lords, was but a temporary measure, and has not been renewed since the death of Lord Gifford,* so that the appeals are as numerous as ever. It is doubtful whether a similar step would have continued to be advantageous to the public, even were a judge to be met with who would always be disposed to discharge such important functions without receiving any remuneration. * * * * *

It is not to be dissembled, that the uncertainty which prevailed as to the judges who had to decide causes in the dernier resort proceeded from a defect of good government; and I do not think that the good Scots, who had been desirous of appealing to Lord Eldon, were altogether satisfied at finding another magistrate in his place to hear their cases.

Neither do I see any resemblance between these temporary measures and the creation of the supplemental sections of our courts, when the causes are in arrear.† In France the judges are too numerous for an appeal to be made with a view to obtain the decision of any particular judge. Besides this, it is customary (and this even forms part of the system of organization of our tribunals) to create new sections, or to suppress others, according as the public service requires, and, as you know, usage is everything with the people.

* Few persons are ignorant of the measures which Lord Lyndhurst has been obliged to take to expedite the hearing of appeals. Sir John Leach and Sir William Alexander not being peers, and consequently not having a deliberative voice, fill characters inferior even to those which the ancient *Conseillers Rapporteurs* did formerly in the parliament of Paris. * * * * * * * * *
—*Note by the Editor.*

† See *Dupin, Lois concernant l'Organisation Judiciaire.—Note by the Editor.*

LETTER XX.

The more I become enlightened upon the origin of the jurisdiction exercised by the House of Lords in civil causes, the more I am astonished that the English tolerate a system subject to so many inconveniences.

It is generally known that after our Parliaments were made stationary, and the gentlemen of the robe were introduced there, the functions of these assemblies became* judicial, and that they very rarely exercised a legislative power. In England the contrary is the case. From time immemorial the Parliament has been principally occupied in the creation of laws, and it is only the House of Lords that has assumed the right of judicature.

The commencement of this usurpation remains hid in the obscurity† of antiquity; but it will suffice for you to know, that the Lords formerly claimed a right to decide not only appeals but also original causes.

Another thing which will doubtless appear to you very extraordinary is, that the House of Lords has not enjoyed the privilege of adjudicating causes without interruption. Whole centuries have passed over without their having exercised their judicial functions either in appeal or in the first instance; and between the commencement of the fifteenth century and the beginning of the seventeenth few

* See the works of *Meyer*, *Bernardi*, *Henrion de Pensey*, and *Jousse*, quoted in former Letters. See also *Boucher d'Argis*, *Histoire abregeé de l'Ordre des Avocats*. —*Note by the Editor.*

† In Hale's Jurisdiction of the House of Lords, and in the Preface, written by Mr. Hargrave, to that work, all the authorities which relate to the origin and history of the jurisdiction now exercised by the House of Peers in civil causes are to be found collected.—*Note by the Editor.*

traces are to be found of this jurisdiction.* But since the time of James the First many examples have been collected of original causes decided in the House of Lords, in consequence of petitions presented by the parties.

During the Protectorate it does not appear that this House exercised any judicial act. Cromwell had noticed the absurdity of investing with the functions of judges the members of an assembly unacquainted with jurisprudence, and therefore adopted the more sensible plan of creating a Court of Appeal,† composed of magistrates who had cultivated the study of the law.

After the restoration of Charles the Second, the Legislature, instead of profiting by the good example set them by Cromwell, abolished the court of appeal, which he had instituted, and allowed the House of Lords to resume its ancient rights. There are also to be found in the archives of this House, during this reign, different decisions, in civil causes, pronounced by it in the first instance.

But, towards the end of the seventeenth century, controversies arose respecting the pretended right which the House of Lords had arrogated to itself. The discussions on this subject were very warm, and Sir Matthew Hale, a judge worthy of being placed in competition with our De l'Hopital and D'Aguisseau, maintained that, according to the constitution of the country, the House of Peers ought to have no judicial functions in civil cases.

It is tolerably certain, that if the Lords of former days

* The Parliamentary Rolls of a remote period are full of proceedings of every kind. Vide *Rotuli Parliamentarii*, and *Ryley, Placita Parliamentaria*.—*Note by the Editor*.

† This court had cognizance only of appeals from the Court of Chancery. Appeals from the other tribunals being very uncommon, it is probable enough, that when they occurred, Cromwell appointed commissioners expressly to decide them.—*Note by the Editor*.

had been able to foresee the kind of spectacle which the House now exhibits, where their descendants are obliged to assist, they would have been eager to divest themselves of their judicial duties. But they only called to mind the period when the King and his Barons presided over the courts of justice, and decided all the suits of the kingdom. Their judicial functions, which they regarded as hereditary, interested them more than the public welfare, and they were unwilling to renounce them for fear of diminishing their dignity.

The sequel was, that in spite of the arguments and just remonstrances of Hale, the Peers succeeded in their designs. But this victory is but of little service to the Peers of our days, to whom the privilege has become a task so troublesome, that to oblige them to attend more regularly at the sittings, a very considerable fine is levied upon those who neglect it.

It is true that the House now exercises a much more limited jurisdiction than formerly, not hearing causes in the first instance, nor appeals from all the tribunals. But notwithstanding this, the appeals carried to the House are much too numerous.

You will doubtless have made the observation, that the English Peers now act the same part as our Barons did at the period when jurisprudence having become a science, they had need of Counsellors* to fix their decisions, in order that they might not give judgments contrary to the laws. But our ancestors soon remedied this inconvenience, by separating the legislative from the other functions, so that our Parliaments became simply tribunals of justice.

The English cannot make the same suppression, that is

* The Author means to speak of the *Gens des Lois*. Before they had a deliberative voice, they were called *Conseillers Rapporteurs*. The Peers bore the title of *Conseillers Auditeurs*.—*Note by the Editor.*

to say, deprive the House of Lords of its legislative functions, but it seems to me very practicable to abrogate its judicial functions.

LETTER XXI.

In the time of our Parliament there were no appeals from their decrees, for few cases then existed in which recourse could be had to the Council* of the King; and for many reasons, which it is needless to recapitulate, no inconvenience resulted from this order of things.

But after having created so many tribunals of appeal in the place of the Parliaments†, and particularly after having made so great an alteration in the laws, the legislature was very soon convinced of the necessity of forming a sovereign court to annul the proceedings of the other tribunals, when forms might be violated, and to quash every judgment which might contain an express contravention of the law, and by this means to produce an uniformity in all the courts.

The National Assembly,‡ in consequence, created the Court of Cassation. The magistrates of this tribunal, being taken from different provinces of the kingdom, are perfectly conversant with the customs and localities§ which

* See *Henrion de Pensey de la Autorité judiciaire en France*. Vol. ii. c. 31. *Meyer Institutions Judiciaires*. Vol. iv. p. 412. *Bernardi de l'Origine et des progrès de la legislation Française*, p. 342.—*Note by the Editor.*

† The *Cours d'Appel* now bear the name of *Cours Royales*. Their number, that of Corsica included, is twenty-seven. For a long time the Parliament of Paris was the only Parliament. In 1501 there were seven Parliaments. At the period of the Revolution there were thirteen.—*Note by the Editor.*

‡ See the Decree of the National Assembly of the 27th of November, 1790. —*Note by the Editor.*

§ It is the principle here explained which has influenced France, and caused it to grant to its Colonies the privilege of nominating to the Court of Cassation. —See the Decree of the National Convention, of the 1st day of the 2nd month, of the 2nd year of the Republic.—*Note by the Editor.*

may influence the affairs litigated in these same Provinces, and serve to explain them. No tribunal is, therefore, more admirably constituted for the decision of appeals than this Court, the judges being fully capable of appreciating the motives which have dictated the decrees, even when these motives may be veiled or completely disguised.

This Court has not the cognizance of facts; it decides only upon the decrees, and sends back the substance of the matters to the inferior tribunals. It would be impossible for it to follow a cause from its commencement without being overwhelmed by the weight of the business with which it would be loaded. It was, therefore, wise to limit its functions to the surveillance of the conservation of the laws, and the guaranteeing of the judicial forms.

To increase still more the influence of the tribunal of Cassation in judicial affairs, the obligation of giving the reasons of their opinions is imposed upon the judges. This measure makes the Courts below acquainted with the maxims adopted by the Supreme Court.

They endeavour to conform themselves accordingly, that they may not see their judgments reversed; and in the judgments delivered, with the reasons upon which they proceed, the advocates discover the basis of a jurisprudence which interprets the existing laws, and fills up the void in our legislation.

For different reasons a Supreme Court is less necessary in England than in France. The small number of tribunals renders the preservation of uniformity in the forms and decisions much more easy. The judges in general enjoy much more consideration than those of our inferior Courts. They always give the reasons of their judgments, the same as the Court of Cassation. Their sentences are published by the counsel, sometimes by themselves; and become rules for governing the future decisions of the tribunals when similar cases again present themselves; at least, as long as they are not reversed by a decree of the House of Lords.

If the number of judgments delivered by the inferior Courts is considered, it will be found that it is comparatively very rarely that resort is had to the House of Lords, and still more rarely that that House reverses the decrees of other tribunals; the assembly being generally composed of the same judges as have already decided in the first instance.

It is essential for the advocates to read not only the works containing the ancient decisions of the tribunals, which commenced with the monarchy, and which still have the same authority as laws, but they must also read the works which appear periodically, and which contain all the modern decisions; so that each new interpretation, every new rule produced by a new conjuncture of circumstances being spread through all parts of the kingdom, they are commented upon, debated, and acknowledged as just and correct; or if the contrary be the case, measures are taken to obtain the reversal of the decrees which have given rise to them.

It is incontestable that so long a train of decisions, founded upon each other, joined to the necessity of their being studied, must contribute to produce an uniformity in the decrees, (without mentioning the small number of tribunals.) Nevertheless it appears to me obvious, that every country which desires its laws to be interpreted and administered uniformly, and which, besides this, is eager to avoid all conflict and contradiction in the proceedings and decrees of the different tribunals, ought for this purpose to establish a Supreme Court. If then, the English should deprive the House of Lords of its judicial functions, I think that it would be indispensable, in order to render that separation advantageous to the public, to create another Court. My next* will contain the sentiments of several distinguished barristers of this city, concerning a new Supreme Court in the room of the House of Lords, (an English Court of Cassation.)

LETTER XXII.

SUCH would be my plan for a Court of Appeal, to be substituted for the Upper House of Parliament.

This Court should be composed of judges who had already presided in the tribunals of equity and common law, and who, having sat there for a certain number of years, should retire from them at an age when the too great fatigue of labour had not enfeebled them, or rendered them incapable of being of service to their country when placed in a Court of the highest rank, but the duties whereof should be less laborious. A Court composed according to this sketch, and, moreover, sitting at the same time with the other Courts, would enjoy a consideration infinitely greater than that of the House of Lords, and would be equal to the disposal of all the judicial business.

Besides its judicial functions, this Court would have leisure for the surveillance of the laws, and might, from time to time, make propositions to the legislature for such alterations as might appear to it calculated to ameliorate them. The legislature also, it seems to me, might have recourse to this tribunal, in preference to a committee of the House, to draw the bills intended to make innovations upon the general and permanent laws of the country; instead of their being, as now, brought into the House by

* This Letter is lost.—*Note by the Editor.*

persons ignorant of the existing laws, and passed at once into laws without the consequences being foreseen, which are often so calamitous, that they are forced to be repealed or amended as soon as possible.

The Chancellor, by virtue of his office, might perhaps be made a member of this tribunal. But when we consider the number of divorce cases, claims to vacant peerages, &c. wherewith the House of Lords is surcharged, and which it is not in the habit of discussing in the absence of the Chancellor; when we recollect also the other judicial duties which would remain allotted to the Chancellor, even after he had been relieved of the ordinary functions of the Court of Chancery,* we shall see that it would not be expedient to admit him among the number of the magistrates of the High Court of Appeal I have imagined.

To proceed now to appeals from the colonies, I have been given to understand, as I have before told you, that this government is about soon to propose certain plans with a view to this kind of suits being determined in the last resort in the colonies in which they were instituted,† or, at least, in some adjacent colony, so as to avoid, by this means,

* In the fragment of another Letter, the author has given some details upon the proposition so often brought upon the carpet, of separating the office of President of the House of Lords from that of the Chancellor. It appears that if this proposition did not originate with Mr. Pitt, it, at least, was received favourably by him. But it is said, that Lord Eldon had the address to dissuade him from putting it into execution.—*Note by the Editor.*

† As well as the editor can recollect, during the last session of Parliament, Lord Harrowby said that it would be desirable to see a court of last resort established in the colonies: but he added, for reasons nearly similar to those mentioned in the text, that the thing was impracticable. This may be true with regard to the generality of our colonies; but it may be worth while to consider whether it would not be practicable to form a tribunal of last resort in the East Indies, where the population, riches, and climate enable us to have tribunals and judges of a different character from those who are placed in the other colonies; and where, on several accounts, besides the distance which separates the parties from England, appeals to the Privy Council are most oppressive.—*Note by the Editor.*

the delays and immense expense which the presentation to the King's Privy Council occasions.

Were such a measure practicable, it would undoubtedly be attended with great advantage: but when the difficulty, not to say impossibility, is considered of finding judges possessed of the requisite information, or even a moderate knowledge of the laws of the generality of the colonies, and besides this, when regard is had to the enormous value of the property which is sometimes contested before their tribunals, it would not be either just or prudent to take away the right of appealing to an effective tribunal in England. The establishment of a Court in the colonies for deciding suits in the last resort, would not give any great satisfaction, and would neither hasten nor, except in a very small degree, diminish the expense of the suits. I advise the English then to follow our example, by adopting all measures which may tend to diminish unnecessary appeals, and to cause the appeals which do take place, to be carried before the High Tribunal of Appeal of which I have spoken, instead of before the Privy Council. They would do well also to place amongst the number of the judges of this Court, (as we have done* in France with regard to the Court of Cassation,) some magistrates who should be versed in the laws of the different colonies.

Indubitably voices will be raised against the creation of a High Tribunal of Appeal in the room of the House of Lords, as a measure carrying too great innovation into the constitution of the country. No one is more attached to ancient institutions than I am, and I should be the last to vote for their abolition, did I see any means of reconciling

* See a Note to the preceding Letter. In 1826 two commissions were appointed by the French government, of which, one was to be employed upon the political, and the other upon the judicial organization of the colonies.—*Note by the Editor.*

them with the changes have which taken place in society, or if any other expedient than their suppression could be discovered for remedying the evils which are occasioned by their preservation.

But, it seems to me, that, whilst I propose to the House of Lords to abandon a jurisdiction which is so burdensome to itself, I ought not to be considered as a man who desires to make an attack upon the constitution of this country. It is within a few years that the Peers themselves renounced their pretensions, derived from their ancestors, to the privilege, not only of hearing causes in the first instance, but also of pronouncing in the last resort upon appeals from the maritime and ecclesiastical tribunals, the colonies, &c. Why then should the divesting the Peers of their present rights of jurisdiction on appeals be regarded as an innovation upon the constitution of the country?—particularly since it is easy to prove that this exercise of jurisdiction on the part of the Peers, independently of the House of Commons, is itself an usurpation, and an innovation upon the constitution.*

The Peers of this kingdom have a privilege which is granted to them by statutary law, and which they might render more serviceable to their country than this right of deciding appeals. An ancient statute enjoins them to appoint, in each session of parliament, a committee composed of members of their body, to make inquiries touching the delays which may exist in the tribunals of justice, and to propose means for remedying them:† and to this end also the statute gives them the power of reviewing the archives

* At a more remote period than what the author speaks of, the House of Commons took no part in the judicial functions of Parliament.—*Note by the Editor.*

† Vide *Selden's Privileges of the Baronage of England when they sit in Parliament*, cap. 6.—*Note by the Editor.*

of the different Courts, and of ordering the judges to attend before them.

Let the Peers then abandon a privilege which is as troublesome to them as it is injurious to the good administration of justice, but let them assume another right, which, used with moderation and prudence, may conduce to the amelioration so long desired, and so absolutely necessary in the judicial organization of this country. Let them not forget, that an alteration which has for its object the hastening of the decision of suits, and the diminishing of their expense, instead of being considered as an innovation upon the constitution, would, on the contrary, be but the fulfilment of the Great Charter, by which the King has promised that there shall neither be denial nor delay of justice.*

* "Nulli negabimus aut differemus rectum vel justitiam."—*Magna Charta.* —*Note by the Editor.*

APPENDIX C.

THE LETTERS ON THE COURT OF CHANCERY.—A WRITER IN THE THIRD NUMBER OF THE FOREIGN QUARTERLY REVIEW.—MR. HUMPHREYS'S BOOK ON THE ENGLISH LAWS OF REAL PROPERTY.—FOREIGN CODES.

THE writer of an article in the last number of the Foreign Quarterly Review has thought fit to assert that the author of these Letters "has contrived, in making a great display "of extensive reading, French, German, and Italian, to lose "sight of the only useful object of study, and writes himself "Anti-Tribonian, with evidently little consideration of the "principles for, or against which he conceives himself to "contend."

The reviewer must refer to that portion of the Chancery Letters which treat of the subject of codification to which the writer of those Letters is opposed, and of which, I am told, the reviewer is an advocate. Now, it is not impossible that the author of the Chancery Letters may, in common however with many other persons, have adopted erroneous notions upon this subject; but when the reviewer charges him with an ignorance of the principles for or against which he contends, it is obvious he has passed judgment without ever having condescended to read the Letters that relate to codes, or, if he had read those Letters, that he could never have understood them.

The question of the expediency of abrogating the laws of a nation and substituting a code in their stead, embracing all that is worth preserving in the old, has only been recently agitated in this country; but it has for many years engaged the attention of the most celebrated continental jurists, (especially in Germany,) and some extremely valuable works have appeared, embodying all the arguments which it is possible to adduce for or against so important a change in the jurisprudence of a state.

The suffrages, however, of the most learned professors, as well as of some of the most able practical lawyers, have been given against the introduction either of a permanent code, or of one which should have within itself a principle of revision, so as to adapt it to the ever-varying wants of a great civilized people.

The works of some of the most eminent of the adversaries of codes are cited in the Chancery Letters, and their arguments detailed at some length.* The reviewer will find there the names of Hugo and Savigny, and other founders of the historical school, names which, although they may be unknown to him, are deservedly celebrated in

* The expediency of the modern codes was questioned even before the period mentioned in the Chancery Letters. *Filangieri's* work, entitled "*La Scienza della Legislazione,*" appeared about the year 1785. He eulogizes the attempts of Catherine the Great, and Frederick the Great, to introduce codes into their respective dominions. He seems, however, to have been more aware of the difficulties attending such a measure than the Reviewer and his friends, "Qualche "volta dunque basta riparare l'antica legislazione, qualche volta bisogna mu- "tarla interamente. La prima di queste intraprese non è molto difficile; ma "quanti ostacoli s'incontrano nella seconda." The notion of a permanent system of laws he considered to be visionary, and proposed the appointment of a Censor to make those alterations which the lapse of time and change of circumstances must inevitably require. Filangieri's book called forth *Schlosser's* sensible work, entitled, "*Briefe über die Gesetgebung überhaupt und den Ent- "wurf des Preusischen Gesetzbuchs insbesondere,*" which was frequently cited in the late controversy in Germany, by the historical lawyers. Experience has shown that Schlosser was right.

every country of Europe. He will find, too, that the author of these Letters supports the doctrine he inculcates, namely, the gradual improvement of particular portions of the law by the application of sound principles of jurisprudence, and the amendment, classification, and consolidation of the statutes, in preference to the sweeping away of our whole judicial system, and the establishment of a pocket code of the reviewer and his friends in its place, by the history of the principal codes of Modern Europe, nay, of that ancient code so much admired, and so little understood by many of our most zealous reformers, I mean the code of Justinian. He will find that the defects of that code have been unfolded to the public view by a Cujas and a Donou, so far back as the sixteenth century; and that for 150 years past the great object of the professors of the civil law has been to supply those defects by a study of such parts of the Jus Ante-justinianeum as have, in spite of Justinian's barbarous enactment, come down to us; and that the recent discovery of the Institutes of Gaius bids fair to make Germany better acquainted with the Roman law than Rome was herself in the degenerate times of the latter emperors.

Nor is this all that the reviewer will find in those Letters. He will there find that numerous as are our statutes and our reports, they are nothing when compared with what have been produced in France within the last twenty years, forming a supplement to the Code of Napoleon, which would not make so convenient a manual to go down to posterity with the hero and legislator as the neat little duodecimo now before me, a book which it is as absurd and ridiculous to hold up to the English public as containing the laws of France, as it would be to affirm that a Catechism supplies the place of a theological library. He will find, too, that so numerous are the volumes of the *Bulletin des Lois*, and of *Arrêts* of the different tribunals, that even the admirers of the Code admit the necessity of its being remodelled, and it has been more than once proposed that a compilation should be made from the adjudged cases and opinions of eminent jurists upon the construction of different articles of the Code, to be called, in honour of the reigning monarch, the Carlovingian Pandects; and, in addition to all this, the reviewer will find in the Chancery Letters, that the Code Napoleon has not superseded the necessity of studying the endless volumes of the civil law.*

The reviewer's censure of the author of the Chancery Letters is preceded by an eulogy of Mr. Humphreys's well-known book. The reviewer tells us, that that gentleman has in his work drawn amply from the stores of his acquaintance with the systems of other nations. Nothing can be more prejudicial to a writer than indiscreet praise, and I feel convinced that Mr. Humphreys would be the first man to disclaim this unmerited eulogy. The suggestions for the reform of some glaring faults in our Law of Real Property coming, as they do, from an individual of learning and experience in that branch of the profession, are of course entitled to attention, and have, in my humble judgment, deservedly met with the approbation of the public; but few, except the reviewer, would think of ascribing to Mr. Humphreys a familiar acquaintance with the foreign codes.† Indeed Mr. Humphreys himself, in his Letter to

* "Jamais vous ne saurez le nouveau code civil si vous n'étudiez que ce "code:" such are the words addressed to the Academy of Legislation by one of the authors of the French code, as quoted in a book which happens now to lie open before me, "*Histoire du Droit Romain suivie de l'Histoire de Cujas. Par* "*M. Berriat Saint Prix.*"

† Since this Appendix was written I have derived much gratification from the perusal of *Dr. Reddie's Letter to the Lord Chancellor, on the expediency of the Proposal to form a new Civil Code for England.* I cannot but recommend that pamphlet to the attention of the Reviewer. Dr. Reddie, I believe, studied under Hugo, and may be supposed, therefore, not to be altogether ignorant of the foreign codes, and their *working qualities.*

Mr. Sugden, does not scruple to state how little he knew upon the subject. After observing that Mr. Sugden had expressed himself rather strongly as to the excess of law-books, and of litigation, which had already inundated France from its Code, he adds, "on these subjects, however, we "can both of us personally be but imperfectly instructed. "Nothing short of close and repeated inquiries on the spot "could afford any accurate result." And *it is said*, that Mr. Humphreys has immediately afterwards given a very apt illustration of what he has stated, by falling into a whimsical error; from which it should seem that even inquiries made on the spot cannot always be relied on. Mr. Humphreys informs us, that he had been recently honoured with an interview at Brussels by M. Van Maanen, the minister of justice, who bore no inconsiderable part in framing the constitution and the laws of the kingdom of the Netherlands; and from whose assurance he felt warranted in stating, that their code, which enjoyed the advantage of posteriority over that of France, worked well: and he tells us, after the publication of his Letter to Mr. Sugden, that he perused the civil code of the Netherlands, and then traversed that country in almost every direction, which he found cultivated like a garden, with a peasantry thoroughly at its ease, owing to the admirable *working quality* of the new code.* Now *it is said*, that this code has not come into operation; that by a fundamental law of the new monarchy of the Netherlands, the Code Napoleon was, for political reasons, to be abolished, and a new code established in its stead; but that no part of the new code was to take effect until the whole should be finished; and that although the government has been engaged in the formation of the code ever since the year 1814, yet that the only

* See the Preface, and the 218th page of Mr. Humphreys's book, second edition.

parts completed are the *Code Civil*, the *Code de Commerce*, and the *Code d'Organisation Judiciaire*; that the *Code Pénal* was to be the subject of discussion in the Session of the States-General held last year, and that it has not yet been finished and approved, and that if it were finished and approved, the *Code de Procedure Criminelle* would still remain; and that the Code Napoleon, with certain temporary modifications, is still in force in the kingdom of the Netherlands.

How far these *on-dits* are correct, I will not pretend to determine; that they are not altogether without foundation will appear from the following extract from the last part of that excellent periodical work, published at Paris, *Thémis ou Bibliotheque du Jurisconsulte*.—" Royaume des " Pays-Bas.—Les derniers titres du *Code Civil* et le *Code* " *de Commerce* ont été adoptés, pendant la session de " 1825-1826: on doit discuter pendant la session prochaine " le *Code d'Organisation Judiciaire*. Il faut se rappeler, " que tous les Codes doivent être achevés avant qu'aucun " d'eux devienne exécutoire. Mais quelques lois particu-" lières ont dejà remplacé certaines dispositions des Codes " Français; qui pour le surplus continuent à régir le roy-" aume des Pays-Bas."

The passage is contained in an article that professes to give the latest intelligence as to the progress made in the formation of codes, in different countries of Europe and America.*

* M. Blondeau, who is known to more than one member of the Chancery Bar, is the writer of the article from which this extract is taken. I have never been able to procure any copy of the *new* civil code of the Netherlands, except one formed of the different numbers of that code as they have from time to time made their appearance in the *Journal Officiel du Royaume des Pays-Bas*. This code does not at all correspond with Mr. Humphreys's quotations from the *Belgic Code*. I have not the Code Napoleon, as modified for the Belgic provinces, but if M. Blondeau is correct, it will probably be found that Mr. Humphreys, both in his conversation with M. Van Maanen and in his criticism, has mistaken *that* code for the *new* Civil Code of the Netherlands.

But it is time to return to the Letters on the Court of Chancery. It may seem extraordinary were I to take leave of the reviewer without noticing another charge, although of infinitely less importance, which he has brought forward against the unfortunate author of that work, "who "has thought fit for no reason that *he* (the reviewer) can "imagine, to disguise his sentiments in French words en- "grafted on English idiom."

Now it is impossible to peruse half a dozen pages of the Letters in question without perceiving that no one could possess the information there detailed as to the Court of Chancery, except a barrister practising in that Court; and that the letter-writer and editor are fictitious personages, introduced by the English author for the purpose of more conveniently conveying to the public his sentiments as to the abuses and absurdities existing in our great equity tribunal. It is very natural, therefore, for the reader, never accustomed perhaps since he left College to compose in a foreign tongue, to suspect that such a work, written by one of his countrymen, must abound in Anglicisms; but one can hardly believe that a person having so moderate an acquaintance with the French tongue as the reviewer evidently possesses, should publicly denounce the style of the Letters as English, without once consulting a native of France, or any other individual more capable than himself of forming a judgment upon the subject. This, however, is what the reviewer, seated upon the tripos of criticism, has thought proper to do. A very little inquiry would have taught him that the book in question had been almost as much read at Paris as in London, and that although the errors of the press are, for the reasons stated in the Preface, and for others which it is not necessary to enumerate in this place, unusually numerous, yet that the work is not composed "in French words engrafted on English idiom." Indeed it is not likely, after fourteen years of uninterrupted intercourse between the two nations, any one would venture to publish such French as the Reviewer pronounces the Chancery Letters to be. The Letters undoubtedly contain many errors and inaccuracies of language, but they are such as a Frenchman would commit who was not over scrupulous in composition. Similar errors are to be found in the present work, and in the works of most of our juridical writers composed in their native tongue.

With regard to the author's motive for publishing in French, there are few persons who have read the first and the last letters who have not discovered it, although they have not, like the reviewer, known who was the author. Many persons think that the author has allowed himself to be swayed by false notions of delicacy, and that he would have acted more wisely had he published in English. The motive, however, for giving the work to the learned public only, even if it be erroneous, cannot possibly do him any discredit. All the first and the last Letters, with some trifling exceptions, were written whilst Lord Eldon held the Seals, and were intended for one of the public papers. His Lordship, however, resigned before any one of them was printed, and the author amused himself in the Long Vacation by adding the notes and the letters respecting the foreign codes, and published the work in its present form at the end of last October. A very few copies were printed, and nearly the whole were presented to the author's professional friends.

APPENDIX D.

LORD COLCHESTER'S OPINION AS TO THE PROPRIETY OF WITHDRAWING FROM THE LORD CHANCELLOR THE ORDINARY BUSINESS OF HIS COURT.

SINCE the foregoing pages went to press my attention has been drawn to the preface to a work written and published by Mr. Abbott, now Lord Colchester, as long ago as the year 1795, entitled, "*Jurisdiction and Practice of the Court of Great Sessions of Wales upon the Chester Circuit.*" The principal object of the preface is to show that the Welsh judicature ought to be abolished, and the common law and equity jurisdiction transferred to the Courts of Westminster Hall, and the number of English judges augmented, to discharge the increase of circuit duty: and many precedents are cited, from our history and statutes, to show that jurisdictions which were useful in their origin have been suppressed, as by change of times they have become pernicious. "The justices in eyre were superseded by the more effectual office of justices of assize. The Star Chamber, a Court next in rank to Parliament itself, eminently useful in its origin, and regular in its proceedings, was, for the gradual abuse of its power, at last abolished by stat. 16 Car. I. c. 10. The Court of the President and Council of the North was put an end to by the same statute. The Court of Wards and Liveries was abolished by stat. 12 Car. II.

c. 24. The Court of the President and Council of Wales and the Marshes, restrained by stat. 16 Car. I. c. 10, was abolished by 1 W. & M. sess. 1. c. 27, and the counties palatine of Hexham and Pembroke were extinguished by stat. 27 Hen. VIII. c. 26. and 14 & 17 Eliz. c. 13." Mr. Abbott observes, that, in point of economy, there would be an advantage to the public if two additional English judges were appointed in lieu of the establishment of eight inferior judges for Wales; but, he adds, that it would be more eligible if three were appointed, and the reasons he gives in support of his opinion so strongly corroborate what has been advanced in some parts of this work that I shall give them in his own words. He states, that the three additional judges might "render most eminent service to the public, by accelerating the progress of causes in the highest Court of Equity, and sitting constantly there under the same sort of commission as now authorizes certain of the judges to sit there occasionally in the absence of the Lord High Chancellor. For his time is, and must be, necessarily and continually employed in attending upon his Majesty's affairs in council and parliament, and in dispensing the royal favour for the public service, by selecting fit persons to supply vacant benefices in the Church, and to fill all the seats of justice in the superior courts, as well as in those numerous and important tribunals where the commission of the peace is executed by magistrates whose appointment is wholly intrusted to his vigilance, and whose removal depends singly upon his pleasure. Modern times having gradually involved the interests of almost every individual in the nation within the equitable jurisdiction of Chancery, the magnitude of its labours seems to require this additional aid for their despatch. And the custody of the Great Seal embracing so large a circle of other duties, this first magistrate and great officer of the crown might be expected gradually to withdraw his presence from the actual administration of ordinary justice; appearing there only when called upon to represent the King in his visitorial authority over eleemosynary corporations of royal foundations, or to exercise the King's prerogative in matters of lunacy, or his summary jurisdiction as general guardian of all infants, or to pronounce upon the contested legality of patents submitted to the sanction of the Great Seal, or to sit in judgment upon the great questions of commerce which arise out of the laws of bankruptcy, and interposing his equitable authority only in the decision of appeals and rehearings: from whence this further advantage must follow, that, after causes had undergone by these means such repeated and solemn consideration in the Court of Chancery, it would become less frequently necessary to encounter the expense, delay and inconvenience of resorting to the appellate jurisdiction of the House of Lords."

THE END.

LONDON:

PRINTED BY C. ROWORTH, BELL YARD,

TEMPLE BAR.

Printed in Dunstable, United Kingdom

91220088R00258